Formulation of Appropriate Laws: A New Integrated Multidisciplinary Approach and an Application to Electronic Funds Transfer Regulation

Paul F. White · Sardar M. N. Islam

Formulation of Appropriate Laws: A New Integrated Multidisciplinary Approach and an Application to Electronic Funds Transfer Regulation

Springer

Dr. Paul F. White
Barrister-at-Law
Victorian Bar – Australia
Associate Director
Law & Economics Program
Victoria University
Australia
pwhite@vicbar.com.au

Prof. Sardar M. N. Islam
Professor, CSES, and Director
Law & Economics Program
Victoria University
Australia
sardar.islam@vu.edu.au

ISBN 978-3-642-09123-0 e-ISBN 978-3-540-72047-8

Cover design: WMXDesign GmbH, Heidelberg, Germany

Printed on acid-free paper

9 8 7 6 5 4 3 2 1

springer.com

Foreword

Formulation of Appropriate Laws: A New Multidisciplinary Modelling Approach and an Application to Electronic Funds Transfer Regulation.

Efficient laws have profound positive social, economic, political and welfare effects. As a consequence, the formulation of efficient laws is a central issue in the study, practice and implementation of laws. Fragmented approaches to the formulation of laws such as 'comparative law analysis' and 'welfare economic analysis of laws' exist in the current literature; they even occasionally rear their heads in the practice and implementation of laws. However, what these authors offer and what is needed, is an integrated approach to help formulate efficient and socially desirable laws – an approach that not only incorporates 'comparative law analysis' and 'welfare economic analysis of laws,' but also takes into consideration other various dimensions of human welfare that are affected by new laws and legal reform. This book presents such an approach using the Electronic Funds Transfer (EFT) regulation in Australia as its vehicle of analysis. The two-pronged approach offered in this book can be applied to formulate efficient laws that maximise the social welfare of the country, irrespective of social, political and economic organisations of the country under study.

As such, this book makes several distinct contributions to the literature in law as it:

1. develops a new integrated multi-disciplinary approach using quantitative methods to formulate appropriate laws;
2. applies recent developments in welfare economics;
3. provides a quantitative empirical analysis of legal rule formulation;
4. undertakes a very comprehensive study of the regulatory issue of EFT; and
5. prescribes a set of appropriate, efficient, and socially desirable regulations in an optimal regulatory framework.

Given the limited number of research books dealing with this topic, this book makes a significant contribution to enrich the literature in this area. I believe that students, researchers, academics, practitioners, and policy makers in the areas of law, finance, banking, economics and development management will benefit form its scope and content. I commend the authors for this valuable contribution to the literature in law, economics and finance.

April 2008

Professor Nicholas Mercuro
Professor of Law in Residence
Michigan State University College of Law
East Lansing, Michigan USA

Preface

The formulation of efficient laws (that is, appropriate legal rule formulation) is a central issue in the study, practice and implementation of laws since efficient laws have profound positive social, economic political and welfare effects. Fragmented approaches to the formulation of laws, such as 'comparative law analysis' and 'welfare economic analysis of laws' exist in the existing literature and sometimes in the practice and implementation of laws. An integrated approach, which embeds these 2 approaches as well as other considerations of other dimensions of human welfare that are affected by laws, is necessary in formulating efficient (socially desirable) laws. In this book, such an approach is developed with an illustrative application to electronic fund transfer regulation in Australia. This approach can be applied to formulate efficient laws, which maximise social welfare of the country, irrespective of the legal, social, political and economic organisations of the country under study.

Electronic Funds Transfer ('EFT') as a modern, global consumer payment method continues to expand rapidly by comparison with credit cards and traditional paper-based forms of payment.

The core issue in EFT addressed in this book is a controversial one: the fair allocation of liability between the consumer and financial institution in the event of a disputed or unauthorised EFT transaction. The purpose of this study is considered especially apposite in view of the Australian Securities and Investments Commission's ('ASIC') imminent review of the self-regulating Australian *EFT Code of Conduct* ('EFT Code') and both the increasing incidence of reported unauthorised EFT transactions and in non-compliance by EFT financial institutions with the *EFT Code*. It is also an important study because of the rapid recent growth in EFT transaction volume and the continued expansion of EFT products and services compared to other payment instruments, which are in a corresponding decline. Moreover, there has been no previous study or review of the current Australian *EFT Code*, which was revised in 2002.

In the EFT payments system, consumers are exposed to risks quite different from those in traditional payments instruments. These include flaws in the various methods employed by financial institutions for the distribution of EFT cards and PINs, problems adducing unequivocal evidence in the event of unauthorised use of the instrument and systemic errors and technical malfunctions in processing EFT transactions. Furthermore, the distinct nature of electronic authentication using an electronic device and secret code makes the general common law principles dealing with handwritten signature authentication in the case of paper instruments (eg, by analogy with a forged cheque) particularly unhelpful.

In order to address these controversies, this book presents a *new integrated multi-disciplinary analysis of EFT regulation in Australia* in an attempt to identify the efficacy of current EFT regulatory arrangements as well as to appraise the merits of different EFT regulatory options to attain a more optimal and efficient regulatory regime for the future. The adapted multi-disciplines include *comparative law method, economic criteria and regulation theory methods, as well as ethical, social and administrative considerations.*

The two (2) EFT regulations which are the subject of this comparative study are the Australian *EFT Code* and the *US EFT Act*. The latter was chosen for comparative purposes as it is a rare example of a formal legislative response to the above core issues and risks, which the EFT system in the USA has in common with Australia.

Unlike the *US EFT Act*, for example, which has a relatively simple and administratively convenient approach to apportioning fault, the self-regulating Australian *EFT Code* essentially shares the burden of proof between the financial institution and the consumer in most instances. The consequence of the *EFT Code's* ambiguous, undefined and multi-layered legal tests and guidelines for determining the allocation of liability to either consumer or financial institution is that it leaves the Australian Banking and Financial Services Ombudsman, as the independent and preferred adjudicator of Australian EFT disputes, with the difficult and arbitrary task of hearing contrasting arguments and weighing the inconclusive evidence led by both sides before then seeking to reach a fair and equitable finding on the 'balance of probabilities'. Indeed, the practical application of the *EFT Code* is extremely difficult and confusing, as the Ombudsman regularly observes in its annual reports and is almost always evident in its actual case examples.

The task undertaken in this book to research and analyse these difficult and complex regulatory issues is both helped and hindered by another important issue: the lack of literature on consumer EFT regulation. Helped, because it represents a unique opportunity to embark upon such a study afresh, and, hindered, because little benefit can be derived from previous studies and hence there are no foundations upon which to build or progress the debate, the research and the analysis.

Accordingly, the significant gaps in this area provide a rare occasion to explore these contemporary and contentious issues using the multi-disciplinary techniques and approach proposed in this book.

As is argued in this book, the current regulatory arrangements in Australia are ineffective on several grounds. In particular, in: (i) efficiently settling disputed or unauthorised EFT transactions; (ii) ensuring compliance by financial institutions; and (iii) legal enforcement of its provisions

Ultimately, in consequence of this study, it is concluded that (a) in order to design and formulate an efficient or optimal regulatory regime, a more rigorous analysis beyond a straight legal studies approach needs to be undertaken, and (b) to improve consumer confidence and institutional compliance, as well as to arrest rising fraud and illegality, there is an urgent need for a comprehensive review and reform of EFT regulation in Australia. In this sense, the multi-disciplinary research and analytic approach adapted in this study is an integrated approach with the intention that it will not only drive the debate on an appropriate EFT regulatory framework forward, but ultimately with its 48 findings and 25 specific recommendations, also serve as a workable framework with some actual pragmatic criteria on which to assess different EFT regulatory and policy options. The proposed and applied approach *is a general one*; it can be applied to all legal issues in all countries irrespective of their socio-political-economic and legal conditions and systems.

This book will be useful to barristers, solicitors, judges, researchers, academics, policy makers and other practitioners of law.

The authors are especially grateful for the materials and generous time and assistance of the Federal Reserve (USA) and Australian Securities and Investments Commission (Aust.), as well as Prof Benjamin Geva.

Our special and particular thanks also go to Prof Colin Clark and Prof Neil Andrews for their extensive comments and help with editing, together with Dr Danielle White and Alex Manzoni for their assistance with editing and proofreading of this, our exciting and groundbreaking book.

April 2008

Dr. Paul F. White
Prof. Sardar M. N. Islam

Table of Contents

List of Charts

List of Figures

List of Tables

List of Cases

Australia

Balmain New Ferry Co Ltd v Robertson (1906) 4 CLR 379
Brandi v Mingot (1976) 12 ALR 551
Briginshaw v Briginshaw (1938) 60 CLR 336
Commonwealth Bank v Reno Auto Sales Pty Ltd [1967] VR 790
Commonwealth Trading Bank of Australia v Sydney Wide Stores Pty Ltd (1981) 148 CLR 304
International Harvester Co of Australia Pty Ltd v Carrigan's Hazeldene Pastoral Co (1958) 100 CLR 644
Jones v Dunkel (1959) 101 CLR 298
Kennison v Daire (1986) 160 CLR 129
Rejfek v McElroy (1965) 112 CLR 517
SGIC v Laube (1984) 37 SASR 31

United Kingdom

Greenwood v Martins Bank Ltd (1933) AC 51
Ingram v Little [1961] 1 QB 31
Kepitigalla Rubber Estates Pty Ltd v The National Bank of India Ltd (1909) 2 KB 1010
Lewis v Averay [1972] 1 QB 198
London Joint Stock Bank Ltd v Macmillan (1918) AC 777
Olley v Marlborough Court Ltd [1949] 1 KB 532
Parker v South Eastern Railway Co (1877) 2 CPD 416
Price v Neal (1762) 3 Burr 1354, 97 ER 871
Tai Hing Cotton Mill Ltd v Liu Chong Hing Bank Ltd and Others (1986) AC 426; (1985) 2 All ER 947

United States of America

Bisbey v DC National Bank, 253 App. DC 244, 793 F2d 315 (DC Cir, 1986)
Evra Corporation Inc. v Swiss Banking Corporation, 673 F 2d 951 (1982)
Feldman v Citibank, 443 NYS 2d 43 (Civ Ct, 1981)
Kramer v Chase Manhattan Bank, NA 235 AD 2d 371 (1997)
Kruser v Bank of America, 281 Cal Rptr 463 (Cal App 5th Dist, 1991)
Ognibene v Citibank Inc, NY City Civ Ct 446 NYS 2d 845 (1981)
Pickman v Citibank, 443 NYS 2d 43 (Civ Ct City of NY, 1981)
State v Citibank, 537 F Supp 1992 at 1994 (SDNY, 1982)

List of Statutes and Codes

Statutes

Australia

Australian Securities and Investments Commission Act 2001 (Cth)
Banking Act 1959 (Cth) and accompanying *Banking (Foreign Exchange) Regulations* (1974)
Cheques Act 1986 (Cth)
Currency Act 1965 (Cth)
Electronic Transactions Act 1999 (Cth)
Evidence Act 1995 (Cth)
Financial Transaction Reports Act 1988 (Cth)
Trade Practices Act 1974 (Cth)

Denmark

Payment Cards Act (1984)

United States of America

Electronic Funds Transfer Act, 15 USC § 1693 (1978) and
Regulation E, 12 CFR § 205 (1981)

Codes

Australia

Code of Banking Practice (1993)
Electronic Funds Transfer Code of Conduct (original, 1989)
Electronic Funds Transfer Code of Conduct (revised, 2002)
Uniform Consumer Credit Code (1996)

United Kingdom

Code of Banking Practice (1992)

Glossary of Terms

ABIO	Australian Banking Industry Ombudsman (now Banking and Financial Services Ombudsman)
ACCC	Australian Competition and Consumer Commission
APSC	Australian Payments System Council
ASIC	Australian Securities and Investments Commission
ASIC Act	*Australian Securities and Investments Commission Act 2001* (Cth)
ATM	Automatic Teller Machine
CBP	*Code of Banking Practice* (1993) (Australia)
Consumer	The person in whose name the EFT account is held
EFT	Electronic Funds Transfer
EFT Account	The personal bank account of an identifiable consumer for personal (not business) use and maintained by the financial institution, which can be accessed electronically
EFT Card	The access device in the form of a card with a magnetic strip which contains the consumer's account information (also known as an 'EFT Debit Card')
EFT Code	*Electronic Funds Transfer Code of Conduct* (2002) (Australia)
EFTPOS	Electronic Funds Transfer at Point of Sale
EFT Working Group	Refers to the various working groups and task forces established by the Commonwealth Government of Australia to investigate EFT regulation
Electronic Banking	The range of modern banking and financial services that utilise electronic equipment, including telephone banking, Internet banking, ATMs, EFTPOS and stored-value cards (also known as 'e-banking')
Federal Reserve	The Federal Reserve Board of the USA (the central bank in the USA)
Financial institution	The institutional provider of EFT products and services
NCEFT	National Commission on Electronic Fund Transfers (USA)
PIN	Personal Identification Number
RBA	Reserve Bank of Australia (Australia's central bank)
TPA	*Trade Practices Act 1974* (Cth)
TPC	Trade Practices Commission
US EFT Act	*Electronic Funds Transfer Act*, 15 USC § 1693 (1978) (USA)

Chapter 1. Introduction

'In fact, the most striking trend within the retail payments sector over the last decade is the rapid decline in the use of cheques in Australia, from more than 80% of the dollar value of non-cash retail payments in 1995 to less than 30% in 2002. At the same time, the electronic [payments] system has expanded rapidly…rapid growth in overall EFT debit card usage of about 10% per year'. [1]

'[Compliance and monitoring data from the Australian regulators] exhibits an increasing number of EFT transactions reported as "unauthorised"…the adverse trend is evidenced by the incidence of complaints of unauthorised EFT transactions increasing dramatically from 14 per million EFT transactions in 1995 to 41 per million in 2002'. [2]

'Despite EFT debit's rapid growth and prominence, the determinants and repercussions of EFT debit use have largely escaped academic scrutiny'. [3]

'The approach for regulating unauthorized [EFT] consumer transfers [under American legislation] is entirely different [to self-regulating codes of conduct]...and is worth considering elsewhere'. [4]

1.1 Context and overview

An important area of study of law is legal rule formulation – that is, the development of a framework for formulating efficient laws which maximise fundamental determinants such as: social welfare through improved law and order, economic efficiency and development, resolution of conflicts among parties resulting in social harmony and fairness and reduced agency costs. In the existing literature, this exercise is performed by the comparative law analysis method and welfare economics analysis of laws. However, the existing approaches are fragmented and fail to incorporate all the essential considerations necessary to

---

1 Reserve Bank of Australia, Bulletin: The Changing Australian Retail Payments Landscape (2003) 1-2.

2 Australian Securities and Investments Commission, Compliance with the Payments System Codes of Practice and the EFT Code of Conduct (2003) 59, and from the detailed analysis of data as part of the literature review in Chapter 2 of this book.

3 Federal Reserve Bank of New York, Why Use Debit Instead of Credit? Consumer Choice in a Trillion Dollar Market (2004) <http://www.newyorkfed.org/research/economists/zinman/2842_debit_or_credit.pdf> at 7 October 2004.

4 Benjamin Geva, Bank Collections and Payment Transactions (2001) 410, 421.

embed in a method for formulating efficient laws. This limitation of the existing methods for legal rule formulation is seriously prevalent in emerging fields and issues in law such as the law or regulation of 'Electronic Funds Transfer' (EFT).

As the above introductory quotations indicate, the rapid growth in EFT as a modern consumer payment instrument has been attended by an increasing incidence in the number of disputed or unauthorised EFT transactions in both numerical and proportional terms. Yet, as the Federal Reserve Bank of New York observes (above), the many complex and controversial governance and regulatory issues arising from these marked trends have largely been overlooked at academic level.[5]

In addressing these difficult contemporary issues, this book builds on the limited existing legal literature concerning EFT regulation and presents an extended multi-disciplinary approach to assessing EFT regulatory options, including comparative law method to analyse the distinctly different EFT regulations of Australia and the USA,[6] economic criteria and regulation theory methods, as well as administrative, social and ethical considerations.

The central, common problem, which the regulations of Australia and the USA attempt to address, is the fair allocation of liability between the financial institution and consumer for disputed, unauthorised consumer EFT transactions. Although taking markedly divergent paths, the regulatory responses of Australia and the USA followed a shared concern: the inapplicability of the paper-based legal principles founded in the common law[7] and the initial one-sided allocation of risk in consumer electronic banking contracts, which were perceived to be inadequate and heavily in favour of the financial institutions who drafted them.[8] Thus, notwithstanding the vastly different economic scale and Federal/State regulatory structures in the USA compared with Australia, the USA is the only relevant common-law-country example of a statutory response to essentially the same EFT problems.

In terms of context within the broader field of electronic commerce ('e-commerce') regulation, the focus in this book is on consumer EFT regulatory challenges and issues. Thus, it should be stated at the outset, that many of the issues raised in this book, such as identity fraud, may be equally significant in commercial e-contracts where electronic signatures or digital authentications are used (this is discussed in more detail in Section 2.1 and the attending Footnote 78).

---

5 Federal Reserve Bank of New York, above n 3.

6 Given that only the USA and Denmark have been identified as having specific legislation governing consumer EFT, it is submitted that because only the USA operates within a comparable, common law-based legal system (Denmark operating under a civil law-based system, with its statute having a commercial rather than consumer focus), the USA provides the most striking comparison given they approach the same EFT problems as Australia, but with a markedly different regulatory response.

7 See, eg, Greg Tucker, 'Regulation of Electronic Banking' (1990) 64 Law Institute Journal 706; and Geva, above n 4, 392-421.

8 See, eg, Report of the Working Group Examining the Rights and Obligations of the Users and Providers of Electronic Funds Transfer Systems (1985) 27.

In this context, it may be advanced that consumer EFT encompasses a wide variety of existing and planned payment system products designed to provide an alternative to traditional paper-based means of paying for consumer goods and services.[9] The features of all such electronically-initiated products vary considerably and a precise definition is therefore not possible (however, in Section 1.3 pertinent definitions are presented).

In using retail payment instruments, consumers are exposed to many types of risk, including flaws in the various methods employed by financial institutions for the distribution of EFT cards and personal identification numbers ('PIN'/'PINs'), unauthorised use of the instrument and systemic errors and technical malfunctions in processing transactions.[10] In general, EFT products give rise to the same types of risk that other traditional payment instruments do (eg, such as those for a forged cheque), although the degree of any particular risk may vary considerably because of differences in operating characteristics among the payment instruments.[11] Indeed, the distinct nature of electronic authentication using an electronic device and secret code makes the general common law principles dealing with handwritten signature authentication in the case of paper instruments (eg, by analogy with a forged cheque) particularly unhelpful.[12]

Although it is submitted that both consumers and issuers of EFT payment instruments have incentives to themselves mitigate the risks associated with using these products, some consumer risks are addressed by industry standards, and, in some very rare instances by formal laws, including those that are the subject of the comparative legal analysis in this book: the Australian *EFT Code of Conduct* ('*EFT Code*')[13] and the *Electronic Funds Transfer Act* in the USA ('*US EFT Act*').[14]

Essentially, the overarching and common goal of both the *EFT Code* and the *US EFT Act* is to protect the integrity of the EFT payments system in the respective countries.[15] Broadly speaking, the regulations seek to reduce uncertainties for both consumers and financial institutions regarding liabilities related to electronic payments. Both seek to provide protection against unauthorised or erroneous electronic transactions that access consumer accounts, by setting guidelines to allocate liability for unauthorised EFT transactions as well as imposing documentation and record-keeping requirements to assist consumers in detecting and remedying disputed problems. The regulations also require that

9 Board of Governors of the Federal Reserve System of the USA, Report to Congress on the Application of the Electronic Funds Transfer Act to Electronic Stored-Value Products (1997) 2.

10 Ibid 2-3.

11 Ibid.

12 See, eg, Tucker, above n 7; and Geva, above n 4.

13 Electronic Funds Transfer Code of Conduct (1989) (revised 2001, amended 2002).

14 Electronic Funds Transfer Act, 15 USC § 1693 (1978) and Regulation E, 12 CFR § 205 (1981).

15 See, eg, Australian Securities and Investments Commission, Discussion Paper on an Expanded EFT Code of Conduct (1999).

providers of EFT services disclose certain information regarding the terms and conditions of these services and inform customers of any changes in terms.

However, that is where the similarities end. For it is in the substantive provisions governing unauthorised EFT transactions in the *EFT Code* (clause 5) and *US EFT Act* (§1693(g) and §205 of *Regulation E*, which implements the Act) that the marked differences in approach exist. Whereas the USA regulation squarely places the burden of proof on the financial institution in the event of a disputed, unauthorised EFT transaction, it is submitted in this book that the *EFT Code* does not clearly assign either (i) a definitive apportionment of liability or (ii) an unambiguous burden of proof on either the consumer or financial institution; it merely purports to fasten liability on the consumer if the financial institution can prove that the consumer contributed to an EFT loss 'on the balance of probabilities'. Moreover, it does not supply any guidance as to how to 'weigh the evidence' of each when an evidentiary stalemate occurs. Although it should be noted that the *EFT Code* does endeavour to set out a sensible regime of liability between financial institutions and consumers where the fault is clear. Conversely, the *US EFT Act* (15 USC § 1693) makes no allowance for the degree of fault or consumer negligence or carelessness with an EFT card and PIN. The *US EFT Act* simply places liability at the foot of the financial institution unless there is a delay by the consumer in reporting loss, theft or misuse. Accordingly, it is submitted that it is easier to adjudicate and administer and avoids all disputes and problems in relation to evidentiary stalemates in apportioning fault than that of the *EFT Code*.

The problematic consequence of the *EFT Code's* ambiguous guidelines for determining the allocation of liability to either consumer or financial institution is that it leaves the Australian Banking Industry Ombudsman ('ABIO'),[16] as the independent and preferred adjudicator of disputes, with the difficult and arbitrary task of hearing arguments and weighing the evidence of both sides before then seeking to reach a fair and equitable finding on 'the balance of probabilities'. Indeed, the practical application of the *EFT Code* is extremely difficult and confusing, as the ABIO regularly observes in its annual reports.[17]

It is also noted that both the *US EFT Act* and the *EFT Code* are silent on a customer's paper-based right of 'countermand' under EFT. In respect of the distribution of EFT cards and PINs, the *EFT Code* does provide some minimum requirements for financial institutions, whereas the *US EFT Act* does not cover the matter at all. The *US EFT Act's* dispute resolution provisions appear more favourable to the consumer with provisional re-crediting of the customer account if the dispute is not resolved within 10 days.

The underlying question of how to apportion loss for unauthorised transactions is exceedingly difficult, short of adopting the simplified and administratively convenient no-fault, loss-imposition approach taken by the USA regulators. The

---

16 Note that during the completion of this book that the ABIO changed its name to the 'Banking and Financial Services Ombudsman', but will continue to be referred to throughout this book as the ABIO, the acronym by which it is still widely known.

17 See, eg, Australian Banking Industry Ombudsman, Annual Report, 1995/1996, 25.

complex facets of EFT regulation concern the extent to which consumers need or deserve to be protected from third party fraud, faults on the part of financial institutions, and consumers' own carelessness.

The Australian and USA regulations are administered by the Australian Securities and Investments Commission ('ASIC') and the Federal Reserve Board of the USA ('Federal Reserve'), respectively. ASIC and the Federal Reserve are responsible for ongoing review of the regulations and to monitor their compliance.[18] Clearly, though, both ASIC and the Federal Reserve must also balance consumer protection with the compliance costs necessary to provide this protection, and, to the extent practicable, demonstrate that the consumer protection provided by the regulation outweighs the compliance costs imposed upon consumers and financial institutions.[19]

It is submitted in this book that formal government regulation (ie, in the form of legislation) may be warranted when the unfettered operations of the private sector fail to achieve an economically efficient outcome.[20] That is, in the presence of so-called 'market failure'.[21] Government responses to market failures, although having the potential to improve market outcomes, may have unforeseen, and sometimes adverse, consequences.[22] The economic assessment criteria and regulation theory considered in this book (the reader is referred to Section 1.6 for an introduction to the methodology dealt with in detail in Chapter 3), are based on the implication that government regulation has the potential to both equally foster or hinder technological progress and the development of new products by influencing private sector incentives to invest in research and development activities and private sector choices among alternative technologies. In deciding whether, and, if so, how to regulate EFT products, policymakers must therefore carefully assess the potential effect of their decisions on the evolution of these new products and the extent to which they achieve market acceptance. For choices made today may significantly influence the payment options available to market participants in the future.[23] Consumers using EFT products would generally be expected to acknowledge some risks in return for protection against some risks, even in the absence of explicit government regulation.[24] To induce consumers to substitute EFT products for more familiar paper-based payment alternatives, providers need to make EFT products attractive to consumers and to make potential customers aware of the characteristics of their products.

In Australia, the great variety in existing and planned EFT products had meant that a single set of formal consumer protections was inappropriate for all

---

18 Eg, see generally, Australian Securities and Investments Commission, Discussion Paper, above n 15; and Board of Governors of the Federal Reserve System of the USA, Report to Congress, above n 9.

19 Board of Governors of the Federal Reserve, Report to Congress, above n 9, 4.

20 Ibid 2.

21 Ibid.

22 Ibid.

23 Ibid.

24 Ibid.

electronic banking products.[25] However, in 1998, ASIC commissioned a new working group comprising ASIC staff, legal experts, banking industry and consumer advocate representatives ('EFT Working Group') to investigate the appropriateness of the then current *EFT Code* regulations, which were implemented in 1989.[26] The EFT Working Group's 1999 Discussion Paper[27] successfully put forward options for expanding the previous *EFT Code of Conduct* so that it covered all consumer electronic funds transfer transactions and not just Automatic Teller Machines ('ATM'/'ATMs') and Electronic Funds Transfer Point of Sale ('EFTPOS') transactions, as was the case. The EFT Working Group's objective was to make the Code 'technologically neutral',[28] to the extent possible, so that the same protections would apply regardless of whether an EFT transaction involved, for example, the use of an ATM, the telephone or the Internet.

Importantly, though, the EFT Working Group had not sought to review the *EFT Code* generally, or its approach to unauthorised ATM and EFTPOS transactions in particular, by reference to the *US EFT Act*. Indeed, the EFT Working Group specifically rejected the USA approach,[29] where, essentially, the user is only liable for delays in reporting lost or stolen devices or failing to report unauthorised transactions shown on a periodic statement. Rather, the project was confined to substantially retaining the approach of the previous *EFT Code*, but amending it to cover all forms of consumer EFT technologies as well as some amendments which take account of recent developments in the areas of privacy and dispute resolution.[30] The EFT Working Group's approach, which was ultimately adopted in the revised *EFT Code* (which became effective 1 April 2002),[31] was to divide the Code from its former 2 parts into 3 parts. The new third part extended coverage to transactions 'which effect funds transfers to or from or between accounts at institutions by remote access through electronic equipment'.[32] For example, consumer EFT transactions involving telephone and computer banking, and funds transfers using stored value products, such as smart cards and digital cash.

In view of the escalating incidence of unauthorised EFT transactions and non-compliance with the *EFT Code* by financial institutions, arguably the EFT Working Group missed a unique opportunity to consider fully whether formal legislative regulation along USA lines may be appropriate for Australia. Accordingly, this book is concerned with evaluating the efficacy of current

---

25 Ibid 4-5.

26 Pursuant to: Treasury and the Australian Competition and Consumer Commission, Electronic Funds Transfer Report (1988).

27 Australian Securities and Investments Commission, Discussion Paper, above n 15, 14-16.

28 Ibid.

29 Australian Securities and Investments Commission, Second Draft Paper on an Expanded EFT Code of Conduct and Commentary (2000) 27.

30 Ibid 9-11.

31 Electronic Funds Transfer Code of Conduct (1989) (revised 2001, amended 2002).

32 Australian Securities and Investments Commission, Second Draft Paper on EFT, above n 29, 9-11.

consumer EFT regulatory arrangements in Australia using an extended, integrated multi-disciplinary approach. This integrated multi-disciplinary approach Incorporates critical comparative law method, together with recognised economic assessment criteria and regulation theory (the reader is referred to Section 1.6 below where the proposed research methods are introduced).

Ultimately, though, given the significant increase in the incidence of unauthorised EFT transactions in Australia in recent years,[33] and, in non-compliance by financial institutions with the *EFT Code* at large,[34] it would seem necessary that above all else, the fundamental EFT problem of how to apportion loss (where there is an absence of evidence or the evidence of both parties is deadlocked) even if not be legislated for, then at least be more clearly outlined in the imminent comprehensive review of Australia's *EFT Code* by ASIC.

As stated at the outset, to address these controversial issues, this book presents a multi-disciplinary methodology and subsequent analysis. The first method adapted is the critical comparative law method to undertake a comparative legal analysis of the current 'self-regulation' of the consumer EFT system in Australia by means of an industry code of conduct, the *EFT Code*, with the USA that has approached the regulation of EFT in marked contrast via broad, substantive legislation in the form of the *US EFT Act*. Given that only the USA and Denmark have been identified as having specific legislation covering EFT, it is submitted that because only the USA operates within a comparable, common law-based legal system (Denmark operating under a civil law-based system and whose legislation appears to be more focused on commercial rather than consumer EFT use), the USA provides the most striking comparison given they approach the same EFT problems as Australia, but with a markedly different regulatory response.

Further, there is not only a dearth of literature on a comparative approach to international consumer EFT regulation (refer to the literature review in Chapter 2 where this assertion is supported in detail), moreover, there is no published research on a particular and substantive comparative analysis between the contrasting Australian and USA regulation of unauthorised consumer EFT issues. The pre-existing literature is also incomplete in that the focus has typically been on a narrow 'legal studies' approach to analysing EFT regulatory issues and does not properly take into account comparative law, economic, social, ethical or administrative considerations, which, as is argued in this book, can be of utility in designing or formulating a more efficient or optimal set of rules for EFT. Moreover, the literature review in Chapter 2 has revealed significant gaps in the legal studies approach as well, with the limited prior research being dated and exhibiting a disparate and domestic-only focus, prepared largely in isolation by the relevant stakeholders involved. Accordingly, there is a need for a broader, more thorough approach to analysing the many controversial and complex EFT regulatory issues. This book attempts to draw together these strands using multi-disciplinary techniques including comparative law method, economic criteria and

[33] Ibid 6.

[34] Ibid 56, 63.

regulation theory methods, as well as administrative, social and ethical considerations.

1.2 Aims of the research in this book

In view of both the deterioration in EFT financial institution compliance and consumer complaints and the rise in use of consumer EFT services in Australia with a marked shift away from traditional paper-based payment methods,[35] and the limitations of the pre-existing legal studies method, the aims of this multi-disciplinary, comparative study are:

- to develop an extended, integrated multi-disciplinary approach, incorporating: the above comparative legal analysis, economic efficiency and loss allocation criteria, a regulation cost/benefit analysis and also taking account of administrative, social and ethical considerations;
- to critically review the adequacy of general paper-based principles of the common law as they relate to unauthorised consumer EFT transactions;
- to examine the rationales for government regulation of unauthorised consumer EFT transactions and the economics of liability allocation;
- to undertake a detailed comparative legal analysis of the substantive provisions of the *EFT Code* and *US EFT Act* using actual case examples concerning unauthorised EFT transactions from the Australian Banking Industry Ombudsman ('ABIO') and litigated cases in the USA; and
- to report specific recommendations, on the basis of the findings from this research, to better address the regulation of unauthorised consumer EFT transactions in Australia based on the multi-disciplinary methods and analysis.

1.3 Definitions

EFT emerged as a new technology in the mid 1970s in the USA and the early 1980s in Australia. A technology essentially joining banking, communications and computer systems. The term loosely covers a system which is replacing paper symbols of value such as cheques, withdrawal slips and other payment vouchers with 'invisible' symbols capable of being processed by computers.[36]

Geva usefully defines an EFT as follows:[37]

---

35 See, eg, Australian Securities and Investments Commission, Report of Compliance with the Payments System Codes of Practice and the EFT Code of Conduct, 1999/2000 (2001).

36 Australian Consumers Association, EFT in Australia: Issues and Problems (1984) 1.

37 Geva, above n 4, 392.

> [A]n electronic funds transfer is one that is initiated when a bank customer, acting as a sender, transmits payment instructions to the sending bank's computer from a terminal. Such communication from the customer to the computer of the customer's bank can take place from:
> (1) a public access terminal, usually either an automated teller machine (ATM);
> (2) a point-of-sale (POS) terminal at a retail establishment; or
> (3) an exclusive-access terminal used solely by one sender and located at the sender's place of business or home, which could be the sender's own computer or, at the other extreme, a simple telephone or television set.

In the USA, § 1693a(6) of the *US EFT Act* defines the term 'Electronic Funds Transfer' as meaning any:

> [T]transfer of funds, other than a transaction originated by check, draft, or similar paper instrument, which is initiated through an electronic terminal, telephone instrument or computer or magnetic tape so as to order, instruct, or authorize a financial institution to debit an account.

The definition of an EFT transaction in the Australian *EFT Code* is set out in clause 1.2. It would appear to be more cumbersome and less specific than that in the USA:

> A funds transfer is the transfer of value to or from an EFT account [an EFT account is defined elsewhere in the Code] including between two EFT accounts or between an EFT account and another type of account.

A more explicit definition was in clause 1.1 of the previous *EFT Code* (1989) which, although excluded newer technology such as Internet and telephone banking, nevertheless provided a more concise and explicit definition: [38]

> [T]his code applies to transactions intended to be initiated by an individual through an electronic terminal by the combined use of an EFT plastic card and a personal identification number (PIN).

The coverage of both the *US EFT Act* and the *EFT Code* does not apply to credit cards (other than the extent to which they are used as EFT cards).

For each EFT transaction, the sender (or consumer's) instructions are typically authenticated by means of an access device (eg, a secret code or PIN), either alone, or more usually in conjunction with a physical device, such as an EFT card, which is inserted at the terminal. Cards are primarily used at publicly accessed ATMs or EFTPOS terminals and in each case authentication is immediately followed by verification by the financial institution (eg, a bank) according to its own security procedures. Thereafter, the financial institution proceeds to execute the instructions and carry out the EFT transaction.[39]

---

[38] Electronic Funds Transfer Code of Conduct (original, 1989).

[39] See, generally, the discussion in Geva, above n 4, 392-6.

The present study, though, is more particularly concerned with an 'unauthorised EFT transaction'. This occurs when the EFT transaction is initiated, and subsequently authenticated by the financial institution, but without the authority of the consumer and which is nevertheless carried out.[40] It follows that an unauthorised EFT transaction must emanate from someone, a third party, who assumed control of the access device unlawfully or bypassed the access device altogether. Such a person may be known to the true consumer or may be a total stranger.[41] Therefore, any effective entry of the access device or card and use of the correct code or PIN, even where it may be carried out by an unauthorised person to whom it may have become available unlawfully, appears to the financial institution as a valid authentication. Thus, as Geva notes,[42] electronic authentication is a means of *legitimising* the action of that person, but not of *identifying* him or her as a manual signature on a cheque does because it is individual to the signer. In addition, it should be said that 'unauthorised electronic funds transfers' ought to be distinguished from properly authenticated instructions containing unauthorised or unintended contents. In principle, discrepancies in the contents of otherwise properly authenticated payment instructions are at the customer's risk and responsibility.

Two further important and controversial terms also require definition. Central to this book' inquiry are: (i) the 'burden (or onus) of proof'; and (ii) the related term of establishing proof 'on the balance of probability' in the event of an unauthorised EFT transaction.

For 'burden of proof', under the common law adversarial or accusatorial system, this is the duty of one party (usually the party bringing proceedings against another) to make out the case against the other party and to prove to the tribunal of fact (ie, the court or adjudicator) that the case has been established.[43] Thus, the burden of proof arguably has two key components: (i) the evidential burden; and (ii) the legal burden. The evidential burden denotes which party has the burden of adducing evidence and hence the burden of establishing a prima facie case on that issue. Central to this book is the examination of the contrasting approaches taken in Australia and the USA to assigning this burden between the financial institution and consumer. The legal burden is a 'persuasive burden' on that party to satisfy the tribunal of fact to make a finding in good conscience on the 'balance of probability'. The 'balance of probability' is the prescribed test for proving an unauthorised EFT transaction in the Australian *EFT Code* (clause 5). This difficult and problematic threshold test (as discussed in detail in Chapter 4) may be defined as follows:[44]

---

40 Ibid.

41 Ibid 394.

42 Ibid 395.

43 M Aronson and J Hunter, Litigation: Evidence and Procedure (6th ed, 1998), 698-9, 716-23; and, see, J D Heydon, Cross on Evidence (7th Australian ed, 2004); Butterworths, Concise Australian Legal Dictionary (2nd ed, 2000) 44, 60; and the Definitions provisions of the Evidence Act 1995 (Cth).

44 Aronson and Hunter, above n 43, 716-23; and see Rejfek v McElroy (1965) 112 CLR 517; and Briginshaw v Briginshaw (1938) 60 CLR 336.

[T]he weighing up and comparison of the likelihood of the existence of competing facts or conclusions. A fact is proved to be true on the balance of probabilities if its existence is more probable than not, or if it is established by a preponderance of probability or to the reasonable satisfaction of the tribunal of fact.

1.4 Research problem and conceptual framework

Using comparative legal and economic analysis methods, how can the Australian EFT Code of Conduct more appropriately balance the rights and obligations of users and providers of EFT in the event of an unauthorised consumer EFT transaction?

A diagrammatic presentation of how this research problem will be addressed is as follows:

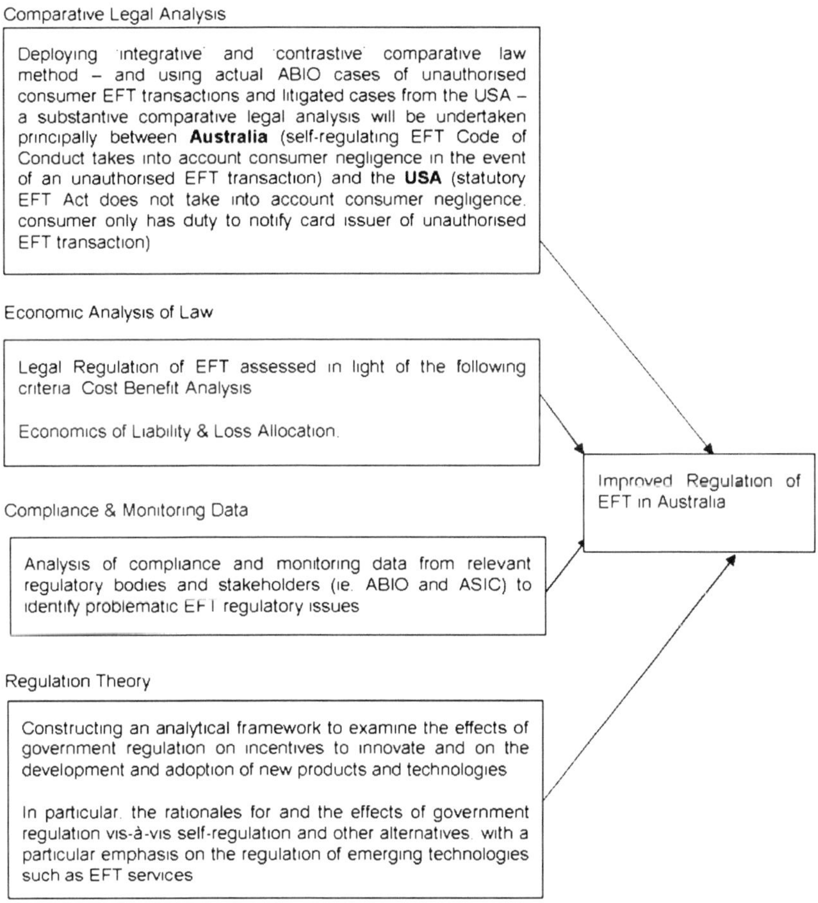

Figure 1.1. Conceptual Framework to Address the Research Problem

The above Figure 1.1 illustrates the integrated multi-disciplinary research methods and data that will be employed in this study in order to assess various regulatory options and ultimately to construct an efficient or optimal regulatory framework. In particular, using an adapted critical comparative law method, a comparative analysis of the substantive provisions of the *EFT Code* and *US EFT Act* will be undertaken (see Chapter 4).

A further in-depth analysis of EFT regulatory options using other disciplinary criteria will also be carried out (see Chapter 5). Namely, by employing economic efficiency criteria, regulation cost-benefit considerations, examining the rationales for government regulation, exploring whether 'market failure' is prevalent in the EFT system, a discussion of possible consumer protection alternatives, and, finally, examining the roles of ethics, administrative feasibility and social acceptability in formulating financial rules.

1.5 Contributions of this book

Acknowledging the significant increase in the use of consumer EFT payment methods in preference to paper-based payment methods and the continued rise in the incidence of unauthorised EFT transactions in Australia, it is submitted that this book will lead to a significant contribution to knowledge in this field because it will be the first study to:

- employ a multi-disciplinary approach (ie, comparative law, economic analysis, regulation theory, administrative and social feasibility and ethical methods) to the common core problem of regulating unauthorised consumer EFT transactions;
- undertake a detailed comparative legal analysis of the divergent regulatory approaches of Australia and the USA;
- utilise current EFT case examples, monitoring and compliance data sourced from the relevant stakeholder and regulatory bodies;
- examine consumer EFT regulatory issues in the context of policy considerations and the rationales for government regulation; and
- advance findings and recommendations for improved consumer EFT regulation in Australia using comparative law method, economic efficiency/ liability allocation criteria, regulation cost/benefit analysis, ethical and other considerations.

The quest for better loss allocation rules in EFT regulation in Australia is particularly relevant because the *EFT Code* is overdue for review by its regulator, ASIC (clause 24.1(a) of the revised *EFT Code* (effective 1 April 2002) stipulated that ASIC would undertake a review within 2 years). Accordingly, this book will be the first review of the revised *EFT Code* and the first to do so using multi-disciplinary tools.

Moreover, despite the new Australian *EFT Code's* firm intention to address pre-existing EFT financial institution compliance and consumer complaint problems, ASIC's latest 2003/2004 report highlights a further dramatic rise in the incidence of reported unauthorised EFT transactions by consumers (in both absolute and proportional terms), as well as a significant increase in non-compliance by financial institutions with the *EFT Code's* requirements.[45]

It is also telling justification for this book that in the USA, the central bank, the Federal Reserve, contends that despite EFT debit's rapid growth and prominence, the determinants and repercussions of EFT debit use have largely escaped academic scrutiny.[46]

1.6 Research method and the new multidisciplinary approach

The research method (described in detail in Chapter 3) adopted for this book is an extended, integrated multi-disciplinary approach incorporating: (i) critical comparative law; (ii) an economic analysis of law (based on cost benefit analysis (discussed in Chapter 5)) and regulation theory; and (iii) a consideration of ethical principles, administrative feasibility and social desirability in formulating rules.

In existing studies of law, these methods are either partly adapted or completely overlooked in a particular research work. In the present study, all of these methods are adapted in an integrated way. In this sense, the multi-disciplinary research approach adapted in this study is an innovative and integrated approach with the intention that it will drive the debate on an appropriate EFT regulatory framework forward.

First, the comparative law method adopted reflects the belief that, for this problem, similar yet divergent consumer EFT regulation systems can benefit from each others' experience. That is, having identified a 'common core problem'[47] shared by Australia and the USA, the preferred comparative law approach is one that could be described as the 'critical comparative law' approach; one that not only seeks to identify the differences, but observes the possibilities for some convergence.[48] Thus, common elements are sought ('integrative comparative law') just as much as differences stressed ('contrastive comparative law').[49] Further, it becomes apparent that because a legal rule operates well in one legal system it does not necessarily mean that it will operate equally well in another. Of particular

[45] See, eg, Australian Securities and Investments Commission, Report of Compliance with the EFT Code of Conduct, 2003/2004 (2005).

[46] Federal Reserve Bank of New York, above n 3.

[47] M Bussani, 'Current Trends in European Comparative Law: The Common Core Approach' (1998) 21 Hastings International and Comparative Law Review 785.

[48] R B Schlesinger, 'The Past and Future of Comparative Law' (1995) 43 American Journal of Comparative Law 477.

[49] Ibid.

interest also is the inherent tension between formal and informal regulatory approaches to a common core problem.

The second method: economic analysis of law and regulation theory, is concerned with whether the application of formal legislative regulation (ie, USA-style regulatory provisions) to EFT in Australia is meritorious. Beginning with an examination of the economic rationales for government regulation and the economics of liability allocation, this book presents an analytical framework for evaluating the effects of regulation on incentives to innovate and on the development and adoption of new technologies.

In applying economic criteria or analysis to law, various available mathematical and quantitative methods may be adapted, including the following: discounted cash flow or cost-benefit analysis, statistical methods, game theory, dynamic and statistical optimisation methods.[50] From all these available alternatives, the discounted cost-benefit method will be adapted in this study, given the suitability of this method for designing optimal EFT regulation in Australia.

In this book, the cornerstone of a methodology for economic efficiency is loss allocation theory and how losses which may flow from unauthorised or erroneous EFT transactions are distributed between the account institution and the user.[51] This book adopts the starting premise that a regime for allocating losses arising from unauthorised EFT transactions should, if it is possible to do so efficiently, distribute those losses between the user and the account institution, according to the circumstances of the loss.

In order to give careful consideration to an improved regulatory regime for unauthorised consumer EFT transactions in Australia, this book employs the economic principles generally espoused by Cooter and Rubin.[52] These principles are distilled from an economic efficiency approach to liability and loss allocation rules.

This book then moves on to consider another relevant analytical economic framework for effective EFT regulation: to examine the utility and effects of government regulation for better consumer protection, as well as on incentives to innovate and on the development and adoption of new products and technologies (ie, a preliminary regulation cost/benefit analysis).[53] In particular, the rationales for, and the effects of, government regulation, with a particular emphasis on the regulation of emerging technologies such as consumer EFT services.[54] To this end, the economics of technological advancement is considered[55] and how this may

---

50 See, eg, S M N Islam and C S Y Mak, Normative Health Economics – A New Pragmatic Approach to Cost Benefit Analysis, Mathematical Modelling and Applications (2006).

51 See, eg, Australian Securities and Investments Commission, Discussion Paper, above n 15.

52 R D Cooter and E L Rubin, 'A Theory of Loss Allocation for Consumer Payments' (1987) 66 Texas Law Review 63.

53 See, eg, K E Case and R C Fair, Principles of Economics (1989).

54 Board of Governors of the Federal Reserve, Report to Congress, above n 9, 7.

55 See, eg, R M Solow, 'Technical Change and the Aggregate Production Function' (1957) 39 Review of Economics and Statistics 312, 312-320.

influence the rate of economic growth generally.[56] Yet the book will at all times seek to contemplate the economics of EFT product and technological developments in light of the regulatory challenges posed.[57]

That is, in terms of the rationale for formal government regulation, EFT can readily be viewed as affording a convenient, low-cost alternative to traditional banking yet still require some form of government regulation where there is so-called 'market failure'[58] due to both 'internal' as well as 'external' costs and benefits[59] which may accrue to parties both directly and not directly involved in the EFT system.[60]

The questions then posed are: is government intervention itself able to remedy market failure?[61] And are there any possible unforeseen or adverse consequences?[62] Thus, even when it could be argued that market failure necessitates some form of government intervention, it must still be seen in the context of both its costs as well as its benefits.[63] The economics of requiring EFT providers to disclose and disseminate additional notices and information relating to EFT regulation is also briefly addressed.[64]

The economic assessment also addresses the likelihood of regulatory compliance costs being transferred to, or recovered from, EFT consumers.[65] In the event that they cannot economically or feasibly do so, whether that of itself may lead to EFT providers limiting or ceasing to provide a full array of EFT services both current and intended.[66]

As part of the economic analysis of EFT regulatory measures, this book will also briefly draw on some qualitative and quantitative evidence regarding experience with the *US EFT Act*[67] and an empirical study from the USA concerning the costs of regulation by formal legislative means.[68] These results will be extrapolated for Australian conditions and are considered to be of utility in anticipating the likely effects of the imposition of a formal regulatory regime for EFT in Australia.

---

56 Ibid.

57 Board of Governors of the Federal Reserve, Report to Congress, above n 9, 7.

58 Case and Fair, above n 53, 295.

59 Ibid.

60 Ibid.

61 Board of Governors of the Federal Reserve, Report to Congress, above n 9, 10-11.

62 Ibid.

63 Ibid.

64 Ibid.

65 See, eg, Case and Fair, above n 53.

66 Board of Governors of the Federal Reserve, Report to Congress, above n 9, 10-11.

67 F J Schroeder, 'Compliance Costs and Consumer Benefits of the Electronic Funds Transfer Act: Recent Survey Evidence' (Report for the Board of Governors of the Federal Reserve System, 1985) 143.

68 See, eg, G Elliehausen, 'The Cost of Banking Regulation: A Review of the Evidence' (Working Paper for the Board of Governors of the Federal Reserve System, 1997); and J M Boyle, 'A Survey of the Mortgage Banking Industry Concerning the Costs and Benefits of Regulation' (Report for the USA Federal Trade Commission, 1982).

Using the above economic criteria, different policy options will be considered, including the option of relying on market forces,[69] and, whether, in light of the rapidity of new EFT products and services becoming available, that additional or more formal regulation is premature.[70]

A consideration of ethics, administrative feasibility and social acceptability in formulating EFT rules is also discussed.

This study also employs the recognised business research method known as the 'structured interview method'[71] to collect original data from the publications and staff of the six (6) major Australian financial institutions (ie, the principal EFT financial institutions in Australia) to supplement the secondary data collected for this multi-disciplinary qualitative study (this method is described in detail in Section 3.6 of Chapter 3). The 6 major Australian financial institutions dominate the Australian EFT market (ASIC's latest 2003/2004 report states that they account for 91% of all EFT transactions in Australia; see Chart 2.2 in Section 2.6 of Chapter 2). These are: the National Australia Bank, the Commonwealth Bank, the ANZ Bank, Westpac Bank, St George Bank and the Bendigo Bank. The results are discussed and analysed in Sections 4.1, 4.2 and 4.3 of Chapter 4, which focuses on the regulatory requirements governing the availability of EFT terms and conditions of use, continuing disclosure of EFT terms and conditions of use and the issuance of EFT cards and PINs. The tabulated results are appended to this book at Appendix 1.

1.7 Scope

As indicated, the recently revised *EFT Code* (2002) has extended its coverage to Internet and telephone banking transactions as well as to stored-value cards and credit cards in certain circumstances. However, in the absence of any meaningful data on either the use or the incidence of unauthorised transactions under these extended uses, this book focuses on EFT debit cards deployed in ATMs and EFTPOS terminals using a PIN as the authentication means, where the vast majority of transactions and problematic legal issues arise.

In evaluating the different approaches by the USA and Australia to the treatment of liability in the event of a disputed, unauthorised consumer EFT transaction, this book has principally drawn from the two relevant regulations directly: the *US EFT Act* (1978) and Australia's *EFT Code* (2001).

Whilst this book is not concerned with an exhaustive comparative analysis of all international EFT regulation measures, it does draw some limited comparisons with relevant regulations in other countries. As stated earlier, it is submitted that

---

69 See, eg, Board of Governors of the Federal Reserve, Report to Congress, above n 9.

70 Ibid.

71 J Collis and R Hussey, Business Research – A Practical Guide for Undergraduate and Postgraduate Students (2nd ed, 2003).

the USA provides the most striking comparison given they approach the same core EFT problems as Australia, but with a markedly different regulatory response.

1.8 Outline of the book

The balance of this book is organised as follows.

In Chapter 2, the prior literature on comparative consumer regulation of unauthorised EFT transactions will be examined, together with an overview of the risks and subsequent development of EFT regulation in Australia as well as identifying the key stakeholders and regulators and their role in the EFT system. This chapter also examines the inadequacy of the common law's general principles governing paper-based payment methods in dealing with EFT issues.

In Chapter 3, a new multi-disciplinary research method employed for this book will be discussed. This forms the analytical framework for examining the divergent regulatory responses of Australia and the USA using comparative law, economic criteria, ethical, administrative and social criteria and regulation theory methods.

In Chapter 4, a thorough comparative analysis of the substantive provisions of the Australian and USA regulations governing unauthorised EFT transactions will be presented. This section also uses actual case examples from the ABIO, together with litigated cases from the USA, to analyse the practical application and relative utilities of the contrasting regulatory approaches to apportioning liability.

Following the comparative legal analysis in Chapter 4, in Chapter 5, an analysis of EFT regulation in light of other multi-disciplinary criteria will be undertaken. Namely, using recognised economic (loss allocation, efficiency and cost/benefit) criteria, examining the rationales for government regulation, and, finally, a consideration of administrative, social and ethical principles in formulating EFT rules.

In Chapter 6, a more efficacious regulatory framework for the regulation of unauthorised consumer EFT transactions in Australia is put forward incorporating the research findings and advances some specific recommendations.

The summary and conclusion to the book will be presented in Chapter 7.

1.9 Conclusion

In this chapter, the foundations for the research undertaken for the present book are laid. The research problem, conceptual framework and research questions are introduced. Then the key basic definitions are presented, the research and contributions are justified, the new approach to legal rule formulation and research methods are briefly described and justified, and, finally, the scope and structure of the book are outlined. On these foundations, the book will proceed with a detailed description of the research.

Chapter 2. The EFT System and Regulatory Framework

As briefly discussed in the previous introductory chapter, there are limitations in the existing literature both in discussing EFT regulatory issues, generally, and in evaluating EFT regulatory options, in particular. The paucity of existing literature on EFT regulation omits any comparative and economic analysis, is somewhat dated, domestic-focused and mostly prepared in isolation by the various institutional stakeholders involved. EFT's emerging dominance of the payments system in Australia and internationally requires an extended contemporary approach to discussing and evaluating regulatory issues and options as part of the quest for a more efficacious regulatory system (which is described in detail in Chapters 3, 4 and 5).

Accordingly, this chapter is structured as follows: In Section 2.1, the prior literature on EFT regulation is discussed and its limitations are highlighted. The history and emergence of EFT as a preferred payment method is examined in Section 2.2 and in Section 2.3 the risks in the consumer payments system generally, and for EFT in particular, are discussed. The focus in Section 2.4 is on whether pre-existing paper-based common law and contractual principles, as between banker and customer, have relevance and application to EFT payments. The advent and evolution of the Australian *EFT Code of Conduct* is considered in Section 2.5. The role of ASIC as Australia's peak financial regulator is examined in Section 2.6 as well as examining the adverse trend prevalent in the ASIC EFT monitoring and compliance data. The discussion in Section 2.7 concerns the difficult role of the ABIO as the principal adjudicator of EFT disputes between financial institutions and consumers, while in Section 2.8, the Australian *Code of Banking Practice* is briefly reviewed to the extent that it relates, in small part, to the *EFT Code* and is also a self-regulating instrument. The role and relevance of the legislative force of the *ASIC Act* is considered in Section 2.9. In Section 2.10, the background and scope of the *US EFT Act* is examined and the conclusion to the chapter is presented in Section 2.11.

2.1 Prior literature and its limitations

The research undertaken for this book indicates that there is not only a dearth of literature on a comparative approach to international consumer EFT regulation, moreover, there is no published research on a particular and substantive comparative analysis between Australian and USA regulation of consumer EFT issues. Indeed, the relevant literature identified in Australia and the USA is largely domestic-focused, is fragmented and prepared by the relevant stakeholders in relative isolation reflecting their vested interests.

Accordingly, this research attempts to draw the strands together and proceeds by considering the aspects and adequacy of the current regulation of unauthorised EFT transactions in Australia, under its voluntary *EFT Code*, principally by reference to the relevant provisions of the *US EFT Act* and also:

- actual terms and conditions of use distributed by financial institutions;
- common law;
- Australian Code of Banking Practice (1993);
- other relevant Australian legislation (namely, the *Australian Securities and Investments Commission Act 2001* (Cth));
- other relevant overseas regulation of consumer EFT;
- 3 Commonwealth Government Working Group Reports on EFT ('the EFT Working Group') of 1985, 1986 and 1999;
- former Australian Payments System Council's ('APSC') and current Australian Securities and Investments Commission's („ASIC') annual reports up to and including 2005;
- summary of issues and example cases contained in the annual reports of the Australian Banking Industry Ombudsman ('ABIO'); and
- academic journal articles and industry commentaries of partial relevance.

Of this literature, only the 1999 EFT Working Group Discussion Paper[72] and a limited review of the *EFT Code* conducted for the ABIO published in a journal article by Sneddon,[73] have, in small part at least, contributed to debate in this area.

The EFT Working Group's 1999 Discussion Paper successfully put forward options for expanding the previous *EFT Code of Conduct* so that it covered all consumer electronic funds transfer transactions and not just ATM and EFTPOS transactions, as was the case. The EFT Working Group's objective was to make the *EFT Code* technologically neutral, to the extent possible, so that the same protections would apply regardless of whether a transaction involved, for example, the use of an ATM, the telephone or the Internet. Importantly, though, in its 1999 Discussion Paper, the EFT Working Group had not sought to review the *EFT Code* generally, or its approach to unauthorised ATM and EFTPOS transactions in particular, by reference to the *US EFT Act*. Indeed, in that Discussion Paper, the EFT Working Group specifically rejected the US approach, where, essentially, the user is only liable for delays in reporting lost or stolen devices or failing to report unauthorised transactions shown on a periodic statement. Rather, the project was

---

72 Australian Securities and Investments Commission, Discussion Paper, above n 15.

73 Martin Sneddon, 'A Review of the Electronic Funds Code of Conduct' (1995) 6 Journal of Banking and Finance Law and Practice 22.

confined to substantially retaining the approach of the previous *EFT Code*, but amending it to cover all forms of consumer EFT technologies as well as some amendments which take account of recent developments in the areas of privacy and dispute resolution.

The EFT Working Group's approach in its 1999 Discussion Paper, which was ultimately adopted in the revised *EFT Code* (effective 1 April 2002), was to divide the Code from its former 2 parts into 3 parts. The new third part extended coverage to transactions 'which effect funds transfers to or from or between accounts at institutions by remote access through electronic equipment'. For example, consumer EFT transactions involving telephone and computer banking, and funds transfers using stored value products, such as smart cards and digital cash.

Although the expanded coverage of the *EFT Code* to embrace related EFT access means is to be welcomed, the EFT Working Group report does not bear significantly on the scope and substance of this book.

This book also significantly differs from Sneddon's limited 1995 review of the *EFT Code*, which was based on 1994 EFT data and was prepared on behalf of the ABIO (including privileged access to the ABIO files and resources). It also predates the arrival of the recently revised *EFT Code* which came into effect on 1 April 2002. Indeed, it is noted that the new *EFT Code* has yet to be rigorously reviewed in any literature let alone subject to a detailed comparative analysis with markedly different regulation such as that provided in the *US EFT Act*.

Whilst Sneddon's research was similarly concerned with the *EFT Code's* approach to liability for unauthorised consumer EFT transactions, it was essentially restricted to a domestic-only review of the *EFT Code's* initial 5 years' operation. Sneddon did, though, share the proper conclusion that the *EFT Code* was inadequate by not clearly assigning a 'burden of proof' on either the financial institution or consumer and in not providing any guidance in the event of an 'evidentiary impasse' when a disputed EFT transaction has occurred. Sneddon's focus was on 'unclear' cases of whether the consumer contributed to a loss such as instances where the correct PIN is used at first attempt in an alleged unauthorised EFT and also where the consumer may have been involuntarily observed keying in the PIN to an EFT access terminal. Sneddon surmised that the *EFT Code* was ambiguous in assigning the burden of proof in these two instances.[74]

Moreover, it will be shown that the incidence of alleged unauthorised consumer EFT transactions has increased markedly over the intervening 10 years since Sneddon's paper was released.

---

[74] Ibid 37. See, also, the very brief commentary on the *EFT Code's* evidential problems in A L Tyree, *Banking Law in Australia* (3rd ed, 1998) 335, where Tyree similarly concludes that the ABIO's 'weight of information available' test in deciding EFT disputes to be logically flawed and supports the simple, straightforward USA approach. Therein, Tyree also refers to instances where the banks adduce evidence of the "correct PIN being used at first attempt" as the fundamentally flawed "one shot rule".

Elsewhere, this book extends the work of Tucker,[75] Geva[76] and White[77] in examining the adequacy of the general principles of the common law by analogy to a forged cheque in its application to an unauthorised EFT transaction.

Both Tucker and Geva concluded that the paper-based legal principles developed over several centuries are inadequate and particularly unhelpful for electronically-based transactions. Geva usefully articulated that the fundamental reason for this inadequacy has to do with the vastly different means and legal nature of 'authentication'.[78] Geva contended that electronic system access and the ensuing authentication using an EFT card and code is unlike a handwritten or manual signature on a paper-based instrument which is individual or peculiar to the signer and carries the mandate for the bank to effect payment.[79] Geva further stated that the electronic authentication is only a means of '*legitimising*' an action, but is not necessarily a valid '*identifier*' of the true customer.[80] This issue is explored further in Section 2.4.

In addition, White considered that EFT gives rise to entirely different systemic issues in the event of an unauthorised EFT transaction vis-à-vis the physical and legal position with cheques. In particular, problems with evidence of payment, liability for unauthorised transactions, computer malfunctions, security of the EFT system, loss of stop payment rights and errors in accounts.[81] These observations also predate the current regulatory arrangements under the revised *EFT Code* and are extended further in Section 2.4.1 of Chapter 2 and in Chapter 4.

---

75 Tucker, above n7.

76 Geva, above n 4, 394-5.

77 P F White, 'A Critique of the Self-Regulation of Electronic Funds Transfer in Australia' (MBus Minor Thesis, Victoria University of Technology 1997) 9.

78 Geva, above n 4, 394-5. Note also that 'electronic' or 'digital' authentication (eg, electronic signatures) and the consequences of their misuse have also been the subject of extensive discussion in e-commerce literature over the past decade. Many of the issues raised in this book – such as identity theft and identity fraud – are equally significant in commercial e-contracts where electronic or digital authentications have been permitted by legislative amendment under the Australian federal Electronic Transactions Act 1999 (Cth) as a result of traditional commercial requirements of a deed or seal not able to be replicated in an electronic environment. Indeed, technologically 'neutral' language appears to have been a significant legislative aim in drafting in Australia over the past 10 years, which has also produced tension in trying to treat paper and electronic documents as equivalents. For further discussion on e-commerce authentication and identity issues, see, eg, A L Tyree, The Law of Payment Systems (2000) 86-7, 151-2; and Leif Gamertsfelder, 'The Commonwealth Electronic Transactions Bill 1999: Ailments and Antidotes' (1999) 1 The Journal of Information Law and Technology 1.

79 Geva, above n 4, 394-5.

80 Ibid.

81 White, above n 77, 9.

2.2 Emergence of EFT

The USA led the way with the introduction of automatic teller machines ('ATM'/'ATMs') in the early 1970s by Bank of America and Citibank. The network of ATM's grew slowly at first, then eventually across the nation, together with Electronic Funds Transfer Point of Sale ('EFTPOS') terminals, by the end of that decade.[82]

In Australia, the first ATM was introduced by the Bank of New South Wales (now Westpac) in May 1980 and the first EFTPOS terminal in March 1984 also by Westpac.[83]

As a result, from an Australian perspective, consumers enjoy the convenience of EFT technology in the form of ATMs inside and outside banking hours to deposit, withdraw and transfer funds. In supermarkets, service stations and in an increasing number of retail outlets, payment for goods can be effected simply by swiping a card through EFTPOS terminals.[84]

In Australia, for instance, ASIC records that the number of EFT transactions rose from 996 million in 1995 to in excess of 1.64 billion in 2002[85] and a further rapid rise to 2.53 billion in 2004.[86] Indeed, the Reserve Bank of Australia ('RBA') recently observed that:

> In fact, the most striking trend within the retail payments sector over the last decade is the rapid decline in the use of cheques in Australia, from more than 80% of the dollar value of non-cash retail payments in 1995 to less than 30% in 2002. At the same time, the electronic [payments] system has expanded rapidly...rapid growth in overall EFT debit card usage of about 10% per year. [87]

This 'striking trend' has paralleled the experience in the USA. The preference for EFT services in the USA is evidenced by recent 2002 figures for use of EFT debit cards. The USA central bank, the Federal Reserve, observed that EFT debit cards have surpassed credit cards to become the most common form of card payment.[88] Overall, EFT debit was used for over 15.5 billion EFTPOS transactions totalling $700 billion in the year 2002. This represented about 35% of all EFT payment transaction volume and 12% of EFTPOS non-cash payments. Indeed, the Federal Reserve noted that EFT debit card's ascension has been sudden, with 47% of

---

82 Ibid.

83 W S Weerasooria, Banking Law and the Financial System in Australia (4th ed.1996) 124.

84 White, above n 77, 9.

85 Australian Securities and Investments Commission, Report of Compliance with the Payments System Codes of Practice and the EFT Code of Conduct, 2001/2002 (2003) 56.

86 Australian Securities and Investments Commission, Report of Compliance with the EFT Code of Conduct, 2003/2004 (2005).

87 Reserve Bank of Australia, Bulletin, above n 1, 1-2.

88 Federal Reserve Bank of New York, above n 3.

households using it by 2001, up from just 18% in 1995.[89] Moreover, the Federal Reserve predicts continued strong growth for EFT debit, while forecasting relatively weak growth in other payment mechanisms.[90]

Despite all this growth in, and preference for, EFT services in the USA, it is notable that the consumer problem of greatest concern across all modes in USA payment systems, indeed, the problem of greatest concern overall, is fraudulent transactions, and particularly identity theft.[91] In fact, 39% of consumer complaints to the USA Federal Trade Commission in 2003 were for identity theft, and consumers in the USA rate it as their highest priority among consumer issues, although the incidence of identity theft in *credit* cards actually has begun to level off. On the other hand, EFT debit card fraud in the USA is growing rapidly.[92]

The problems of EFT debit consumers are similar to those of EFT debit consumers in Australia, particularly with respect to the allocation of loss due to unauthorised use, identity theft and fraud.

Indeed, as stated, it is also telling for the justification of this book and its currency that the Federal Reserve also contends that despite EFT debit's rapid growth and prominence, the determinants and repercussions of EFT debit use have largely escaped academic scrutiny.[93]

As for consumers, there are also many advantages in favour of the financial institutions in the shift to electronic banking and the move towards the so-called 'cashless society'.[94] After the substantial initial capital investment in the technology, they are finding EFT much less expensive to operate than the traditional labour and paper-based systems."[95] Moreover, all major Australian and USA financial institutions are now actively scaling down their retail branches, thus heightening their reliance on electronic banking.[96]

Whilst the benefits of EFT to both financial institutions and consumers are clear, there are significant disadvantages for consumers in the progressive change to an electronic payments system.[97] For EFT brings with it risks quite different from those involved in a paper-based system.[98] In particular, problems with the issuance of EFT cards and PINs, evidence of payment, liability for unauthorised transactions, computer malfunctions, security of the system, loss of stop payment

[89] Ibid.

[90] Ibid.

[91] A S Rosenberg, Better than Cash? Global Proliferation of Debit and Prepaid Cards and Consumer Protection Policy (2005) Thomas Jefferson School of Law, San Diego USA <http://law.bepress.com/expresso/eps/766> at 29 January 2006.

[92] Ibid.

[93] Federal Reserve Bank of New York, above n 3.

[94] Federal Bureau of Consumer Affairs (Australia) A Cashless Society? Electronic Banking and the Consumer (1995) ch 7.

[95] L Procter, 'Reforming the Australian Payments System: The State of Play' (1993) 3 The Australian Banker 135, 135-40.

[96] White, above n 77, 9.

[97] Ibid.

[98] Ibid.

('countermand') rights and errors in accounts are among the central concerns of EFT consumer groups here and abroad and are the subject matter of this book.[99]

However, unlike the USA, which has specific legislation to regulate EFT, Australia has entered the age of electronic banking without any specific legislation.

2.3 Risks in the consumer payments system[100]

The consumer payment mechanisms available to consumers in Australia and the USA are subject to numerous risks that could result in harm to the consumer. First, some types of payment instruments have value in and of themselves, and the *loss* of these instruments through theft or other circumstances results directly in financial loss to the consumer. Second, the *unauthorised use* of an instrument or unauthorised access to an account could also lead to the consumer's financial loss. Third, an *error* may occur in the processing of a payment resulting in loss to the consumer. Fourth, a payment instrument may be *dishonoured* by the issuer or drawee. Finally, a consumer may unexpectedly be *unable to use* a particular payment mechanism, either because of technological problems or because the mechanism is not acceptable to the payee.[101]

A consumer who loses a bearer instrument will incur a direct financial loss.[102] The primary example of a bearer instrument is currency, which is legal tender. If a consumer loses currency, it will be replaced.[103] If currency is stolen, the consumer generally has no recourse outside of pursuing a civil or criminal action against the thief.

Credit and EFT debit cards generally have no value in and of themselves.[104] Consumers can usually get replacement credit cards and EFT debit cards quickly, under the rules that apply to each particular card's system. Financial institutions provide this service to make their products more attractive. Consumers may lose the entire balance on an EFT card and PIN if they are lost, stolen, or damaged. These risks are similar to the risk of losing currency, and consumers can reduce the risk by safeguarding their EFT card and PIN.[105] However, the conditions that may be damaging to a card (and the type of damage caused, such as demagnetisation) may be less obvious to consumers than the conditions that would damage currency.

---

99 Ibid.

100 This section draws both directly and extensively from the Board of Governors of the Federal Reserve, Report to Congress, above n 9, and from White, above n 77.

101 Board of Governors of the Federal Reserve, Report for Congress, above n 9, 29.

102 Ibid.

103 Ibid 30.

104 Ibid.

105 Ibid.

Consumers also face the risk of financial loss due to unauthorised use of a payment instrument, which may or may not result from the instrument being lost or stolen.[106] Unauthorised use is a relatively common problem for several types of payment instruments, such as cheques, EFT debit cards and credit cards.[107] For example, if blank cheques are stolen, the consumer is not liable on any cheque the consumer has not signed, placing the onus on the consumer's bank to inspect the drawer's signature. If a cheque is stolen and the payee's endorsement is forged, the ultimate liability falls on the bank that first accepts the cheque for deposit. If the cheque is returned to the bank of first deposit, that bank may seek restitution from the customer whose account was credited. Whereas with EFT cards, often an unauthorised user needs only the information from the card and not the card itself. Thus, consumers who are particularly concerned about theft or unauthorised use may choose to use payment instruments with refund capabilities, and they may be willing to pay for this extra degree of security in cases involving larger amounts of funds.

If an error occurs in the processing of a payment, the payment may be made to the wrong party or for the wrong amount.[108] With currency, the consumer generally has control over who receives the payment and how much is tendered.[109] For example, the consumer could make an error in the amount of currency tendered, but an error that is not detected by the consumer or the payee at the time of the transaction may be difficult to prove or correct later.

With cheques, various types of errors could occur.[110] For example, a consumer could mistakenly write a cheque for the incorrect amount. If the payee received payment for more than the amount actually owed, the drawer would likely have a claim for restitution against the payee. Similarly, the payee likely would continue to have a claim on the underlying obligation if the cheque were written for less than the amount owed.[111] Another type of cheque-related error could occur if a consumer's bank debits the consumer's account in error for more (or less) than the actual amount of a cheque.[112] Generally, it could be expected that discrepancies between the amount of a cheque and the amount charged to an account are corrected once either the bank or the consumer identifies the error.[113]

Malfunctions also could occur in the use of EFT cards. Such disruptions or malfunctions could cause a temporary inability to complete a payment or could cause financial losses.[114]

---

106 Ibid 31-2.
107 Ibid 31.
108 Ibid 32.
109 Ibid.
110 Ibid.
111 Ibid 32-3.
112 Ibid 32.
113 Ibid.
114 Ibid 33.

Consumers may face the risk that a particular payment instrument will be dishonoured by the issuer or drawee. Payment instruments may also be returned because of the default of the issuer or drawee. These risks generally do not exist with currency.[115]

It should also be stated that for various reasons, a consumer might be unable to use a particular payment mechanism.[116] This situation would not necessarily result in a financial loss to the consumer but might unexpectedly prevent a consumer from discharging a debt or obtaining goods or services, result in late fees or other penalties, or at the very least, cause embarrassment.[117]

A consumer might be unable to use a payment instrument because of a defect in the instrument. For example, a credit card or EFT debit card might have a demagnetized strip or a damaged chip, causing the card to be rejected by a card-reading machine. To encourage the use of their products, banks and other financial institutions generally provide replacements for damaged cards relatively quickly. By comparison, a damaged cheque may be delayed in the collection process if it cannot be handled by a cheque-sorting machine, but usually it is ultimately collected.

Consumers typically reduce risks that they will be unable to make payments by carrying more than one form of payment with them. In doing so, they must weigh the benefits of maintaining access to additional payment options against any inconvenience and fees involved in doing so.

2.4 Regulating liability for unauthorised EFT transactions

As stated in the literature review in Section 2.1, among the most controversial of EFT issues is liability in the event of an allegedly unauthorised EFT transaction. Because this area is so contentious, it is important to consider the policy foundations for allocating liability between consumers and financial institutions.

As already mentioned, an unauthorised transaction is one that is likely to profit a party other than the consumer. As will be evident shortly in the substantive analysis undertaken in Chapter 4, Australia and the USA have a markedly different regime for allocating losses arising from unauthorised EFT transactions. It will be submitted that neither properly take into account the circumstances of the loss. But, first, it is of utility to look at the historical common law banker-customer implied terms, which underpin the contract between bank and customer in both common law countries.

115 Ibid 33-4.
116 Ibid 35-6.
117 Ibid 35.

2.4.1 Historical perspective: a comparison with cheques

Some common law principles derived from paper-based payments (most commonly, cheques and bills of exchange) could possibly apply by analogy to EFT transactions. Briefly, these principles provide the following 'implied terms'.

- A financial institution is bound by a duty to properly recognise its customer's signature and so obey the mandate of its customer with an authority to debit the customer's account granted by a customer properly drawing his or her cheque and there are funds available to meet the cheque.[118] It is established that once the customer informs the bank of an anomaly in payment of a cheque, it is for the bank to prove that the customer erred.[119]
- A customer must take all usual and reasonable precautions in drawing his or her cheques so as to prevent fraud on a banker.[120] However, there is no higher standard imposed on a customer. The bank may not debit the account of the customer even if the customer has been careless in keeping the cheque-book.[121] For instance, there is no duty to take such precautions in the overall management and operation of the account (for example, in the storage of cheque books as opposed to the mere drawing of a cheque), nor does the customer have any duty to 'discover' forgeries.[122] There is, however, a duty by a customer to notify the bank immediately of any forgeries 'known' to the customer.[123]

Therefore, as the EFT working Group did observe: long before electronic account access, the common law had developed rules to distribute this loss in the case of banks acting on forged mandates. In broad terms, a forged signature was a nullity giving a bank no mandate from the customer. The customer was not liable for a forgery, unless the customer was estopped from denying the signature in limited circumstances, or had ratified the signature.[124] Thus, a financial institution acted on forged instructions at its own risk.

Whatever might have been the position for EFT reached under the common law by analogy to cheque cases discussed under (a) and (b) above, a consumer's 'mandate' has changed from a signature on paper to a PIN, which is an identifying feature 'external' to the consumer. But as Tyree inquired: is a card-PIN combination really just the substitution of one form of identification for another? This is so when the transaction proceeds according to the expectation of the parties, but the situation is very much different when the transaction goes wrong,

---

118 London Joint Stock Bank Ltd v Macmillan (1918) AC 777.

119 Commonwealth Trading Bank of Australia v Sydney Wide Stores Pty Ltd (1981)148 CLR 304.

120 Ibid.

121 Kepitigalla Rubber Estates Pty Ltd v The National Bank of India (1909) 2 KB 1010.

122 Tai Hing Cotton Mill Ltd v Lie Chong Hing Bank Ltd and Others (1986) AC 426, (1985) 2 All ER 947.

123 Greenwood v Martins Bank Ltd (1933) AC 51.

124 See, eg, Price v Neal (1762) 3 Burr 1354, 97 ER 871.

usually because of a misappropriation of the means of identification.[125] As stated earlier, Geva contends that electronic authentication is only a means of *legitimising* the action of that person, but not of *identifying* him or her as a manual signature on a cheque does because it is individual to the signer.[126] Accordingly, this technological development has had the following two significant effects on allocating liability for acting on unauthorised transactions:[127]

- It effectively displaced years of case law on the liability of financial institutions for acting on unauthorised transactions. It permitted institutions to create new rules for allocating liability by contract; and
- The choice of technology used often made it difficult, if not impossible, for parties, by ex post facto examination of the transaction, to gather evidence to evaluate whether an instruction was unauthorised or had been altered. There are two further aspects to this point:
  - It is often impossible to distinguish an unauthorised instruction from an authorised instruction (for example, if a 4-digit PIN is the authentication mechanism, the PIN is identical whether keyed in by an authorised or unauthorised user whereas a forged signature may be examined at the time of the transaction and afterwards to differentiate it from a genuine signature); and
  - The transaction audit trail does not necessarily collect data that is helpful in distinguishing authorised from unauthorised use.

Understandably, financial institutions were, and are, concerned about the scope for customer fraud created by these developments. Both these developments enabled card-issuing institutions to shift risk onto consumers. First, the consumer had no records to prove a transaction was not authorised, whereas the financial institution's records usually showed that the correct authentication mechanism was used (but not by whom). Secondly, the new rules on liability allocation were determined by contract between the financial institution and consumer.

2.4.2 Written terms and conditions of use

In Australia and the USA, contracts with individual customers typically made consumers liable for any transaction authenticated by use of the EFT card and PIN, regardless of loss or theft of the EFT card or surreptitious observation of the PIN.[128]

---

125 A L Tyree, Banking Law in Australia (3rd ed, 1998) 330.

126 Geva, above n 4, 395.

127 Section from: Australian Securities and Investments Commission, Discussion Paper, above n 15, 27.

128 Ibid; and see A L Tyree, Digital Cash (1997) 137.

In most Western countries, there was a consumer/political reaction to this initial one-sided allocation of risk in consumer electronic banking contracts. This was based on the recognition that:[129]

- Consumers do not have the ability or sophistication to negotiate balanced liability allocation rules with financial institutions; and
- The 4 or 6-digit PIN chosen by financial institutions as a cost-effective mass-distribution authentication method for consumers is a relatively weak and inherently insecure authentication procedure, compared with other authentication mechanisms such as biometric identifiers (eg, voice or eye identification). It is liable to be guessed or surreptitiously observed over the shoulder at an EFT terminal or discovered from a written record kept by the consumer as an 'aide memoire', and then misused by a third party to perpetrate unauthorised transactions. If a financial institution chooses to use a lower cost authentication method with a higher risk of facilitating unauthorised use, the financial institution should bear some of that risk rather than pass it all onto the consumers.

As a result, in the 1970s and 1980s, that contractual risk allocation for consumer banking transactions was reversed or revised by self-regulation or legislation in many Western countries, most notably in the USA with the *US EFT Act* (1978) and the Danish *Payment Cards Act* (1984), or less formal regulation such as the EFT Codes of Conduct in Australia and New Zealand and the *Code of Banking Practice* (1992) in the United Kingdom. It could be said that these generally produced a more balanced or pro-consumer risk allocation. Indeed, this trend has continued with the European Commission's Recommendation of 30 July 1997, *Boosting Customers' Confidence in Electronic Means of Payment in the Single Market.*[130]

Accordingly, the history of electronic remote account access products in Western countries shows that freedom of contract and industry self-regulation alone had not produced fair and acceptable liability allocation rules in consumer contracts.[131] If this view is correct, it would then follow that regulation or regulatory persuasion of some form has been required to redress the balance in institution-authored contractual allocations, while ensuring financial institution institutions are protected from customer fraud.

[129] Australian Securities and Investments Commission, Discussion Paper, above n 15, 28.

[130] European Commission's Recommendation: Boosting Customers' Confidence in Electronic Means of Payment in the Single Market (1997) COM (97) 353.

[131] Australian Securities and Investment Commission, Discussion Paper, above n 15, 28-29.

2.5 Evolution of the EFT code of conduct

The issues involved in the proliferation of consumer EFT technology have prompted much debate at government, banking industry and consumer levels.[132]

As far back as 1981, the *Campbell Committee of Inquiry into the Australian Financial System* acknowledged the then recent advent of electronic banking and the increasing importance EFT systems could assume in the Australian payments system.[133] The Committee considered that the development of such systems posed important policy and regulatory questions on the rights and obligations of the different parties involved in EFT transactions. However, the Committee admitted that it had not undertaken sufficient work to determine whether there was a need to regulate. Its recommendation that a taskforce comprising representation from the Commonwealth Government, the States and the Territories be established to assess the impact of EFT systems was not taken up.

The EFT issue was again revisited in the 1983 *Martin Group Review of the Australian Financial System* with the Review concluding that while legislation was premature, a Payments System Council was a necessary implementation to deal with the broad issues of EFT.[134]

Prior to the advent of the first *EFT Code*, 3 government-sponsored bodies produced reports discussing the need to regulate the relationship between financial institutions and EFT consumers. The first initiative was a report prepared at State level, the *Draft Guidelines for Consumer Protection in EFT Systems*, prepared by the New South Wales and Victorian consumer affairs ministries (SCOCAM: Standing Committee of Consumer Affairs Ministers),[135] the contents of which went on to become the basis of the initial *EFT Code of Conduct* in 1989.

At the national level, the Commonwealth Government finally sought to investigate the growing debate and need to assess regulation by establishing an interdepartmental Working Group chaired by Treasury, to assess the operation of the EFT system, and, more particularly, to examine the rights and obligations of the users and providers of EFT systems. The Working Group produced a detailed report in 1985[136] and a second, updated report in 1986.[137]

The Working Group took the view that legislation was not warranted at that time and that whilst some uniform practices should be established by financial

---

[132] See, eg, White, above n 77.

[133] See Commonwealth, Committee of Inquiry into the Australian Financial System, Final Report (1981).

[134] See Commonwealth, Review of the Australian Financial System, Final Report (December, 1983).

[135] Commonwealth, Standing Committee of Consumer Affairs Ministers, Draft Guidelines for Consumer Protection in Electronic Funds Transfer System (January, 1986).

[136] Report of the Working Group Examining the Rights and Obligations of the Users and Providers of Electronic Funds Transfer Systems (October 1985).

[137] Second Report of the Working Group Examining the Rights and Obligations of the Users and Providers of Electronic Funds Transfer Systems (September 1986).

institutions offering EFT products and services, the necessary measures could be left to the financial institutions themselves to implement.

However, in an effort to forestall SCOCAM's momentum towards uniform State-based legislation, the Working Group invited SCOCAM to collaborate with the Working Group.[138] The combined State and Commonwealth group then produced a voluntary code known officially as the *Recommended Procedures to Govern the Relationship between the Users and Providers of EFT Systems*. In essence, this so-called 'unofficial code' was in terms similar to that of the SCOCAM Draft Guidelines and was endorsed by the Commonwealth and all State and Territory Governments.

Another major report released in 1986 was the report of the Australian Science and Technology Council ('ASTEC') to the Prime Minister.[139] This was a comprehensive document dealing also with the social and economic implications of EFT systems, but shared the combined Working Group's conclusion that EFT legislation would be premature in Australia.

In December 1988, the then Trade Practices Commission ('TPC') (now the Australian Competition and Consumer Commission ('ACCC')) released a report entitled: *Finance Industry Code of Conduct on Electronic Funds Transfer Services: An Assessment by the Trade Practices Commission*.[140] The report made a number of suggestions to modify the draft *EFT Code* and the way in which it should be monitored and administered.

The final *EFT Code* was the product of this somewhat protracted and fragmented process.

Upon implementation of the *EFT Code* in December 1989, the first subsequent report was a review of the initial 6 months of the *EFT Code's* operation: a *Report by the Treasury and* (the then) *the Trade Practices Commission on the Operation of the EFT Code of Conduct*.[141] Its specific purpose was to examine how effectively EFT financial institutions had implemented the *EFT Code* arrangements in its first 6 months. It recommended changes to tightening the procedures governing EFT card and PIN distribution were endorsed and incorporated into the *EFT Code* which was updated to reflect these amendments in January 1991. Nevertheless, the Report otherwise concluded that 'substantial progress has been achieved by financial institutions and their associations towards implementing the *EFT Code* arrangements, including monitoring and reporting procedures'.[142]

The Treasury and TPC review also properly acknowledged that it was still too early to adequately assess compliance with the *EFT Code* and that another review should be undertaken based on 'several years experience'.[143] Despite several

138 A L Tyree, Banking Law in Australia (2nd ed, 1995) 284.

139 Australian Science and Technology Council, Towards a Cashless Society (May 1986).

140 Finance Industry Code of Conduct on Electronic Funds Transfer Services: An Assessment by the Trade Practices Commission (1988) 1-15.

141 Commonwealth, Report by the Treasury and the Trade Practices Commission on the Operation of the EFT Code of Conduct (1989) 1-5.

142 Commonwealth, Report by the Treasury and the Trade Practices Commission on the Operation of the EFT Code of Conduct (July 1990) 2.

143 Ibid.

prognostications by the ACCC, that review was not undertaken for almost 10 years until July1999.

Finally, in July 1999, the EFT Working Group released a draft expanded *EFT Code* in a Discussion Paper,[144] which put forward options for expanding the previous *EFT Code* to cover all consumer electronic funds transfer transactions and not just ATM and EFTPOS transactions, as was the case. The new 'draft code' took account of the comments received in submissions and meetings with all stakeholders.

The EFT Working Group stated that a crucial distinction had to be drawn between services, which through electronic equipment effect payment by funds transfers to or from or between accounts at institutions using remote access to accounts (the focus of the former *EFT Code*), and new electronic payment products which effect payment by the transfer of pre-paid value (eg, stored value card balances or digital coins), but do not involve access to, or the transfer of funds to or from, accounts at account institutions. Payments using these new electronic payment products can be likened to payments by the physical transfer of currency which do not involve the adjustment of accounts at account institutions to effect the payment.

The key objective of the draft was to create a 'technology neutral' *EFT Code* which covers all forms of consumer electronic funds transfer transactions (ie, to apply to all electronic funds transfers to or from or between accounts at institutions by remote access through electronic equipment). For example, in addition to ATM and EFTPOS transactions, it covers telephone and Internet banking, credit card payments over the Internet as well as stored value products such as smart cards and digital cash. Its recommendations were fully adopted in the revised *EFT Code* (effective 1 April 2002).

2.6 Australian Securities and Investments Commission ('ASIC')

Financial institution compliance with the *EFT Code* is monitored by the Australian Securities and Investments Commission ('ASIC'), a Commonwealth Government regulatory body. ASIC has been monitoring the *EFT Code* since 1998, assuming control from the Australian Payments System Council ('APSC'), an arm of the Reserve Bank of Australia.

ASIC requires that all EFT card issuing institutions report annually on various aspects of EFT by completing a detailed annual check list of 69 questions covering each clause of the *EFT Code*. In the 1999/2000 review year, ASIC stated that compared to the previous reporting period (1998/1999), the incidence of

144 Australian Securities and Investments Commission, Discussion Paper, above n 15, 36.

reported non-compliance has increased in the case of the EFT Code.[145] Indeed, ASIC stated in its review that the largest number of disputes (of all ASIC monitored payments system codes) related to PIN-based EFT transactions.[146]

ASIC also noted that the number of complaints under the EFT Code increased significantly with financial institutions reporting a total of 106,719 complaints in 1999/2000, compared with a total of 73,125 complaints in 1998/1999.[147] This represents an increase from 42 complaints per million transactions in 1998/1999 to 64 complaints per million transactions over the reporting period. About two-thirds of the EFT complaints (67,193) in 1999/2000 related to system malfunctions, and most of these were resolved in favour of the consumer. Twenty-eight per cent of EFT complaints (30,375) involved unauthorised ATM and EFTPOS transactions.[148]

Of particular relevance to this book, was the data on complaints about unauthorised transactions. The data exhibited an increase from the previous reporting period overall, however, trends varied between banks, building societies and credit unions. The majority of these complaints were resolved in favour of the financial institution; the most common reason being consumer negligence with their PIN.[149] In fact, in the ASIC reporting year 2001/2002, there was a large increase in the number of cases where the consumer was considered liable, and the liability was a result of negligence with the PIN. This equated to an increase of 20.1%.

Indeed, ASIC estimated that the number and incidence of complaints about unauthorised EFT transactions has increased by at least 75%.[150] ASIC also suggested that the number of complaints about unauthorised transactions had increased from no more than 10 complaints per million transactions in 1998/1999 to 18 complaints per million EFT transactions in 1999/2000[151] and to 41 per million in 2001/2002.[152] While these statistics may appear insignificant (especially when compared to cheque payments),[153] the ASIC data illustrates that the trend is increasing not just in absolute terms, but in proportional terms.

In its recently released compliance report (December 2005),[154] ASIC qualifies its findings with the following comments:

---

145 Australian Securities and Investments Commission, Report of Compliance with the Payments System Codes of Practice and the EFT Code of Conduct, 1999/2000 (2001) 4.

146 Ibid.

147 Ibid 6.

148 Ibid.

149 Ibid.

150 Ibid 63.

151 Ibid.

152 Australian Securities and Investments Commission, Compliance with the Payments System Codes of Practise and the EFT Code of Conduct, 2001/2002 (2003) 59.

153 Weerassoria above n 83, 114.

154 Australian Securities and Investments Commission, Report of Compliance with the EFT Code of Conduct, 2003/2004 (2005) 2.

Since the revised EFT Code came into operation in 2002 there have been problems associated with data collection and quality. Because of this, only limited comparisons are made with previous reporting periods and these are highly qualified. ASIC is working with subscribing institutions to improve the quality and comparability of monitoring data.

Despite the data collection problems, as in previous years, reported levels of compliance with the *EFT Code* remain high overall. The reported numbers of complaints per million transactions was 55 although the lack of data provided in some instances means that this figure may be under or over stated and making trend comparisons on this issue would be unwise.

Notwithstanding this express qualification, ASIC still observed a marked deterioration in compliance by EFT financial institutions in the 2003/2004 reporting year, together with a significant corollary increase in the incidence of reported unauthorised EFT transactions up to 63 per million EFT transactions (compared with 41 per million in the previous reporting period 2001/2002). Indeed, ASIC formerly reported its concerns that EFT financial institutions were in breach of many of the *EFT Code's* requirements and that they have now been forced to intervene and directly coerce EFT financial institutions to comply.[155]

In terms of aggregate EFT transaction data, ASIC reported that EFT financial institutions reported 2.5 billion EFT transactions in the year to 31 March 2004.[156]

As Chart 2.1 below exhibits, ATM and EFTPOS transactions far exceeded other types of EFT transactions. However, ASIC noted that several institutions (particularly larger institutions) had difficulty reporting telephone and Internet transactions.[157] Therefore, telephone and Internet transactions are probably understated in Chart 2.1.

The source of data for both Chart 2.1 and Chart 2.2: Australian Securities and Investments Commission, *Report of Compliance with the EFT Code of Conduct, 2003/2004* (2005).

155 Ibid.

156 Ibid 18.

157 Ibid.

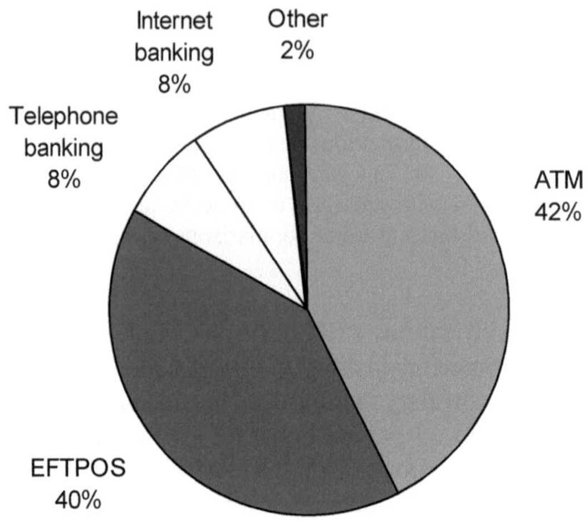

Chart 2.1 Total number of EFT transactions

As indicated in Chart 2.2 below, the *major banks* reported most (80%) of the EFT transactions recorded during this period.

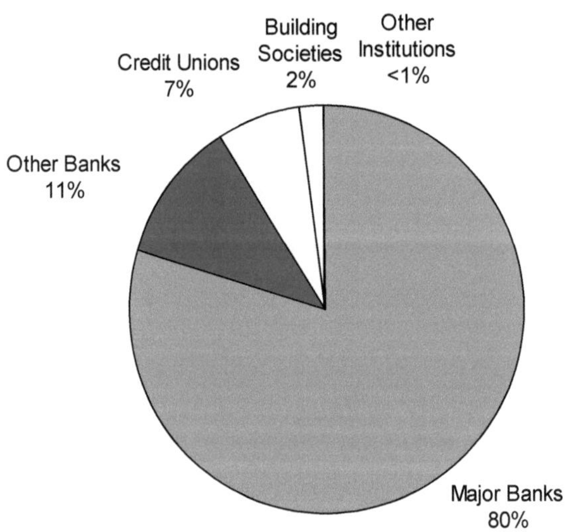

Chart 2.2 Total EFT transactions by institution type

Notes to chart:

As indicated in Chart 1, some institutions, including some of the *major banks*, experienced difficulty providing accurate EFT transaction statistics.

2.7 Australian Banking Industry Ombudsman ('ABIO')

The office of the Australian Banking Industry Ombudsman ('ABIO') commenced on 18 June 1990 and provides an independent mechanism for the resolution of banker-customer disputes.[158] Offering a free service to customers, the ABIO was the first self-regulatory financial body operating on an industry-wide basis in Australia. It was modelled on a comparable adjudicating body in the United Kingdom. After England, Australia became the second country globally to have such a body.[159]

Pursuant to clause 11 of the *EFT Code*, the responsibility for handling complaint investigation and resolution procedures rests, in the first instance, with the financial institution. Should the consumer still remain dissatisfied, external avenues are available. In particular, the independent ABIO is the industry's preferred body to assist in EFT dispute resolution according to the Reserve Bank of Australia's payment system regulation arm, the APSC.[160]

The ABIO is available (free of charge) if the dispute cannot be resolved between the financial institution and consumer and is within the ABIO's terms of reference. The ABIO's terms of reference limit the size of a 'dispute' relating to a 'banking service' to $150,000 (where 'dispute' is defined as a deadlock between the individual and senior management of a member bank and EFT is considered a 'banking service').[161]

The ABIO scheme was created to provide individual customers of member banks with access to an independent avenue of redress when they had a complaint about one of those banks. It was intended to provide a kind of 'appeal process' and research indicates it has been highly effective in improving the banks' practices in handling customer complaints.[162] However, the ABIO is not intended to be an avenue of appeal where a dispute has already been heard before a competent court or tribunal and a judgment given on its merits.[163] The rationale behind the scheme was the high cost of litigation, as well as the perceived inability of the average customer to contest matters in courts against a bank and the inadequate in-house dispute resolution mechanisms of banks. As an illustration, in the case of *Commonwealth Bank v Reno Auto Sales Pty Ltd*,[164] the bank sued the customer unsuccessfully to recover payment of a sum as little as $250.[165]

Although intended to be 'independent', it is notable that the member banks of the ABIO scheme are its 'owners' by virtue of them being shareholders in a

158 Weerasooria, above n 83, 207.

159 Ibid.

160 Australian Payments System Council, Annual Report 1994/1995.

161 Australian Banking Industry Ombudsman Limited, Annual Report 1995/1996, para 20.

162 M J Oborn, 'Procedures Adopted by Australian Banks for the Resolution of Customer Complaints and the Role of the Australian Banking Industry Ombudsman (1992) 2 Journal of Banking and Finance Law and Practice 268.

163 Australian Banking Industry Ombudsman Limited, Annual Report 1992/1993, para 20.

164 [1967] VR 790.

165 Weerasooria above 83, 207.

company limited by guarantee named the Australian Banking Industry Ombudsman Limited. The company's board consists of senior bankers and its responsibilities include the industry oversight of the scheme and the raising of funds to support it with each bank contributing to the maintenance of the scheme according to the number of its disputes pursued with the ABIO.[166]

In respect of function, the ABIO stated in its 1995/96 Annual Report[167] that dispute resolution can take three (3) forms: (i) during an informal conciliation conference bringing together both parties on neutral ground where, if both parties reach agreement, the ABIO confirms the settlement in writing; (ii) by an ABIO recommendation where a case manager cannot settle the dispute at the negotiated settlement stage at (i) above and both the bank and consumer accept the recommendation; and (iii) a legally binding award made by the ABIO where the bank rejects a recommendation, but the consumer has accepted it.

A section in the annual reports of the ABIO is dedicated to EFT issues and occasionally this includes actual case examples where the ABIO has resolved a dispute. Recent Annual Reports indicate that the ABIO continues to have difficulty resolving cases when it requires the ABIO to 'weigh the evidence' of the financial institution and the consumer where there is inconclusive evidence surrounding an allegedly unauthorised EFT transaction. Some of the ABIO's recent cases and results have been reported in Chapter 4 of this book when the practical application of the *EFT Code* and *US EFT Act* are considered in detail.

2.8 Code of Banking Practice

Following the apparent early success of the *EFT Code* in protecting consumers' rights, consumer bodies sought a general banking code of practice for individual customers. The call was answered with a *Code of Banking Practice* ('*CBP*') in November 1993. In terms of its origin and development, the process was quire similar to that of the *EFT Code* being the result of a joint task force comprising Treasury and the Trade Practices Commission (now the ACCC) representatives. However, consumer advocates argued that the Australian Bankers' Association 'hijacked' the process by releasing its own draft Code of Practice, a variation of the task force draft, which they asserted became the final form of the Code.[168]

The *CBP* applies specifically to 'banking services' (which includes EFT transactions under the Definitions in s 1.1). While its reach includes EFT transactions, the *CBP* does not have the coverage of the *EFT Code* (for example, it does not apportion or limit liability for disputed EFT transactions or carry an unqualified requirement that financial institutions make terms and conditions of use available before a 'banking service' is first used, nor a time frame for dispute resolution as the *EFT Code* does). Rather than fully incorporate the contents of the

[166] Ibid 208.

[167] Australian Banking Industry Ombudsman Limited, Annual Report 1995/1996, 13.

[168] See Weerasooria, above n 83, 222.

previously established *EFT Code* into its text, the *CBP* states that it is to be read subject to the *EFT Code* in the event of any inconsistency: refer *CBP* s 1.4.

Section 1.2 of the *CBP* also states that the *CBP* is to be read subject to any Commonwealth, State or Territory legislation. As the *CBP* could be considered to be the 'parent' document, this presumably would extend to the *EFT Code* which itself makes no such reference. Furthermore, the *CBP* makes reference to non-statute law under s 20.5 which provides that (in the external dispute resolution process) both 'the law' and the *CBP* shall apply to banking services.

The remaining provisions of the *CBP*, where they are relevant to EFT, carry almost identical requirements to that of the *EFT Code* in certain key areas (eg, full and effective written disclosure of contractual information, availability of general information on the bank's obligations to its customer and that a bank must provide an effective dispute resolution mechanism, including an impartial, external process free of charge).

2.9 Relevant legislation: the ASIC Act and the Trade Practices Act[169]

In March 1997, the report of the Financial System Inquiry (the Wallis report) was released. This was a major inquiry into the regulation of Australia's financial system. It recognised that the financial system is undergoing continuous and rapid change, involving, amongst other things, convergence, increased openness, increased competition and globalisation.

These changes are primarily driven by three interlinked forces:

- changing customer needs;
- new technologies and skills; and
- changes to regulation across a broad spectrum.

The report concluded that:

> In the financial system, specialised regulation is required to ensure that market participants act with integrity and that consumers are protected. The financial system warrants specialised regulation due to the complexity of financial products, the adverse consequences of breaching financial promises and the need for low-cost means to resolve disputes.

The federal government accepted this view. In its response to the Wallis report, it stated that there were a number of disadvantages to having a variety of regulatory agencies responsible for consumer protection, including that:[170]

[169] Australian Securities and Investments Commission, Official Website (2006) <http://www.asic.gov.au> at 16 February 2006.

[170] Ibid.

- regulation was inconsistent across the range of competing financial products;
- financial services providers faced a range of different regulatory rules that raised the complexity and cost of compliance; and
- consumers faced inconsistent rules resulting in difficulties in understanding and comparing competing products.

Such reasons led the Government to establish ASIC as the single consumer protection regulator for the financial services sector.

To equip ASIC for its new functions, ASIC was given some additional resources and new legislative powers. Most notably, the previous *Australian Securities and Investments Commission Act 1989* (Cth) was amended to mirror the consumer protection provisions of the *Trade Practices Act 1974* (Cth) ('*TPA*'),

The resultant *Australian Securities and Investments Commission Act 2001* (Cth) ('*ASIC Act*') is considered to be particularly relevant to EFT regulation, as well as the consumer fair trading legislation of each State. As Searles noted, such legislative sanctions 'remain in the background for ultimate use if required'.[171] It should be said, though, that such legislation is in the forefront in terms of setting the limits on what financial institutions generally may exclude by way of liability, and the nature of the statements they make to customers.

As Pengilley[172] and Weerasooria[173] correctly observed of the source provisions in the *TPA*, the *ASIC Act* similarly has broad scope and reach. The simple language of s 12DA of the *ASIC Act* (which duplicates s 52 of the *TPA*) is an avenue to protect customers against 'misleading and deceptive conduct' by financial institutions. Financial institutions clearly fall within the 'financial services providers' definition in s 5. Additionally, it could be argued that even individual bank staff may be liable.[174] The term 'financial services' and 'financial products' can be taken to also cover what was previously defined for 'banking services' in the *TPA*; that is, they include 'a contract between a banker and a customer of the banker entered into in the course of the carrying on by the banker of the business of banking'.

Specifically, s 12DA of the *ASIC Act* prohibits businesses from engaging in conduct in trade and commerce which is misleading and deceptive, or which is likely to mislead or deceive. Moreover, s 12DA is to be generously construed and should not be read down to conform with former common law or equitable requirements'.[175] From the research undertaken for this book, the interpretation of s 12DA in respect of what specifically constitutes a contractual breach between an EFT financial institution and consumer is unclear. However, some conclusions can

---

171 I Searles, 'Self-Regulation as an Effective Alternative to Legislation and Litigation: The Case of Electronic Banking' (1990) 1 Journal of Banking Law and Practice 125.

172 W Pengilley, 'Misleading or Deceptive Conduct and Financial Institutions' (1989) 1 Bond Law Review 157.

173 Weerasooria, above n 83, 259.

174 Ibid.

175 Ibid 260.

be drawn from the general principles of interpretation of s 52 of the *TPA* for 'banking services':[176]

- Misleading conduct involves no question of 'fault' or 'intent' to mislead or deceive;
- A 'lack of awareness by a banker of the consequences of his or her conduct' is not an answer to an allegation that the conduct was misleading or deceptive;
- The term 'in trade or commerce' also includes any misleading or deceptive conduct between a customer and a bank prior to the formation of a formal banker-customer contract;
- 'Silence' and 'half-truths' may constitute a breach where there is a 'duty to speak' or an obligation to reveal facts; and
- Reliance on alleged misleading or deceptive conduct may be rebutted by showing that a customer 'knew the true facts' or 'did not rely on such conduct in entering into the transaction'.

While the literature review undertaken revealed no cases where an action was successfully brought by an EFT consumer against a financial institution, perhaps due to the cost of litigation coupled with a lack of awareness by consumers with *TPA* or *ASIC Act* avenues of legal redress, s 12DA nevertheless clearly provides additional regulation of financial institution conduct. Furthermore, although the *EFT Code* prohibits most of the examples set out below, it is conceivable that the various 'principles of interpretation for banking services' outlined above could also regulate conduct in the EFT context where:

- The financial institution misled or deceived a consumer *before* a contractual EFT relationship was formed;
- The financial institution did not supply the consumer with the terms and conditions of use;
- The financial institution failed to properly notify any changes to the terms and conditions of use; and
- The financial institution made oral or written misrepresentations concerning EFT card and PIN security measures.

The *ASIC Act* would also seem to protect the consumer from 'unconscionable conduct' in the supply (or possible supply) of financial products or financial services under s 12CB of the *ASIC Act* (which duplicates s 51AB of the *TPA*). Pengilley observed that there are some important factors that are to be taken into account in assessing whether or not conduct is 'unconscionable':[177]

---

176 Ibid 257-60.

177 Pengilley, above n 172, 168.

- Relative bargaining strengths of a bank and a consumer;
- Whether conditions are imposed which are not reasonably necessary;
- Whether a consumer is reasonably able to understand relevant documents; and
- Whether undue influence or unfair tactics were used against a consumer.

Based on these factors, it is arguable that s 12CB also regulates attempts by financial institutions to impose additional terms and conditions to elevate consumer liability above that prescribed under the *EFT Code*. Given that 'understanding documents' is one of Pengilley's key principles (above), the failure of the *EFT Code* to require, for example, a definition of key EFT terms, uniform contents or language could also make s 12CB an avenue of protection for a consumer.

Section 12ED of the *ASIC Act* (which duplicates s 74 of the *TPA*) is also particularly important as it implies various conditions and warranties into a transaction including the 'supply of financial products' or 'financial services'. It implies a warranty under s 12ED(1) that services must be carried out with due care and skill. Consider again the example of a transactional error following EFT equipment failure where it is not obvious to a consumer that an ATM or EFTPOS terminal is malfunctioning. Pursuant to s 12ED, financial institutions would be obliged to maintain their EFT systems and equipment with due care and skill.

In addition, s 12ED(2) of the *ASIC Act* imposes a not-excludable warranty that services will be 'reasonably fit for that purpose or are of such a nature and quality that they might reasonably be expected to achieve that result'. The purpose and the result referred to are ones which the consumer makes known to the supplier.[178]

The section comes into operation if the financial services are supplied to a 'consumer' in the course of business and the consumer makes known to the supplier the purpose or the desired result. Where financial services are only used for one purpose, it may be taken that the consumer has made known to the supplier the purposes for which they were acquired.

Section 12ED(2) at first sight imposes a warranty similar to the 'fitness for purpose' warranty familiar from the sale of goods. However, the imposed obligation may be more onerous because of the section's reference to 'result'. It is clear that a customer of a financial institution who uses a payment system is acquiring a financial service to which s 12ED(2) applies.

It seems obvious that a customer who uses a payment system expects to achieve several 'results', among them:

- The customer's account will not be used or debited for payments not ordered by the customer; and
- Payment instructions should be strictly followed, resulting in timely payment of the right amount to the right person.

[178] The following material is both principally and directly drawn from Alan L Tyree, Section 74 TPA and Payment Services (1997) <http://austlii.edu.au/~alan/section74.html> at 5 December 2005.

Although these seem like minimal expectations, Terms and Conditions often include clauses that purport to achieve different results. For example, some Terms and Conditions of computer banking purport to make the customer responsible for all messages received by the bank which appear to have originated with the customer. Terms such as this place the customer at a substantial disadvantage when compared with the terms required by the *EFT Code* (where the customer's liability is limited in the absence of customer fault) or the situation where the customer's signature is forged on a cheque (where the bank bears full liability in the absence of customer fault).

In this context, it is noteworthy that the Attorney General's Expert Group recommended *against* the adoption of Article 13 of the *UNCITRAL Model Law on Electronic Commerce.*[179] This article included rules which allowed the 'addressee' of electronic message to assume that the message originated with the 'originator', even though the message is 'forged'. This would place the addressee in a position more favourable then the position of addressee in a paper-based system and was, for that reason, recommended against by the Expert Group.[180]

The demands of s 12ED are that the service be 'reasonably fit' and that it might be 'reasonably expected' to achieve results. With almost 16 years' experience of the *EFT Code* in operation, including the continual review and monitoring of the *EFT Code*, the *EFT Code* itself may clearly be taken as a guideline to what is 'reasonable' in the provision of a payment service. Of course, since the *EFT Code* is directed at transactions initiated by card and PIN, not all of its clauses will be relevant to every payment system. However, many of the *EFT Code's* clauses concerning disputed transactions, unauthorised transfers and information disclosure are of general application, and clauses which fall short of the standards required in the *EFT Code* might well be challenged as 'unreasonable'.[181]

As the recently updated *EFT Code* attempts to address problems arising from telephone and computer banking, most new payments systems are covered. Accordingly, the *EFT Code* and s 12ED of the *ASIC Act* might be used to encourage reasonable standards in Terms and Conditions of Use.

In s 12EB (which duplicates s 68 of the *TPA*), suppliers of financial services or financial products cannot exclude, restrict or modify the *ASIC Act's* statutory conditions in any term of a contract.

The provisions of the *ASIC Act* (as for the *TPA*) do not appear to cover State-owned financial institutions (where the respective Fair Trading Acts may apply), but would generally appear to have applicability to the majority of EFT financial institutions and so afford consumers a degree of fundamental mandatory protection.

---

179 UNCITRAL Model Law on Electronic Commerce (1996) <http://www.uncitral.org/uncitral/en/uncitral_texts/electronic_commerce/1996Model.html> at 12 March 2006.

180 Commonwealth Attorney General's Department Electronic Commerce Expert Group, Electronic Commerce: Building the Legal Framework (April, 1998) <http://law.gov.au/aghome/advisory/eceg/ecegreport.html> at 24 September 2004.

181 The above material drew both principally and directly from Alan L Tyree, above n 178.

A final observation, though, the problematical status of 'rules' in a code of practice such as the *EFT Code* raises two questions: the extent to which persons are obliged to abide by the rules; and the extent to which the content of those rules is open to scrutiny.

Whilst industry codes may generally restate the law in the *ASIC Act* and Fair Trading Acts in the context of the particular industry, as Woodruffe points out,[182] if the code does not indicate how its provisions relate to legislation, there is a danger that consumers may be misled into believing that the terms of the code are simply advisory and remain unaware or confused about their legal rights. It is important to state that following an examination of some other voluntary or self-regulating codes of practice similar to the *EFT Code*, as a general rule, they do not explicitly relate their provisions to legislative provisions.

2.10 Background and scope of the US EFT Act

As identified earlier, payment-related risks may be addressed by laws, market practices or the actions of consumers themselves.[183] Even when legislative bodies attempt to address consumer payment-related risks by enacting laws, these laws do not usually address the full panoply of risks that exist but rather focus on a subset of risks. Such is the case with the USA's *Electronic Funds Transfer Act 1978*, which addresses primarily risks related to unauthorised use, the detection and resolution of errors, certain types of payment dishonour and the disclosure of terms.[184] The *US EFT Act* does not address the risk of loss or destruction of an instrument (unaccompanied by unauthorised use), which is one of the primary risks associated with EFT cards. It also does not generally address risks related to the inability to use an instrument or privacy matters.[185]

The legislative history of the *US EFT Act* indicates that the US Congress' primary goal was to protect consumers. The *US EFT Act* sought to eliminate uncertainties in the market on the part of both consumers and financial institutions regarding their liabilities related to electronic payments. When the legislation was enacted in 1978, many electronic payment mechanisms – such as ATMs, direct deposits, telephone bill payments and EFTPOS transactions - were relatively new, but were growing rapidly in popularity. The rise in electronic payments was accompanied by a rise in computer–related crimes, and few federal or state laws addressed these problems. The US Congress cited computer crime reports and other anecdotal evidence of consumer and bank losses involving electronic funds transfer services as a reason for establishing consumers' rights. Although providers of electronic payment services argued that the Act was premature and

[182] G Woodruffe, 'Government Monitored Codes of Practice in the United Kingdom' (1984) 7 Journal of Consumer Policy 171, 174.

[183] This section draws both principally and directly from the Board of Governors of the Federal Reserve, Report to Congress, above n 9, 31-41, and from White, above n 77.

[184] Board of Governors of the Federal Reserve, Report to Congress, above n 9, 37-9.

[185] Ibid.

that the electronic payment market should be allowed to develop further on its own, the US Congress believed that establishing a framework of rights and duties for all parties would benefit both consumers and providers.[186]

One of the motivating forces behind the enactment of the law was the report of the National Commission on Electronic Fund Transfers ('NCEFT') of October 1977. The NCEFT undertook a broad assessment of consumer risks in using electronic fund transfer systems that were emerging or being used in a greater degree at that time, including ATMs and EFTPOS. The NCEFT stated in its report that, in general, the appropriate approach to the evolving electronic payment services was to allow their growth to occur free from unnecessary regulation and open to marketplace pressures and consumer demands. However, the report stated that existing law and regulation were incomplete or not applicable to electronic payment services and that some consumer concerns were 'so fundamental that they should be addressed at this time in order to guarantee to consumers a number of basic rights in an EFT environment'.[187] Accordingly, the NCEFT made recommendations for legislation in various areas, including initial disclosures of account terms, documentation of transactions, stop payment, liability for unauthorised transactions, resolution of errors, system malfunctions, compulsory use of electronic fund transfers and unsolicited issuance of EFT debit cards.

Besides the *US EFT Act*, other rules in the form of market practices (such as daily limits on the amount that can be withdrawn from an ATM) have developed to address consumer risks in electronic payments.[188]

The market failure that the Congress appears to have been addressing in the *US EFT Act* is the lack of full information, which may have prevented consumers from adequately assessing the risks of using electronic fund transfer services. Many provisions of the Act are designed to provide consumers with information about the rights and liabilities associated with EFT services. The *US EFT Act* also limits and assesses liability in certain situations and prohibits certain practices. In effect, it imposes contract terms on the parties that may have nothing to do with the availability of information.

A brief analysis of the particular risks addressed by the *US EFT Act* is discussed next.[189]

2.10.1 Unauthorised use

The *US EFT Act* addresses the risk of unauthorised electronic debits to consumers' accounts through two principal means. The first is a limitation on the consumer's liability for unauthorised electronic transfers of funds:[190]

---

186 Ibid.

187 National Commission on Electronic Fund Transfers (USA), EFT in the United States – Final Report of the National Commission on Electronic Fund Transfers (October 1977) 6.

188 Board of Governors of the Federal Reserve, Report to Congress, above n 9, 39.

189 Ibid 37-41.

190 Ibid 39.

Under the *US EFT Act*, the institution may hold the consumer liable for no more than US$50 in most cases. If the consumer fails to notify the institution within two business days after learning of the loss or theft of an EFT debit card or other access device, however, the consumer can be held liable for up to US$500; and if the consumer fails to notify the institution within sixty days after a periodic statement is sent showing an unauthorised transfer, the consumer bears all liability for any further unauthorised transfers after that time.

To impose liability for unauthorised transfers, an institution must meet three conditions. First, the access device involved (eg, the EFT card) must be 'accepted', meaning generally that it must have been requested and received by the consumer before the loss or theft. Second, the institution must have provided a means of identifying the holder of the device; in most cases, through an authentication mechanism such as a PIN. Third, the institution must have disclosed to the consumer the limitations on the consumer's liability under the *US EFT Act*, along with a telephone number and address for notifying the institution of loss or theft (under the *US EFT Act*, consumer negligence is not a prerequisite for consumer liability). An unauthorised EFT, however, generally does *not* include a transfer performed by a person to whom the consumer voluntarily gave a card or an access code.

2.10.2 EFT errors and malfunctions

Another category of risk addressed by the *US EFT Act* involves the possibility of errors or malfunctions occurring in the operation of an electronic payment system.[191] Errors and malfunctions could include: (i) the failure of a transaction to be completed (eg, a deposit at an ATM is not credited to the consumer's account or a payment to a third party is not made); (ii) an EFT transaction executed for an incorrect amount; and (iii) other errors, such as payments made to the wrong party or at the wrong time.

The *US EFT Act* addresses the potential risk of errors primarily by requiring documentation of electronic transactions, which serves to alert consumers to potential errors, and by mandating error resolution procedures. Any EFT transaction initiated at an 'electronic terminal' (including ATMs and EFTPOS terminals, but not telephones or home computers) must be documented by a receipt. The receipt must include the amount, date, and type of transaction; the type of account involved; an identifying number such as the account or card number; the terminal location; and, if a payment to a third party is involved, the name of the third party. In addition, all electronic transactions (including those initiated by telephone or home computer) must be documented on periodic account statements. The statement shows the same items of information that the terminal receipt does and contains other information, such as opening and closing balances for the statement period. The EFT terminal receipt and the periodic

191 Ibid 39-40.

statement enable the consumer to detect errors promptly and to take action to get the problem resolved and prevent recurrences.

The *US EFT Act* also requires that institutions investigate and resolve a claim by a consumer that an error has occurred, such as when an EFTPOS debit card payment to a merchant is shown on the statement as $200 and should have been $20. The institution may complete the process within ten business days after receiving notification from the consumer; alternatively, it may provisionally credit the consumer's account for the amount of the alleged error within ten business days and then take up to forty-five calendar days to resolve the matter.

Another provision addresses errors involving pre-authorised (recurring) transfers by providing the consumer with the right to stop payment. If a consumer has authorised a third party to initiate a series of electronic debits to the consumer's account, the consumer may stop payment of such a pre-authorised debit any time up to three business days before the scheduled date of the debit. If an institution receives a stop-payment order but fails to stop the debit, the institution is liable to the consumer for all damages proximately caused. The *US EFT Act* does not provide a stop-payment right for other types of electronic payments, such as EFT debit card transactions.

2.10.3 Dishonours

The *US EFT Act* protects the consumer from liability when an electronic payment to a third party is not completed as directed by the consumer.[192] For example, if a consumer uses a home banking system to order payment of an electric bill but the institution fails to make the payment, the institution is liable to the consumer for all damages proximately caused by the failure to make the payment correctly.

2.10.4 Disclosure of terms and conditions

At the time that a consumer contracts with an institution for an EFT service, the institution must provide a disclosure of terms and conditions of the service, including the consumer's liability for unauthorised transfers, fees imposed by the institution, the consumer's right to have errors resolved, and the institution's policy regarding release of information to third parties about the consumer's account.[193] If certain terms change adversely for the consumer; for example, if fees increase, the institution must provide a notice at least twenty-one days before the effective date of the change. These disclosure requirements enable consumers to make an informed choice among providers of EFT services and between EFT services and products and other forms of payment. If, for example, a consumer decides that the ATM fees charged by a particular institution are excessive, the

[192] Ibid 40.
[193] Ibid.

consumer may go to a competing institution or decide not to use ATM services at all.

2.10.5 Other provisions of the US EFT Act

Finally, the *US EFT Act* contains provisions that are designed to prevent financial institutions from requiring that consumers use electronic payment mechanisms.[194] The risk of institutions imposing this requirement appears to be low, given the availability of alternative payment mechanisms and the ability of consumers to obtain services from other financial institutions. Nevertheless, the *US EFT Act* attempts to address perceived risks related to consumer choice by placing restrictions on the actions of financial institutions. With limited exceptions, institutions are prohibited from sending an EFT debit card or other EFT access device to a consumer unless the consumer has requested it. In addition, the use of pre-authorised EFT debits as a means of repayment may not be made a condition of extending credit, nor may acceptance of pre-authorised credits (direct deposit) at a particular institution be made a condition of employment or for receipt of government benefits. Furthermore, institutions may not enter into agreements that require consumers to waive their rights under the *US EFT Act*.

2.11 Conclusion

Primarily from the Federal Report to Congress, this chapter drew attention to the limitations in the existing literature concerning EFT regulation and the EFT regulatory debate generally, both the subject of this book. Of the scarce existing literature on EFT regulation, those few sources identified omitted to undertake any meaningful comparative, economic or ethical analysis. In addition, these sources are dated, domestic-focused and largely prepared in isolation by the various institutional stakeholders involved. No literature has attempted a review or analysis of the current, revised *EFT Code*, much less employed a multi-disciplinary approach to the analysis and evaluation of EFT regulation.

After reviewing the limited EFT regulation literature, this chapter examined the rapid emergence of EFT and the myriad regulatory challenges it has posed, which are compounded by the general inapplicability of common law principles for traditional paper-based payment methods. Of particular concern is the escalating incidence of unauthorised EFT transactions and non-compliance with the *EFT Code* as it stands.

Perhaps the most important revelation from this chapter is the quite plausible argument that the *EFT Code* is, in fact, reinforced by the overarching statutory force of all the financial consumer protection provisions of the *ASIC Act*.

[194] Ibid 40-1.

It is also evident that the electronic payments landscape is inherently complex and involves many institutional stakeholders with diverse roles in, and contributions to, the EFT system.

In consequence, an extended, contemporary multi-disciplinary approach to analysing and evaluating EFT regulatory options is needed. This extended multi-faceted technique will be discussed next in Chapter 3.

Chapter 3. An Integrated Multi-Disciplinary Approach

Acknowledging the many limitations and fragmented approaches in the existing literature as discussed in Chapter 2, in this chapter a comprehensive multi-disciplinary methodology is developed uniting critical comparative law, economics of law criteria, regulation theory, ethics as well as administrative and social considerations. This proposed multi-disciplinary approach is considered to be of utility in evaluating the range of different EFT regulatory options, from the prevailing industry self-regulatory regime through to formal statutory regulation or even hybrids of both. It should also be stated that this integrated multi-disciplinary approach is designed to facilitate an evaluation of the efficacy of existing EFT regulation measures, as much as for a forward-looking appraisal of various EFT regulatory options.

This chapter is structured as follows: In Section 3.1, the comparative law literature is explored and discussed, including the different approaches available and it is argued that the critical comparative law method is the preferred approach in evaluating the divergent approaches to EFT regulation in Australia and the USA. In Section 3.2, the case for a hitherto unexplored economics of law approach to evaluating EFT regulatory options is argued, taking in economic efficiency/loss allocation criteria and a framework for both a cost-effectiveness and cost-benefit analysis. The rationales for government regulatory intervention and the possibility of market failure in the EFT system are discussed in Section 3.3. In Section 3.4, the administrative feasibility and social acceptability of amending EFT legal rules in Australia is considered and whether or not ethical standards and norms have any place in formulating financial regulation is debated in Section 3.5, where it is argued that ethical considerations ought to be at the core of financial regulation. In Section 3.6, the structured and closed interview method for a limited survey sample of the relevant retail branch staff of six (6) major Australian banks is described and the conclusion is presented in Section 3.7.

3.1 Comparative law method

Attempting to adopt, or, indeed, adapting, a particular and clear comparative law approach is inherently complex as there appears to be something of a bifurcation into 'comparative legal culture' or 'unofficial law', on the one hand, and, 'foreign law' or 'official law' on the other. At the outset, it must be conceded that, as a result of this, comparative law methodology has even been described as 'meaningless'.[195] In fact, it has been several times pronounced dead; one cause of which was said to be its 'suffocation from narrowness in ignoring unofficial law'.[196]

Acknowledging these inherent tensions and complexities, in order to attempt to formulate a workable comparative law methodology for the purposes of this book, three introductory questions may be posed.[197] The first is: is it true that, traditionally, comparative law has emphasised the differences in institutions, legal structures and substantive rules rather than the common-cores, that is, were divergences overstated in the past? The second question is: can it be said that showing the similarity of some selected single rules in detail, whether as to their substance or as to their function, is enough to negate the 'differences approach' and confirm the 'convergences approach'? The third question is: when 'culture' and 'difference' as facts are the central concerns, should the function of comparative law be the building of bridges, that is to say, should it become 'bridging comparative law', coupled with the acceptance that legal systems and cultural systems can 'live apart together'?[198]

The claim that the grouping of legal systems or what has been described as the 'legal families approach' arose from emphasising differences may be one way of looking at things, since from the point of view of the legal systems put into the same or related groups, this exercise can be presented as arising from recognising similarities.[199] The study of legal transplants is also an indication that scholars have been looking at relationships between legal systems and detecting common features. It is not therefore altogether true that comparative law only emphasised

---

195 Mattei notes the 'disturbing propensity' of comparative scholarship to become either a 'mere discussion of foreign law' or a 'mere parallel exposition of different legal systems': Ugo Mattei, Comparative Law and Economics (1997) 97. Earlier writers, such as Gutteridge, had noted the 'inconsequentialism' of its methodology: 'The process of comparing rules of law taken from different systems does not result in the formulation of any independent rules for the regulation of human relationships or transactions. Gutteridge also contends that not only are there no "comparative" rules of law, but there are no transactions or relationships which can be described as comparative': H C Gutteridge, Comparative Law: An Introduction to the Comparative Method of Legal Study and Research (2nd ed, 1949) 1.

196 Basil Markesinis, 'Comparative Law – A Subject in Search of an Audience' (1990) 53 Modern Law Review 1, 21. For similar criticisms and suggestions for a new taxonomy for comparative law, see also, Andrew Huxley, 'Golden Yoke, Silken Text' (1997) 106 Yale Law Journal 1885, 1924-5; Lawrence M Friedman, 'Some Thoughts on Comparative Legal Culture' in David S Clark (ed), Comparative and Private International Law (1990) 52-5; 'Symposium: New Directions in Comparative Law' (1998) 46 American Journal of Comparative Law 597; and 'Symposium: New Approaches to Comparative Law' (1997) Utah Law Review 255.

197 Esin Orucu, 'Critical Comparative Law: Considering Paradoxes for Legal Systems in Transition' (2000) 4 European Journal of Comparative Law 1.

198 Ibid; and see, eg, K Zweigert and H Klotz, An Introduction to Comparative Law (3rd ed, 1998).

199 Orucu, above n 197, 1.

the differences until recently. As Moccia points out,[200] between the sixteenth to the nineteenth centuries, there was only 'comparative legal history', the comparative law of the time, and it seemed to be most interested in the similarities and not the differences and it is only with rising nationalism and positivism that comparative law discourse started stressing the differences, especially between the civil law and the common law.[201]

There is a standing belief that only a comparative analysis of convergent or similar systems can benefit from each other's experience.[202] The other belief, however, may be that only differences teach us lessons. It would seem more desirable for legal systems in a transitional phase in dealing with the emergence of technology such as EFT in Australia, that there is considerable inspiration from observing a regulatory regime different from our own. In consequence, although taking markedly divergent paths, the regulatory responses of Australia and the USA followed a shared concern: the inapplicability of the paper-based legal principles founded in the common law and the initial one-sided allocation of risk in consumer electronic banking contracts, which were perceived to be inadequate and heavily in favour of the financial institutions who drafted them. Thus, notwithstanding the vastly different economic scale and Federal/State regulatory structures in the USA compared with Australia, the USA is the only relevant common-law-country example of a statutory response to essentially the same EFT problems.

Indeed, Schlesinger successfully points out that 'to compare means to observe and to explain similarities as well as differences'. Schlesinger meritoriously contends that the emphasis is quite properly sometimes on differences and at other times on similarities.[203] Schlesinger refers to periods of 'contractive', which he also calls 'contrastive', comparison with the emphasis on differences alternating with periods of what might be called 'integrative' comparison; that is, a comparison which places the main accents on similarities.[204] Thus, Schlesinger contrasts 'integrative comparative law' with 'contractive or contrastive comparative law'. His conclusion is that the future belongs to 'integrative comparative law'.[205]

Referring to Kant, however, Ward suggests that 'comparativism' is, in fact, too inclined to identify differences, instead of bringing into focus the core-principles within every legal system, jurisprudentially every legal system being at root the same.[206] It is suggested by Ward that the 'same-ness and difference debate' dominates most of 'theoretical comparativism' with the question: 'Are we

200 See, eg, L Moccia, 'Historical Overview on the Origins and Attitudes of Comparative Law' in B De Witte and C Forder (eds), The Common Law of Europe and the Future of Legal Education (1992) 609, 619.

201 Orucu, above n 197, 1.

202 Schlesinger, above n 48, 477.

203 Ibid.

204 Ibid 481.

205 Ibid.

206 I Ward, The Limits of Comparativism (1995) 2 Military Justice Reporter 23, 31.

identifying difference, and cherishing it, or are we trying to suppress it, by effective same-ness?'[207]

Bussani, too, makes some useful observations.[208] One is that even a cursory definition of comparative law tells us that comparative lawyers are looking both at differences and at similarities. The second is that the similarities or common cores that are sought today are limited to the Western world alone. The third point is that the real benefit that can be derived from comparative law is the insight gained by studying and analysing both differences between the *similars* and similarities between *differents*. Finally, the future lies in 'unity in diversity' rather than 'unity through uniformity and standardisation'.[209]

It is therefore submitted that comparative law is not simply a way of contrasting and comparing two legal systems or approaches to regulation in an effort to resolve the dichotomy between them. It may nevertheless reveal ways of appreciating the resultant divergences and harmony may be achieved not only through 'integrative' comparative legal studies, but also through 'contrastive' comparative legal studies. The aim must be to keep the communication and conversation going and allow cross-fertilisation. It could be said then that 'traditional' or 'conventional' comparative law, which rests either side of the viewpoint, has been usurped by what might be termed 'critical comparative law', which sits at the vantage point, commanding all views. Comparativists such as Schlesinger, Ward and Bussani, who could be seen as the seminal advocates of this innovative critical comparative law approach, thus implore that we must analyse and emphasise what is actually there. This could be similarities or differences, or apparent convergence or divergence. Accordingly, the comparative enterprise entails both recognition and appreciation of diversity and search for commonality.

Aims such as 'harmonisation', 'integration' and 'globalisation' show acceptance of the existence of differences but, nevertheless, aspire to produce sameness. Yet the distinctiveness and mutuality should also be emphasised within the concept of 'harmony'.[210]

So in looking at a preferred comparative law method, should the aim be harmonisation or harmony? There is a place for divergence even in a scheme of convergence, as harmony of 'differents' is more fruitful and beneficial to the world of legal learning than efforts to standardise.

What is the meaning of integration? Does harmony mean similarity? Is there a dichotomy between harmonisation and harmony? Harmony is both an objective and an inherent characteristic of any system. Law subsumes harmonisation. The notion of harmonisation of laws in the context of comparative law is, however, considered somewhat obscure. Harmonisation as a concept is a process of bringing about harmony, analogous to that in music.[211] As a method, harmonisation

---

207 Ibid.

208 Bussani, above n 47, 785.

209 Ibid.

210 Orucu, above n 197, 1.

211 Ibid.

becomes a goal for law reform. However, harmony presupposes and preserves diversity. Components retain their individuality but form a new and more complex sound. Consonance as the opposite of discord is a pleasurable combination.[212] Harmony is a relative concept which can also include dissonance. Thus, harmony may be achieved by not only eliminating diversity, but also within diversity.
As already pointed out, when comparing closely related systems it is usually more interesting to explain the differences, while in two entirely unrelated systems it is more interesting to explain the similarities. Yet, it seems a matter of preference, and therefore policy, whether the comparatist highlights the differences or the similarities found.

As considered earlier, in considering the regulation of emerging technologies such as EFT in comparable legal systems, Orucu contends that it is important to be mindful that they are in transition and to differing extents, and, will be more so in the coming decades.[213] He further asserts that the majority of these systems are and will be looking into reshaping their social as well as their legal systems. Therefore, in order to achieve this, according to Orucu, employing the services of comparative law will be of great assistance as comparative law will not only be the major tool for law reform by providing models but it will be pressed to create blueprints for the importer of models and to provide better understanding of changing concepts of nationhood, sovereignty, legal system, law and identity.[214] It may also aid the arbiters in resolving disputes as one of the methods of construction and interpretation. Thus, as Orucu articulates it, comparative law, by providing models and modes of legal reasoning, will supply systems in transition with the possibility of structured change.

In terms of the nexus between comparative law and the economics of law as the preferred methods of utility in this book in the quest for improved regulation of EFT in Australia, it is interesting to note that economists are trying to establish a 'blueprint' by which systems can choose the most efficient solution from the pool of solutions offered by competing systems. In many jurisdictions, there is also the hope that a new *ius commune* (ie, an optimal communion of laws) between common law and civil law systems (eg, in European private law in the form of the revised *UNIDROIT Principles of International Commercial Contracts* of 2004)[215] can develop through the competition of legal rules and an eventual choice of the most efficient or 'best' rule.[216] Thus, the prerequisites for achieving harmony will not be necessarily similarity or regularity, but difference and diversity.

The law and economics movement seems to be in the process of establishing an 'intellectual imperialism', and some comparative lawyers even contend that there is a current movement intending a 'colonisation by law and economics' of a number of legal disciplines; that comparative law has become the special prey for

212 Ibid.

213 Ibid.

214 Ibid.

215 See, eg, UNIDROIT Principles of International Commercial Contracts (2004) <http://www.unidroit.org/english/principles/contracts/main.htm> at 12 March 2006.

216 Ibid.

this colonist.[217] However, as long as comparative law maintains its distinctiveness and this comparative law and economics of law relationship can move beyond 'colonisation' into one of co-partners, then comparative law can only gain in popularity and be seen as indispensable for understanding the role of law in economics and of economics in law.

The comparative law and economics approach aims at building a model for an efficient legal institution and then comparing it with the actual world alternatives offered by different legal systems. It becomes important here to be able to offer explanations for the reasons and the mode of the departure.

From the above comparative law literature, it seems highly probable that as the electronic and digital age become increasingly dominant in commerce and individual lives, a critical comparative law approach, such as undertaken in this book, will not only produce tangible results, but also allow for intellectual vigour which will take comparative discourse further.

Utilising recent actual case examples of disputed, unauthorised EFT transactions from the ABIO, together with litigated cases from the USA, the substantive provisions of the Australian *EFT Code* and *US EFT Act* will be examined using this critical comparative law method in Chapter 4.

3.2 Economic analysis of law

According to Posner[218] and Goetz,[219] the economic analysis of law involves three distinct, but related enterprises: (i) the use of economics to predict the effects of rules (ie, 'price theory'); (ii) the use of economics to determine what legal rules are economically efficient by applying cost benefit analysis, in order to recommend what the legal rules ought to be (ie, 'welfare economics'); and (iii) the use of economics to predict what the legal rules will be (ie, 'public choice').

In consequence, looking at economic analysis of legal rules, one key observation is that economists like Posner and Goetz tend to convert issues from disputes about equity, justice and fairness into disputes about efficiency.[220] That has to do with the predilection of economists with measuring the economic cost-benefit and behavioural effects of legal rules rather than their substantive content and interpretation as lawyers perhaps do. Hence, in evaluating legal rules, a lawyer might ask simply whether a legal rule produces a just outcome in a particular case, whereas an economic analysis might pose the questions: is the legal rule efficient from a cost-benefit standpoint (a rule is efficient if it maximise

[217] See, eg, Markesinis, Huxley and Friedman, above n 196.

[218] See, eg, R Posner, Economic Analysis of Law (1986).

[219] See, eg, C J Goetz, Cases and Materials on Law and Economics (1984).

[220] David D Friedman, Economic Analysis of Law (1987) The New Palgrave: A Dictionary of Economic Theory and Doctrine <http://www.daviddfriedman.com/Law_and_Econ_S97E/Palgrave_L_E.html> at 12 March 2006.

social net benefit) and is it desirable from a behavioural modification perspective?[221]

Ultimately, though, a united legal and economic analysis should increase the depth and probative value in assessing regulatory options for EFT. Conjugating these two previously fragmented disciplines (together with ethical and administrative/social acceptability considerations), may assist a superior and more complete analysis.

Accordingly, the second method: economic analysis of law and regulation theory in this study is concerned with whether the application of more formal legislative regulation (ie, USA-style regulatory provisions) to EFT in Australia is meritorious from an economic standpoint. Beginning with an examination of the economic rationales for government regulation and the economics of liability allocation, this book presents an analytical framework for: (i) a regulation cost/benefit analysis; and (ii) evaluating the effects of regulation on incentives to innovate and on the development and adoption of new technologies. This will be presented in Chapter 5.

3.2.1 Loss allocation and economic efficiency criteria

Fundamentally, a genuine unauthorised EFT transaction profits a third party and leaves a loss to be distributed between two relatively innocent parties: the account institution and the user.[222] This book adopts the starting premise that a regime for allocating losses arising from unauthorised EFT transactions should, if it is possible to do so efficiently, share those losses between the user and the account institution, according to the circumstances of the loss.

In order to give careful consideration to an improved regulatory regime for unauthorised consumer EFT transactions in Australia, this book employs the three (3) economic principles espoused by Cooter and Rubin,[223] which can be distilled from an economic efficiency approach to liability and loss allocation rules: (i) loss reduction; (ii) loss spreading; and (iii) loss imposition.

According to Principles 1 and 2, rules governing unauthorised EFT transactions may be evaluated both on how effectively they spread losses and how effectively they could modify behaviour. That is, Principle 1, has the objective of assigning losses to the 'lowest-cost avoider', thereby minimise the chance of the loss occurring. Principle 2 concerns 'loss spreading', which seeks to minimise the costs to each party by spreading losses as widely as possible. Cooter and Rubin usefully articulate the distinction from loss reduction as: 'loss spreading presumes that a loss has already occurred and assigns liability to the party that can more effectively spread it, but the loss reduction principle assigns liability for the more

221 Ibid.

222 See, eg, Australian Securities and Investments Commission, Discussion Paper above n 15.

223 Principles summarised from Cooter and Rubin, above n 52, 63.

complex purpose of affecting human behaviour'.[224] Principle 3 (akin to that in the *US EFT Act*) is based on the implication that the rules for allocation of liability should be simple, clear and decisive to minimise the costs of administering them. As the EFT Working Group noted,[225] Principle 3 suggests that a no-fault allocation system is better than one that requires the evaluation of fault; and if a fault-based system is used, the obligations on parties should be clear and specific so that a breach of those obligations can be easily determined with little cost.

This suggests that broad standards such as 'the consumer is to take all reasonable steps to safeguard the EFT card and PIN' are less appropriate than specific standards. They are less appropriate because broad standards involve significant judgment and argument as to their interpretation in particular cases.[226] This is expensive, time consuming and somewhat arbitrary.

The Australian *EFT Code* and *US EFT Act* will be compared, contrasted and ultimately evaluated in light of each of these criteria.

3.2.2 Regulation cost-benefit analysis

Another relevant analytical economic framework for effective EFT regulation is to examine the effects of government regulation on incentives to innovate and on the development and adoption of new products and technologies (ie, a preliminary regulation cost-benefit analysis to determine the social welfare effects of a regulation).[227] In particular, the rationales for and the effects of government regulation, with a particular emphasis on the regulation of emerging technologies such as consumer EFT services.[228]

According to the economist, Solow, technological advancement occurs, for the most part, in small incremental steps as firms strive to compete more effectively with existing or potential rivals.[229] Occasionally, technology takes significant leaps forward, fundamentally changing the way households and firms conduct their daily business. Economic research has found that technical progress is an extremely important factor in influencing the rate of economic growth.[230]

Although, it should be said that many new products or technologies may be developed without a clear understanding of how they ultimately will be utilised by users and providers, nor the regulatory challenges posed.[231]

With many financial services now available through ATM networks, over telephone lines or via the Internet, electronic banking, in its various forms, provides a convenient, low-cost alternative to traditional bank visitation. Yet government intervention may be warranted when the unfettered operations of the

---

224 Ibid.

225 Australian Securities and Investments Commission, Discussion Paper, above n 15, 30.

226 Ibid.

227 See, eg, Case and Fair, above n 53, 295.

228 Board of Governors of the Federal Reserve, Report to Congress, above n 9, 7.

229 See, eg, Solow, above n 55, 312-20.

230 Ibid.

231 Board of Governors of the Federal Reserve, Report to Congress, above n 9, 7.

private sector fail to achieve an economically efficient outcome, that is, in the presence of so-called 'market failure'.[232]

Case and Fair also identified the existence of 'internal' as well as 'external' costs and benefits as a key source of market failure.[233] That is, costs and benefits may arise when the production or consumption of a product or service generates costs or benefits that accrue to parties both directly and not directly involved in the production or consumption process. In the absence of government intervention, private parties typically do not have the incentive to produce or consume socially optimal quantities of products or services.[234]

Market failure often provides the motivation for government intervention, but government action alone cannot necessarily solve the problems associated with market failure.[235] Thus, government intervention may prohibit specific behaviours, require certain product characteristics, set or limit prices, or mandate disclosure of information. Government responses to market failures, while having the potential to improve market outcomes, may also have unforeseen and sometimes adverse consequences.[236] Although it should be said that regulatory intervention may not always achieve the desired outcome, even when market failure justifies a regulatory response, the costs as well as the benefits of the regulation must be considered[237] – that is, so that the optimal regulation is derived from an analysis which facilitates the evaluation of the regulation from the perspective of net social benefit or welfare as well.

In markets such as for EFT services where information problems may inevitably arise, ensuring that all market participants are fully informed is not always possible, even with government intervention. Moreover, in requiring firms to provide information to consumers, policymakers must weigh the costs and benefits of such requirements.[238]

For applying economic criteria or analysis to law based on applied welfare economics, various available mathematical and quantitative methods may be adapted, including the following: discounted cash flow or cost-benefit analysis, statistical methods, game theory, dynamic and statistical optimisation methods.[239] From all these available alternatives, the discounted cost-benefit method developed by Islam and Mak (discussed in Chapter 5) will be adapted in this study,[240] given the suitability of this method for designing optimal EFT regulation in Australia. The net present value is considered to be of utility as an adaptable for decision-making about the desirability of a particular rule or law.

---

[232] Case and Fair, above n 53, 295.
[233] Ibid.
[234] Ibid.
[235] Board of Governors of the Federal Reserve, Report to Congress, above n 9, 10-11.
[236] Ibid.
[237] Ibid.
[238] Ibid.
[239] See, eg, Islam and Mak, above n 50.
[240] Ibid.

The formula for the standard net present value is as follows[241] (for full details and discussion of the adapted cost-benefit model for EFT, refer to Section 5.4 in Chapter 5):

$$NPV = \frac{NB_0}{(1+r)^0} + \frac{NB_1}{(1+r)^1} + \ldots\ldots\ldots + \frac{NB_n}{(1+r)^n} \qquad 3.1$$

Which, in turn, is calculated as follows:[242]

$$NPV = \frac{B_0 - C_0}{(1+r)^0} + \frac{B_1 - C_1}{(1+r)^1} + \ldots\ldots\ldots + \frac{B_n - C_n}{(1+r)^n} = \sum_{t=0}^{n} \frac{B^t - C_t}{(1+r)^t} \qquad 3.2$$

Where:
NPV = the net benefits of a law (benefit-cost);
r = discount rate;
n = number of years;
t = year t
B = benefits from the law; and
C = costs of implementation of the law.

Thus, the cost-benefit ratio may be calculated as follows:[243]

$$\mathrm{C-B\ ratio} = \frac{\sum_{t=0}^{n} \frac{B_t}{(1+r)^t}}{\sum_{t=0}^{n} \frac{Ct}{(1+r)^t}} \qquad 3.3$$

Although it is considered beyond both the scope and purview of this book to address in detail the above mathematical modelling of costs and benefits of EFT regulation initiatives, it is nevertheless of some utility to proffer a simplified framework for such an analysis.

In the absence of any particular cost-benefit analysis criteria as applied to EFT regulation, such a framework may assist the systematic evaluation of the relative costs and benefits of different EFT regulatory initiatives so as to provide for more informed decisions on impacts and resource allocation among the different policy options advanced in this book. Potential evaluators may include each of those regulators with responsibility for the various aspects of the EFT system, as well as

241 Ibid.
242 Ibid.
243 Ibid.

those with access to current, meaningful industry-wide banking industry and/or EFT cost-benefit data. Those identified may include: the ABIO, the RBA, ASIC, the ACCC, consumer advocacy groups, the Australian Bankers' Association, or, at the ultimate level, the Australian federal government Department of Treasury. Section 5.4 of Chapter 5 is intended to equip these regulatory evaluators with the techniques and steps required to undertake a full empirical cost-effectiveness analysis and cost-benefit analysis.

3.3 Rationales for regulation

Turning to the policy imperatives and the effects of government regulation[244], market failure may create a legitimate need for government regulation, but policymakers must recognise that such action may influence the behaviour of individuals or firms in unintended and often unpredictable ways. For example, regulatory compliance inevitably generates costs, which may be partially or fully passed on to consumers.[245] A desire to minimise regulatory compliance costs may influence firms' choices among alternative research and development paths and ultimately have an important impact on the specific features of resulting products or services. For example, firms may design new products or services so as to take advantage of regulatory 'loopholes', thereby avoiding actual or anticipated regulatory costs. Alternatively, firms may decide not to offer products or services having certain characteristics because of burdensome regulatory requirements.[246]

On balance, it would seem above all prudent for government to proceed cautiously and to engage in early formal regulation only when the benefit-cost trade-off is particularly compelling.

That is, in essence, whether: (i) variably applying selected *US EFT Act* provisions on the basis of product usage or characteristics is appropriate; and (ii) variably applying selected *US EFT Act* provisions on the basis of the underlying technology's ability to comply with regulatory requirements is appropriate.

It is ultimately concluded that any of these approaches to selective application of *US EFT Act* requirements would, depending on the details, likely impose significant operating costs for some EFT products and could generally give rise to opportunity costs as well. Moreover, there may be the potential to distort market outcomes by differentially affecting the costs of alternative products. As a result, given the absence of any experience with formal regulation of EFT in Australia, it is indeed difficult to assess the extent to which the benefits to consumers from any particular *US EFT Act* provision would outweigh the corresponding costs of compliance. In assessing the potential costs of applying formal regulatory measures to the Australian market, the analysis in this book draws on qualitative and quantitative evidence regarding experience with the *US EFT Act*, including

[244] Section draws in part directly from the Federal Report to Congress, above n 9, 10-12.
[245] See, eg, Case and Fair, above n 53.
[246] Board of Governors of the Federal Reserve, Report to Congress, above n 9, 10-11.

data on compliance costs obtained from a 1981 survey of banks issuing EFT products just 3 years after the legislation was introduced.[247] The discussion also draws on the results of several statistical studies of regulatory costs.[248] These results are considered to be of utility in anticipating the likely effects of the imposition of a formal regulatory regime for EFT in Australia.

In addition, this book will provide an economic analysis of the costs and benefits of several policy options, including the option of relying on market forces to ensure that users of EFT products receive adequate protection, and also discusses legal considerations that may arise in connection with these alternatives.

Further, early or premature formal regulation of EFT in Australia could cause higher regulatory costs than later regulation (if such regulation ultimately is determined to be desirable) because of economies of scale, the cost of revising regulations, and possible opportunity costs. However, early regulation also has the potential to speed up development by promoting standardisation and by removing uncertainty about the applicability of regulation to new products and technologies.[249]

This book also discusses the specific risks to consumers associated with retail payment mechanisms and the way those risks have been addressed not only by regulation, but by market practices as well.[250]

3.4 Administrative feasibility and social acceptability

In addition to, and conjugated with, the above methods, it is also considered meritorious to search for an efficient or optimal regulatory framework for EFT regulation in Australia that is administratively feasible and socially acceptable.

For the institutional participants (ie, the regulators and the EFT product and service providers), having a well-defined acceptable level of compliance with any new regulatory framework ought to provide a simple and administratively efficient model for supervising and complying with it. Thus, it should be possible for regulators and EFT providers, alike, to identify an acceptable level of risk and have these reflected in the new legal rules in order that value issues could be resolved at the time that standards are set, allowing a bank's or regulatory agency's technical staff to monitor compliance mechanically, without having to make case-specific economic, political and ethical decisions. For the public users of EFT products and services, a clearly enunciated acceptable level of risk reflected in any new legal rules would provide a concise focus for evaluating how well its welfare is being protected, saving the public from having to understand the

---

247 Schroeder, above n 67, 143.

248 See, eg, Elliehausen, above n 68; and Boyle, above n 68.

249 See, eg, Board of Governors of the Federal Reserve, Report to Congress, above n 9, 11-16.

250 Ibid.

underlying details of the technical processes and legal provisions giving rise to and addressing those risks.[251]

Of course, a regulatory option must also be assessed in light of the available legal or administrative mechanisms required to administer it – whether it is possible to integrate existing infrastructure, staff and systems to supervise and comply with new regulatory procedures.

Accordingly, an analytical procedure is advanced in this study to attempt to meet these constraints in determining the acceptability of EFT regulation; an efficient or optimal regulatory model that is consistent with institutional capacity and infrastructure and also compatible with public utility and values. Section 5.7 of Chapter 5 will formulate this concept more precisely. It is also followed by a discussion of how it could be implemented procedurally and describes modest compromises to the absolute principle to make it practicable. Embedded in an acceptable EFT regulatory framework, the suggested procedure would offer some chance of making the regulation of EFT in Australia more predictable and satisfying.

Therefore, the proposed EFT regulatory framework advanced in this book will attempt to implement the non-utilitarian principle that a regulation must provide acceptable consequences for everyone affected by it. Pursuing it as far as possible should produce a better regulatory process than current approaches – ones focused on limited legal or economic principles (or no clearly explicit principles at all).

It follows then that if the proposed EFT regulatory framework is attractive, then one might undertake the task of working out its details. That would involve some daunting challenges: for example, estimating with some certainty the magnitude of the risks addressed by the regulation, on the one hand, and eliciting citizens' willingness to trade off diverse costs and benefits, on the other.

It will be argued in Section 5.7 of Chapter 5 that such obstacles are a sign of strength rather than weakness. They are inherent in analytically defining institutionally and publicly acceptable risk regulation and revealed most clearly by an approach that attempts to address them head on.

3.5 Ethical considerations

Another discipline, which also provides some utility in examining appropriate regulation for the EFT system, is that of ethics in financial markets and services.

Financial markets and services may be judged by government, consumers and society at large against considerations of ethics: that embraces notions of fairness, equity, honesty and good faith. These considerations may not necessarily accord with the sort of economic efficiency principles discussed in Section 5.1. Ethics in finance is principally concerned with duty – that is, for the purposes of this book, the mutual duty between the EFT card-issuing institution and the EFT consumer.

---

[251] See, eg, B Fischhoff, Acceptable Risk: A Conceptual Proposal (2005) <http://www.piercelaw.edu/risk/vol5/winter/Fischhof.htm> at 7 March 2006.

Financial ethical considerations thus ought to include, at a minimum, principles for the mutual obligations, fairness in financial transactions and exchanges, fiduciary duties and the welfare of society as a whole.[252]

Many of these ethical issues have been addressed, in part at least, by law and industry regulation. Financial laws range from long established common law banker-customer principles and contract law to federal statutory regulations administered by ASIC and the ACCC to enforce them. Then there are industry codes of conduct such as the *EFT Code* and Code of Banking Practice where industry agrees to set its own rules and enforce them when violations occur. The role of ethics, then, in such a highly regulated, disparate environment may be problematical or at the very least obscured or even overlooked altogether. It could be said that merely obeying or conforming to the relevant rules is sufficient to satisfy ethical obligations: eg, 'if it's legal, then it's morally okay'. However, it could equally be contended that ethical principles already are at the core of much of the financial regulation that exists.

Thus, it is perhaps possible to view the EFT rules governing fraud, unauthorised transactions and liability for system failure and transaction errors as an attempt, in part at least, to enforce ethical standards as much as economic efficiency.

Although it is suggested that ethics represents (or ought to represent) a core consideration in formulating legal rules, it still begs the questions: can ethics be properly compelled and enforced by legal rules? Is legislating for ethical behaviour of itself enough and is it the appropriate response?[253]

Ultimately, though, if the prime objective of EFT regulation is to achieve economic efficiency (as was argued in Section 5.1), then it ought to follow that financial markets may only be truly 'efficient' when its participants have confidence in the fairness and equity of those markets. Perhaps, then, efficiency and ethics are not necessarily mutually exclusive objectives in pursuing an improved EFT regulatory regime.

3.6 Limited survey sample – structured interview method

This study also employs, in small part, the recognised business research method known as the 'structured interview method' to collect original data from the publications and staff of the six (6) major Australian financial institutions (ie, the principal EFT financial institutions in Australia) to supplement the secondary data collected for this multi-disciplinary, qualitative study.

According to Collis and Hussey, in the broader sense, the 'structured interview method' is a method for collecting data associated with either a 'positivistic' or a 'phenomenological' methodology and data collection is taken from selected participants who are each asked questions in order to find out particular aspects of

[252] See, eg, John R Boatright, Ethics in Finance (1999) viii.

[253] Ibid.

what they do.[254] Furthermore, this method may take place in either a 'laboratory setting' or a 'natural setting'.[255] For the purpose of this study, the participant observation takes place in a 'natural setting'. That is, at the head office retail branches of each of the 6 major Australian EFT financial institutions in Melbourne, Australia.

Unlike the *phenomenological* approach, where the interview and questions are 'unstructured' or 'semi-structured' by not having been prepared beforehand to glean what people do in terms of their actions and their behaviour, the *positivistic* approach is preferable for this study as it enables the researcher to prepare *structured, closed questions* which have been prepared beforehand.[256] It also allows the researcher to be directly and fully involved with the participants and affords the researcher a relative degree of control over the data or phenomena being researched.[257] Collis and Hussey state that the aim of the 'structured interview method' is to provide a limited, tailored means of 'comprehending the values, motives and practices of the selected participants'.[258]

This is also considered to be the most appropriate method for the purpose of this study having regard for the limited application of the method in the form of a small survey sample, the relatively inexpensive cost of this research method, the difficulty in gaining any broader access to the institutions concerned, as well as reflecting the extent to which the researcher is comfortable in the role, the amount of time the researcher has available and acknowledging the confined nature of this data collection method as part of the overall comprehensive, integrated multi-disciplinary methods employed in this study. This method is also intended to overcome the problem that the researcher cannot normally control variables in a single natural setting,[259] by observing the behaviour and practices in 6 different settings to facilitate comparisons.

Six (6) major Australian financial institutions are selected for this limited survey sample because, as ASIC reports,[260] these institutions accounted for 91% of Australian EFT transaction volume in the latest ASIC reporting period, the year to 31 March 2004.

The 6 institutions selected are the National Australia Bank, the Commonwealth Bank, the ANZ Bank, Westpac Bank, St George Bank and the Bendigo Bank.

Collis and Hussey suggest that the efficacy of a positivistic approach to a structured interview may be enhanced by using a 'short questionnaire'.[261] Accordingly, three (3) succinct and identical *structured* and *closed* questions are put to the EFT representative officer at each head office retail branch of the 6 respondent banks in Melbourne, Australia. The 3 questions are:

---

254 Collis and Hussey, above n 71, 167-8.

255 Ibid 171.

256 Ibid 168.

257 Ibid 171-2.

258 Ibid.

259 Ibid 168.

260 See, eg, Australian Securities and Investments Commission, Report of Compliance with the EFT Code of Conduct, 2003/2004 (2005).

261 Collis and Hussey, above n 71, 167-72.

1. Do you have a copy of your Bank's EFT terms and conditions of use available?
2. Do you have someone at this branch of your Bank that can personally explain the EFT terms and conditions of use to me?
3. Does your Bank have a formal procedure for issuing EFT cards and PINs?

In recognition of the fact that the six (6) major Australian retail banks overwhelmingly dominate the EFT payments system and transaction volume in Australia (as discussed above), the representatives selected and approached were the designated EFT representative officers at the Melbourne head office retail branch of the six (6) major Australian retail banks.

The results of this limited and closed survey are reported in the detailed comparative legal analysis of the substantive provisions of the EFT Code and US EFT Act in Sections 4.1, 4.2 and 4.3 of Chapter 4, where the regulatory requirements governing the availability of EFT terms and conditions of use, continuing disclosure of EFT terms and conditions of use and the issuance of EFT cards and PINs are discussed and appraised. The tabulated results are appended to this book at Appendix 1.

3.7 Conclusion

As discussed in this chapter, there are hitherto unexplored multi-disciplinary methods, each of great utility, for evaluating EFT regulatory options. The critical comparative law method is the preferred comparative tool for examining the substantive provisions of the Australian and USA regulations. It facilitates not only a contrastive evaluation of the different regulatory responses to a common core problem, but allows for the possibility of convergence and integration as well. The economics of law and regulation theory approaches address several important issues: assessing the allocative efficiency of regulatory options, the benefits and rationales for government intervention, identifying the presence of market failure and enables a framework to be constructed for a rigorous cost-effectiveness analysis and cost-benefit analysis. An ethical approach to formulating an efficient regulatory framework is also a worthy pursuit. Economic efficiency and financial ethics need not be mutually exclusive – the quest for true efficiency may, in fact, embrace ethical considerations. Therefore, an extended multi-disciplinary analysis is needed to comprehensively evaluate EFT regulatory options. This expanded and integrated multi-disciplinary technique is applied in Chapters 4 and 5: the comparative legal analysis of Australian and USA regulations, as well as the limited survey sample, in Chapter 4 and the economic, regulation theory, ethical, administrative, social and other disciplines are applied in the analysis in Chapter 5.

Chapter 4. Comparative Analysis of Substantive Regulations

Deploying the critical comparative law method adopted for this book (discussed in detail in Section 3.1 of Chapter 3), in this chapter a comparative legal analysis is undertaken of the substantive provisions of the markedly divergent Australian *EFT Code* and *US EFT Act*. In particular, the detailed and controversial provisions that purport to regulate liability for unauthorised EFT transactions under both regimes. The related regulation of financial institution disclosure of the terms and conditions of use, the issuance of EFT cards and PINs, ongoing EFT disclosure, liability for EFT system malfunctions, EFT errors, countermand (stop payment) rights and EFT dispute resolution procedures will also be analysed from a comparative perspective.

This chapter is structured as follows: In Section 4.1, a preliminary analysis of the divergent approaches to EFT regulation in Australia and the USA is articulated, through their respective regulation of financial institution disclosure of the terms and conditions of use for electronic banking. A controversial litigated case from the USA is used as a plenary illustration of their contrasting positions. Then, in Section 4.2, the contrasting procedures to be followed in delivering EFT cards or PINs is examined with the discovery of a surprising variety of financial institution practices and a consistent, uniform and secure procedure is argued. The analysis in Section 4.3 is concerned with the disparate provisions governing continuing EFT disclosure by financial institutions – that is, the requirements to provide consumers with crucial EFT transaction evidence in the form of EFT transaction receipts and periodic EFT account statements. Section 4.4 represents the central section of this chapter and presents a detailed comparative legal analysis of the contrasting approach in Australia and the USA for determining and allocating liability in the event of an unauthorised EFT transaction. In this section, actual ABIO disputed cases as well as litigated cases from the USA are used to assist the comparative analysis. In Section 4.5, the complex issue of who bears responsibility for EFT system malfunctions and errors in both jurisdictions is explored and consideration is given in Section 4.6 as to whether EFT can provide countermand or stop payment rights which are available under traditional payment methods. The analysis in Section 4.7 is concerned with the contrasting minimum dispute resolution procedures that are required in Australia and the USA and the conclusion is contained in Section 4.8.

4.1 Overview of regulation of EFT in Australia and the USA

As discussed in brief earlier, in both Australia and the USA, EFT transactions between financial institutions and consumers are governed primarily by the legally binding 'terms and conditions of use' drafted and issued by financial institutions, to which the consumer agrees to be bound when operating a plastic card and PIN via an electronic terminal.[262]

In the USA, the terms and conditions of use refer exclusively to the provisions of the *US EFT Act* in the event of an unauthorised EFT following loss or theft of the card with the onus on the financial institution to disprove fault. The *US EFT Act* is ultimately administered and monitored by the Federal Reserve Board of the USA.

The *US EFT Act*, pursuant to § 1693(d), specifically provides that there be strict disclosure and documentation requirements applicable to financial institutions who provide EFT services to consumers, and, importantly, that these are to form part of the account agreement between the institution (ie, the financial institution) and the consumer.

Similarly, in Australia, under clause 2 of the *EFT Code*, financial institutions must provide a copy of the terms and conditions of use to each EFT account holder. Consumers are to be advised in advance of the relevant charges, daily transaction limits, and other restrictions, descriptions of transactions that may be made, the procedure for reporting a loss, theft or unauthorised use, as well as the means to activate complaint investigation and the dispute resolution process.

It would seem to be in the interests of EFT financial institutions, not to mention avoiding potential conflicts between financial institutions and consumers, for prospective EFT consumers to be given adequate disclosure of the terms and conditions of use *prior* to obtaining EFT services. However, in practice, not all financial institutions have copies of their terms and conditions of use available for perusal prior to signing an EFT account application form ahead of obtaining EFT access.[263] Not only are there variations between financial institutions on the matter of when terms and conditions of use are made available (if at all, as in the case of ANZ Bank: see the tabulated limited survey sample results appended at Appendix 1), financial institutions also have a varied, complex approach to when the consumer is deemed to have accepted the terms and conditions of use, which would seem to be unacceptable and challenges the integrity of the EFT system in Australia.[264] In some instances, they are also quite clumsily drafted and worded.

---

262 See, eg, Electronic Funds Transfer Code of Conduct (original, 1989) cl 1.1.

263 This was the experience when attending upon the head office retail branches of the six (6) major Australian EFT financial institutions in Melbourne, Australia, as part of the limited survey sample ('structured and closed interview method') described in Section 3.6 of Chapter 3.

264 The actual terms and conditions of use cited in the analysis in Section 4.1 draws from the actual EFT terms and conditions of use of EFT financial institutions gathered on 10

For example, the Commonwealth Bank's EFT terms and conditions of use provide that:[265]

This…forms the terms and conditions of the contract between you and us if you decide to open an EFT account. These terms and conditions become binding once we give you (or any other user) and you (or that other user) accept the access method. As from that time, we and you undertake to keep to the terms and conditions.

In consequence, the Commonwealth Bank's EFT terms and conditions of use[266] seek to implement the terms and conditions of use from the time the EFT card is *issued* (not when it is first used as for the majority of the other banks surveyed. Note that the terms and conditions of use of both Westpac Bank[267] and St George Bank[268] appear to be altogether silent on the matter). Indeed, Commonwealth Bank's approach (described above) may give rise to a potential breach of clause 2 of the *EFT Code* which stipulates that the terms and conditions of use must be supplied *before use* (ie, access) with the EFT card. By way of comparison, Bendigo Bank's EFT terms and conditions of use state that:[269]

Acceptance means your (or your authorised user(s) acceptance of these Terms and Conditions in relation to the Bendigo…(EFT)…services evidenced by you or your authorised user(s) access to the Bendigo…(EFT)…services or selection of a PIN by either you or your authorised user(s) to access the Bendigo…(EFT)…services, whichever occurs first.

The EFT terms and conditions of use of the National Australia Bank read in similar terms.[270] However, the reference to '…any use of a card…' is imprecise and raises the problem of 'any use' also possibly including that use initiated by an unauthorised person.

Previously, the National Australia Bank's EFT terms and conditions of use[271] intended a staggered approach to when the terms and conditions of use apply. It was also somewhat ambiguous on what constitutes 'receipt' of an EFT card and/or PIN:

February 2006 as part of the Limited Survey Sample – Structured Interview Data Collection Method.

265 Commonwealth Bank, Transaction, Savings and Investments Accounts – Product Disclosure Statement (01/2006).

266 Ibid.

267 Westpac Bank, Deposit Accounts – Product Disclosure Statement incorporating Terms and Conditions for using your Account (01/2006).

268 St George Bank, Banking Services – Terms and Conditions and General Information (09/2005).

269 Bendigo Bank, Bendigo Phone Banking & Bendigo e-Banking Terms and Conditions (02/2004).

270 National Australia Bank, National Internet Banking – Product Disclosure Statement Including Terms and Conditions (10/2005).

271 National Australia Bank, EFT Terms and Conditions of Use (1997).

The provisions of these Conditions of Use as regards safekeeping of the PIN apply immediately on receipt of your PIN. The full Conditions of Use apply on receipt of the Card.

From these actual examples, it is apparent that financial institutions have different intentions for when the consumer contractually agrees and is bound by the terms and conditions of use. In some cases, it is conceivable that an unacceptable situation might occur where customers are bound when they receive the EFT card and PIN without having been supplied with the EFT terms and conditions of use. EFT account application forms generally only refer the consumers to these terms and conditions, they do not always provide for consumer acknowledgment. The *EFT Code* should either more clearly provide for uniformity on when and how the terms and conditions of use issued by the EFT financial institutions take effect, or take steps to increase its enforcement capabilities under its existing approach.

It is noteworthy, too, that the first report of the EFT Working Group in 1985 recommended that financial institutions not only issue clear and unambiguous terms and conditions of use, but also provide some personal explanation of the key clauses dealing with consumer responsibilities at the time the EFT account application is made.[272] The EFT Working Group also stated that financial institutions should keep and display documents setting out the terms and conditions of use. Given the recent experience that none of these recommendations have been consistently taken up by financial institutions, it would seem reasonable and desirable that the *EFT Code*, at the very least, include the first EFT Working Group's suggestion that some personal explanation be made available on request by the EFT consumer or prospective EFT consumer. Although, it is conceded that it would not be necessary, desirable or even logistically feasible to require all financial institutions extend this level of disclosure of all EFT terms and conditions of use in all instances to all consumers (ie, even extending to additional consumers such as spouses, partners or children). In practice, once adequate disclosure is made to the principal consumer, that consumer is responsible for ensuring his/her nominees utilise the EFT account properly and with knowledge of the relevant terms and conditions of use (eg, in the above Bendigo Bank's and Commonwealth Bank's EFT terms and conditions of use).

Furthermore, under clause 2 of the *EFT Code*, financial institutions must warrant that its terms and conditions of use comply or reflect the requirements of the *EFT Code*, and, moreover, that these terms and conditions are not to provide for or be effective to create liabilities and responsibilities for users (ie, consumers), which exceed or elevate those set out in the *EFT Code*. However, while the *EFT Code* does not have the force of statute law, as advanced earlier in Chapter 2, this warranty may give rise to civil and/or criminal liability under the *ASIC Act*, exposing a financial institution to a substantial fine if its terms and conditions do not comply with the *EFT Code's* requirements. In adopting the *EFT Code*, all financial institutions' terms and conditions of use become part of the financial institutions' contract with the consumer. This forms the contractual nexus and contractual principles will then apply. While adherence to the *EFT*

[272] Report of the EFT Working Group, above n 136, 84-5.

Code is 'voluntary', all suppliers of EFT services are 'encouraged' to comply with it (indeed, some 187 financial institutions, which comprise banks and non-bank financial institutions, according to the latest EFT annual report released by ASIC in December 2005).[273]

The original *EFT Code* was released in December 1989 [274] with the intention of allocating liability in the event of disputes, providing protection and security guidance for customers and stating clearly the obligations of providers of EFT services. As stated, financial institution compliance with the *EFT Code* is monitored by ASIC, a Commonwealth Government regulatory body.[275] Pursuant to clause 10 of the *EFT Code*, the responsibility for handling complaint investigation and resolution procedures rests, in the first instance, with the financial institution. Should the consumer still remain dissatisfied, external avenues are available. In particular, the independent ABIO is the industry's preferred body to assist in EFT dispute resolution according to the Reserve Bank of Australia.

In both systems, litigation is seldom used for relief as quite apart from the uncertainties of litigation, and uneven bargaining power, there may be a lack of consumer awareness and/or that there is rarely a sufficient amount at stake to justify the expense of legal proceedings.[276] However, by way of introduction to a

---

[273] Australian Securities and Investments Commission, Report of Compliance with the EFT Code of Conduct, 2003/2004 (2005) 6.

[274] Electronic Funds Transfer Code of Conduct (original, 1989).

[275] ASIC requires that all EFT card issuing institutions report annually on various aspects of EFT by completing a detailed annual check list of 69 questions covering each clause of the EFT Code. In the 1999/2000 review year. ASIC stated that compared to the previous reporting period (1998/1999), the incidence of reported non-compliance has increased in the case of the EFT Code. Indeed, ASIC stated in its review that the largest number of disputes (of all ASIC monitored payments system codes) related to PIN-based EFT transactions.

[276] Note that given the confines of this book, it is not proposed to explore the USA legal or administrative system in detail, nor the different approaches and practices in litigation in Australia and the USA, suffice to state that both Australia and the USA broadly have in common a similar adversarial common law legal system.

In terms of the differences in litigation practices between Australia and the USA, it may generally be observed that in the USA the losing litigant does not always necessarily pay costs, class actions may be more readily available, and plaintiff lawyers are more prevalent as they can take, by way of contingency fees, a percentage of the verdict which is not permissible in Australia. The result is that in the USA, generally, litigation is possibly more effective as a way of regulating business: see, eg, W Kip Viscusi (ed), Regulation Through Litigation (2002).

There could also be said to be a recognised difference in litigation strategies between institutional repeat players such as the banks and their clients. According to Galanter, the banks are repeat players and may play strategically and sometimes lose cases which they compensate themselves for out of their strategic wins. They also play for the rules and take test cases. Conversely, individual litigants cannot play strategically as they are relative 'one shotter's' in for a single game and sometimes even their lawyers do not share these wider interests: see, eg, Marc Galanter, 'Why the Haves Come Out Ahead: Speculations on the Limits of Social Change' (1974) 9 Law and Society Review 95, 97-114.

more detailed comparative analysis of the substantive regulations of both countries, consider the following working example of an EFT fraud from the USA and how the burden of proof squarely rests with the financial institution to prove consumer fault.

In *Ognibene v Citibank Inc*:[277]

Citibank had an ATM centre with 2 adjacent ATMs separated only by a telephone which provided a direct 'hot line' to Citibank's service centre.

In Ognibene, a third person positioned himself at the telephone and pretended to be making a telephone call to Citibank's service centre complaining about difficulties in using one of the ATMs. Whilst making the non-existent telephone call, he observed a genuine customer at the adjacent ATM inputting the PIN. The third person then pretended that he had been told by Citibank's service centre operator to borrow the genuine customer's card and insert it into the allegedly malfunctioning ATM to see whether or not the ATM would work with another card. He told the genuine customer that he had been so directed and asked if he could borrow the card. The genuine customer accepted the third party's request since the card could only be operated with his PIN. Unbeknown to the genuine customer, the third person used the card and the PIN to extract money.

The court held that the bank was not permitted to debit the customer's account with the amounts fraudulently keyed into the ATM on the grounds that by merely giving his card to the third person to initiate the transfer, the consumer did not thereby furnish the means of access to his account.

The *Ognibene* case above illustrates that handing over an EFT card is not like giving a third party a pre-signed, blank cheque. Giving a fraudulent party a pre-signed, uncrossed blank cheque would be a breach of customer's duty to take reasonable care given that the cheque carries the customer's mandate to the bank to debit his/her account.

Conversely, under Australia's *EFT Code*, *Ognibene* would likely be decided in favour of the bank unless the consumer could show that s/he had been 'shouldered' at the ATM. There are, of course, many variations on the *Ognibene* example (including some recent Australian cases from the ABIO's office, which will be cited in Sections 4.3 and 4.4 and used effectively to compare the different practical applications of the *EFT Code* and *US EFT Act*).

4.2 The issuance of EFT cards and PINs

At present, the delivery method of the EFT access device (the EFT card) and the authorisation number by which a consumer enters the EFT system (the PIN), is not uniform across financial institutions in either Australia or the USA. Recent actual experience and an examination of the procedures surrounding the issue of EFT cards and PINs also revealed a surprising variety of procedural methods and processes across those financial institutions visited upon (principally, the 6 major

---

[277] NY City Civ Ct 446 NYS 2d 845 (1981).

Australian banks: ANZ Bank, Commonwealth Bank, National Australia Bank, Westpac Bank, St George Bank and Bendigo Bank).[278]

At the lower end of the security spectrum are financial institutions who issue EFT cards and PINs, albeit separately by ordinary mail. To a sophisticated or informed thief, it could perhaps be obvious what the envelopes contain and thus it could be argued that this means of delivery is open to interception (eg, a thief or unauthorised person is monitoring the applicant's mail box). Other institutions operate more secure systems requiring either the EFT card or the PIN to be issued from a branch office of the institution against presentation of suitable identification. From a consumer-security perspective, it would seem desirable that the EFT card and PIN both be issued from a branch office.

By way of context and background, the original draft *EFT Code* in 1986 did fasten quite heavy obligations on institutions when issuing EFT cards and PINs. It recommended that a signed acknowledgment be of receipt of the EFT card be obtained by the institution before issuing a PIN, and, where the consumer received the card directly, the institution must satisfy itself as to the identity of the recipient and obtain a signed acknowledgment of receipt. Moreover, the draft *EFT Code* also required that where other signatures of the customer are held by the financial institution, then the financial institution must check those signatures against the signature on the receipt. Furthermore, the draft *EFT Code* also stipulated that PINs may only be delivered by consumers by means of 'personal delivery' through a branch office of the institution or by (presumably personal) delivery by an agent or employee of the institution.

The draft *EFT Code* also stated that explicit warnings must be given to the consumer of the consequences of writing the PIN on the EFT card, keeping the PIN with or near the EFT card or in an obvious place or knowingly disclosing the PIN to third parties including family members.

However, the final form of the original *EFT Code* in 1989 did not include such explicit EFT card and PIN security warnings as a result of concerns expressed by a number of financial institutions, notably those which did not have extensive branch networks and/or which had widely spread customer bases and would have had difficulty obtaining consumer acknowledgments and proper identifications.[279] It is also regrettable that the revised current *EFT Code* did not take the opportunity to remedy the situation. The *EFT Code* does not compel financial institutions to obtain written acknowledgments, identification or confirmation of receipt for either or both the EFT card and the PIN. Presumably, this oversight can only be explained by clause 5.2(c) of the *EFT Code* fastening the burden on the financial institution to establish that the EFT card and/or PIN have been received by the consumer in the event of a dispute over the facts surrounding issuance and subsequent receipt of the EFT card and/or PIN. Therefore, the *EFT Code* has

[278] This was the experience when attending upon the head office retail branches of the six (6) major Australian EFT financial institutions in Melbourne, Australia, as part of the limited survey sample ('structured and closed interview method') described in Section 3.6 of Chapter 3.

[279] White, above n 77, 19.

attempted to apportion the onus of proof if not any real guidance on the safe dispatch of EFT cards and PINs. Although it should be said that discharging any burden of proof under the *EFT Code* is far from straightforward and extremely difficult (again, as the ABIO regularly observes in its annual reports).[280]
Clause 5(c) of the *EFT Code* expressly states that:

The account holder has no liability for:

Losses that arise from transactions which required the use of any device or code forming part of the user's access method and that occurred before the user has received any such device or code (including a reissued device or code). In any dispute about receipt of a device or code it is to be presumed that the item was not received by the user, unless the account institution can prove otherwise. The account institution can establish that the user did receive the device or code by obtaining an acknowledgment of receipt from the user whenever a new device or code is issued. If the device or code was sent to the user by mail or email, the account institution is not to rely only on proof of delivery to the user's correct address as proof that the device or code was received by that person. Nor will the account institution have any term in the Terms and Conditions which deems a device or code sent to the user at that person's correct address (including an email address) to have been received by the user within a certain time after sending.

Interestingly, of all the financial institutions visited upon on 10 February 2006 in Melbourne, Australia, for the purpose of the limited survey sample: structured interview data collection method, only the Bendigo Bank had both: (i) a clear, formal procedure; and (ii) actually sought to have receipt of each of the EFT card and the PIN acknowledged in writing against proper identification.[281] Of the other five (5) major Australian banks, results varied from having no knowledge of the procedure, if any (eg, ANZ Bank, St George Bank and Westpac Bank) to: 'I think we need for you to tell us how you want them sent' (eg, Commonwealth Bank) through to: 'That should all be set out in the terms and conditions booklet' (eg, National Australia Bank).[282]

An actual disputed case adjudicated by the ABIO[283] provides a useful working example of the difficult practical application of this provision of the *EFT Code*:

Ms J was a student, renting a house in Sydney with three other students, and applied to a bank to open an account that could be accessed by card through an ATM. The bank policy was for Ms J to attend a branch and select, at random, a sealed envelope containing a PIN.

Upon that occurring, the teller then entered into the bank's computer a code which was printed on the outside of the PIN envelope. The bank's computer would then generate an

280 See, eg, Australian Banking Industry Ombudsman, Annual Reports, 1992/1993 and 1995/1996.

281 Refer to the results appended at Appendix 1 of the six (6) major Australian EFT financial institutions in Melbourne, Australia, as part of the limited survey sample ('structured and closed interview method') described in Section 3.6 of Chapter 3.

282 Ibid.

283 Australian Banking Industry Ombudsman Limited, Annual Report, 1992/1993, 60-1.

instruction for the card relating to the hidden PIN to be posted to Ms J. Ms J left the branch with the PIN envelope as she was entitled to do and awaited the card by mail.

A week later, $20 was withdrawn from her account via an ATM in Sydney. Two further ATM withdrawals of $500 and $480, respectively, occurred in Queensland. Upon learning of these, Ms J cancelled the card and claimed she had not received it through the post.

The bank initially denied her request for a refund of the money taken from the account on the basis that she must have revealed her PIN to a third party. Ms J claimed to have committed the PIN to memory and not voluntarily disclosed the PIN to anybody.

At conference between Ms J, the financial institution and Ombudsman, the accepted facts were: (i) the card was posted to Ms J, (ii) no acknowledgment of receipt of the card was obtained (with the Ombudsman determining that the disputed use was not evidence of receipt by the consumer), and (iii) whilst the PIN had been retained by Ms J, she had not voluntarily disclosed it to any third person and it could not be safely assumed that she had received the card pursuant to clause 5.2(iii) of the *EFT Code*.

In the circumstances, the Ombudsman decided that the bank must reimburse Ms J for the sums lost plus interest up to the date of payment.

This application of the *EFT Code* by the ABIO would seem to protect a customer who has been sent a card and/or PIN, but has not received it (again, the unauthorised person watching the mailbox). In such instances, under the *EFT Code*, the customer is unlikely to be held liable for losses arising from use of the card and PIN where s/he has no knowledge that the card and PIN had been dispatched and therefore no opportunity to avoid or rectify the position.

By way of comparison, and a major shortcoming of the *US EFT Act*, is that it does not require any detailed procedures be followed in delivering EFT cards or PINs. In consequence, under the strict terms of the no-fault liability provisions of the *US EFT Act* dealing with unauthorised EFT transactions (§1693g), Ms J would still be liable for the first US$50 (the manner in which this figure is arrived at will be explained shortly in the analysis of the substantive regulations in Section 4.4).

4.3 Continuing EFT disclosure

The present position on continuing EFT disclosure required under clause 4 of the *EFT Code* is that financial institutions must issue ATM transaction receipts, point of sale (EFTPOS) transaction receipts, together with periodic account statements.

Clauses 4.1(a),(c) and (d) provide:

At the time of an EFT transaction and unless a user specifically elects otherwise, the account institution will ensure a receipt is issued containing all of the following information:

(i) the amount of the transaction;
(ii) the date and time (if practicable) of the transaction;
(iii) the type of transaction eg, a "deposit", "withdrawal", "transfer", (symbols may be used only if they are explained on the receipt and easily understood abbreviations may be used);
(iv) an indication of the account(s) being debited or credited;

(v) data that enable the account institution to identify the customer and the transaction;
(vi) where possible, the type and general location of any institution equipment used to make the transaction or a number or symbol that enables that institution equipment to be identified;
(vii) in the case of a funds transfer to a merchant in payment for goods or services, the name of the merchant to whom payment was made;
(viii) where possible, and where it is not likely to compromise the privacy or security of the user or the account holder, the balance remaining in the account which is debited in the funds transfer (or, in the case of a deposit, the account which is credited).

(c) Account institutions may choose to provide users with the option to specify at the time of each transaction that a receipt is not required. A charge may not be imposed on a user or an account holder for the issuing of a receipt.
(d) In an EFT transaction where the user does not use institution equipment or an institution system and does not communicate with the account institution or a person acting on its behalf, the account institution is only obliged to use its best endeavours to meet its obligations under paragraph (a).

The transaction receipts required to be issued at both ATMs and EFTPOS terminals take on significance as they provide the consumer with an evidential trail. The transaction receipts normally include details such as the date and time of the transaction, the account number, the card number, the location of the EFT terminal, the nature of the transaction (ie, deposit, withdrawal, account transfer or account balance request) as well as the amount. The transaction documentation obligations of the *US EFT Act* are couched in very similar terms, pursuant to §1693d(a).

For privacy reasons, an account balance is only included on ATM transaction receipts. The periodic statements on account (discussed below) contain details of all transactions affecting an account (including non-EFT transactions) since the date the previous statement was issued. This practice enables the consumer to check and verify the details on the statement against the transaction receipts, but only *if* they are maintained.

Given the evidential value to a consumer, it is curious, indeed, that neither the Australian *EFT Code* nor the *US EFT Act* provisions require that EFT transaction receipts issued at EFT terminals include a receipt number. Making this a specific requirement would enhance the validity of the receipt, and thus the position of the consumer in a dispute, as the receipt number could be checked against the transaction number on a periodic statement and would also be of utility to the financial institution by facilitating a reconciliation of transaction numbers with those on the financial institution's daily EFT transaction reports and logs.

Although, it should be observed that whilst of benefit as an evidential trail, the true evidential effect at law of transaction receipts remains unclear and whether it is admissible in evidence as unequivocal proof of an EFT transaction needs to be clarified. Therefore, a transaction number on a receipt may be of negligible benefit in the event that it is deemed to have no evidentiary effect. Yet, the position is also unsatisfactory from the perspective that it is inconsistent with the *EFT Code's* requirement that periodic EFT account statements show a receipt number or other means (eg, perhaps a symbol or code is envisaged, but this is unclear) to enable the consumer to reconcile the statement entry with the transaction receipt (clause 4.3(iv)).

To enhance the efficacy of these ambiguous *EFT Code* requirements, surely it would be reasonable that consumers must be encouraged to retain EFT terminal transaction receipts (whether numbered or otherwise) in order to check them against the entries on their periodic statements. The *EFT Code*, however, does not go so far. Clause 4.4 merely provides that financial institutions may only *suggest* to consumers that all entries on statements be checked, but with no reference to EFT terminal transaction receipts. Therefore, there is no obligation on the consumer to inspect and authenticate the entries on the periodic statement. Clause 4.4 states:

> Account institutions will suggest to account holders that all entries on statements be checked and any apparent error or possible unauthorised transaction be promptly reported to the account institution. This suggestion will be contained on the account statement. Institutions will not seek to restrict or deny account holders their rights to make claims or to attempt to impose time limits on users to detect errors or unauthorised transactions.

This generally reflects the position for paper-based transactions at common law where there is no duty on the customer to monitor statements and inform the bank of discrepancies in order to prevent fraud.[284] However, the practice of at least one (1) EFT financial institution is quite the opposite. For example, Westpac Bank places a specific obligation on the consumer on page 6 of its terms and conditions of use:[285] specifically, that a consumer must 'check entries on statements and notify the Bank promptly about possible errors or unauthorised transactions'. The reader is then referred to page 43 for more information; however, that page does not contain any information at all regarding periodic statements or the verification of entries on a statement. This would seem to be in clear contravention of the *EFT Code's* clause 4.4, as well as the warranty clause at 2.1, which presumably together would serve to render Westpac's practice illegal, or, at the least, void. While there has been no such disputed cases cited in the ABIO Annual Reports, it would be reasonable to conclude that the ABIO would likely determine that EFT financial institutions could not rely on any such terms and conditions requiring consumers to keep all paper records and that all transactions be reconciled immediately. In addition, relevant provisions of the *ASIC Act* might also be applicable should a financial institution attempt this and breach the warranty requirement under the *EFT Code.*

In relation to periodic EFT account statements generally, clause 4.2(a) of the *EFT Code* provides that:

---

[284] See, eg, Tai Hing Cotton Mill Ltd v Liu Chong Hing Bank and Others (1985) 2 All ER 947.

[285] Westpac Bank, Deposit Accounts – Product Disclosure Statement incorporating Terms and Conditions for using your Account (01/2006).

For an account to or from which EFT transactions can be made, the account institution will provide a record of account activity at least every six months. Account holders are also to be offered the option of receiving more frequent periodic statements. That option is to be brought to the attention of the account holder at the time the access method is first issued. As well, statements are to be available at the request of the account holder.

In contrast, the relevant provision of the *US EFT Act* seems far more practical: §1693d(c) requires that institutions provide a monthly statement if an EFT transaction has occurred in that period or at least quarterly if no EFT transaction occurred. In view of financial institution attempts to insist that consumers retain and reconcile their transaction receipts with their periodic statements, then this approach is sensible. Indeed, §1693d(f) of the *US EFT Act* also usefully provides that all EFT documentation given to the consumer (ie, both EFT transaction receipts and periodic statements) shall be admissible as evidence of an EFT transaction and shall constitute prima facie proof that the EFT transaction was made. Taken together, these requirements of the *US EFT Act* have special meaning as early consumer detection of erroneous or unauthorised EFT transactions based on this documentation will limit the consumer's liability as will be shown in Section 4.4 next.

4.4 Liability for unauthorised EFT transactions

This section is central to the comparative legal analysis of the divergent approaches taken, by Australia and the USA, to disputed, unauthorised EFT transactions. This section presents an analysis of the markedly different approaches when an EFT transaction is initiated allegedly without the authority of the consumer, but which is nevertheless carried out. The fundamental issue to be considered here is the loss or liability allocation between the financial institution and consumer on whose behalf the EFT transaction purported to be initiated.[286]

By way of introduction to the *EFT Code's* approach to regulating unauthorised EFT transactions, it is useful, first, to consider the *US EFT Act*,[287] which creates a concise, three-tier structure for calculating liability.

Under §1693g of the *US EFT Act*, the consumer's liability is set out as follows:

1. Liability no greater than US$50.00 or the amount of the transaction (whichever is less) for unauthorised transactions occurring before notice (of loss or theft of an EFT card and/or PIN) to the institution;
2. Failure to notify the loss or theft of an EFT card and/or PIN within two days of discovery, maximum liability is raised to US$500.00; and
3. If an unauthorised transaction (not previously discovered by a customer) is shown on a periodic EFT account statement, liability is limited to US$500.00 by reporting the

[286] Geva, above n 4, 18.

[287] Electronic Funds Transfer Act, 15 USC § 1693 (1978) and Regulation E, § 205.6 (1981).

discrepancy on the statement within 60 days. Failure to report in 60 days means unlimited liability.

Therefore, the underlying principle is that a consumer in the USA is only liable for authorised EFT transactions as well as for a limited amount of any unauthorised EFT transactions, up to the time of notification to the financial institution. Where such notification is not given within the outside limit of 60 days, the consumer is liable for the entire amount after that 60 days. Importantly, though, is the fact that the consumer's negligence or carelessness with the EFT card and/or PIN in contributing to an unauthorised EFT transaction is not a factor in determining the consumer's exposure to liability.

Hence, Ms J would have been liable for US$50 in the ABIO case (at Section 4.2 above) because she notified the bank within 2 days of becoming aware of the unauthorised transactions.

With this background, how does the Australian *EFT Code* approach the issue of liability for unauthorised EFT transactions? With the exception of the *US EFT Act's* requirement (at 3. above) that a customer check statements for unauthorised transactions and notify any such transactions to the bank within 60 days, the *EFT Code* also, in small part, adopts a tiered approach in determining liability, but in a comparatively cumbersome, legalistic and protracted form. As a preliminary point, it is submitted that such a legalistic and unwieldy approach does not necessarily guarantee certainty and clarity.

At the outset, it is important to also highlight the different definitions of an 'unauthorised EFT transaction' taken by the Australian *EFT Code* vis-à-vis the *US EFT Act*. The *EFT Code's* clause 1.5 is ambiguous and particularly unhelpful and merely states that an unauthorised EFT transaction is one 'not authorised by the user' and 'transactions carried out by the user or by anyone performing the transaction with the user's knowledge and consent' are specifically excluded and thus are deemed 'authorised'. A 'user' is broadly defined in the *EFT Code's* clause 1.5 to be 'the person authorised by the account institution to use the EFT access methods'. Again, this is vague as it may or may not be the EFT account holder and is not necessarily the *actual* user of the EFT access device in a given case. It is therefore most unclear what the position is, for example, with a person other than the consumer who is lawfully in possession of the EFT access means, but has no authority to effect an EFT transaction. Whereas the *US EFT Act's* §1693a(11) comprehensively defines an 'unauthorised EFT transaction' as meaning:

An EFT transaction from a consumer's account initiated by a person other than the consumer without actual authority to initiate such transfer and from which the consumer receives no benefit, but the term does not include any electronic fund transfer (a) initiated by a person other than the consumer who was furnished with the card, code, or other means of access to such consumer's account by such consumer,[288] unless the consumer has

[288] Note: In 'furnishing' the access device (ie, card, code or other means of access), the consumer must have acted voluntarily. Accordingly, where control of the access device is surrendered by the consumer as a result of robbery or fraud, the EFT transaction ini-

notified the financial institution involved that transfers by such other person are no longer authorised, (b) initiated with fraudulent intent by the consumer or any person acting in concert with the consumer, or (c) which constitutes an error committed by a financial institution.

Clause 5 of the *EFT Code*, entitled 'Liability for Unauthorised Transactions', is intended to be an exhaustive statement on consumer liability. The opportunity for financial institutions to extend liability unilaterally by inserting other terms and conditions appears to be limited by the ABIO's interpretation that the terms and conditions cannot 'elevate' a consumer's liability above that under the *EFT Code*.[289] Again, relevant provisions of the *ASIC Act* might also be applicable should a financial institution attempt this and breach the warranty requirement under the *EFT Code*.

4.4.1 No consumer liability

In Australia, pursuant to clauses 5.2, 5.3 and 5.4 of the *EFT Code*, consumers are expressly excluded from liability where agreement is reached between the financial institution and consumer that losses have occurred by:

- The fraudulent or negligent conduct of employees or agents of the financial institution or companies involved in networking arrangements or of merchants who are linked to the EFT system or of their agents or employees.
- From cards that are forged, faulty, expired or cancelled.
- Before the consumer has received his/her card and PIN where the burden of proof rests with the financial institution.
- Losses that are caused by the same transaction being incorrectly debited more than once to the same account.
- Occurring after notification by the consumer that the card has been misused, lost or stolen or that PIN security has been breached.
- Where it is clear that the consumer has not contributed to such losses.

At face value, these exclusions seem reasonable and sensible especially when compared to the *US EFT Act* which does not expressly provide for any exclusions to the 3-tiered liability arrangements under §1693g.

However, it is the last element of the EFT Code's exclusions (clause 5.4) which deserves special attention: the account holder has no liability for losses resulting from unauthorised transactions where it is clear that the user has not contributed to

tiated by the robber or defrauding person is considered to be 'unauthorised'. This was contained in an Official Staff Commentary generously supplied by the Federal Reserve Board of the USA and was effective 2 May 1996. Prior to this interpretation, there was judicial disagreement on what constituted voluntarily furnishing the access device: Feldman v Citibank, 443 NYS 2d 43 (Civ Ct, 1981); Ognibene v Citibank, 446 NYS 2d 845 at 847 (Civ Ct, 1981); and State v Citibank, 537 F Supp 1992 at 1994 (SDNY, 1982).

289 Australian Banking Industry Ombudsman Limited, Annual Report, 1995/1996, 23.

such losses. The EFT Code is silent on who has the burden of establishing this as between the financial institution and consumer and nor does it assist by providing any guidance, process or criteria for how such a conclusion can be drawn to the consumer's benefit. This will become especially apparent when looking at consumer liability next in Section 4.4.2.

4.4.2 Consumer liability

Where the exclusions outlined above in Section 4.4.1 (above) do not apply, clauses 5.5(a) and (b) of the *EFT Code* stipulate in what circumstances the consumer is liable for losses resulting from unauthorised EFT transactions. That is, where it is deemed 'on the balance of probability' that the consumer has contributed to the losses, including, in some circumstances, where the consumer was the 'dominant contributing cause of the losses'.

These multi-layered threshold tests required under the *EFT Code* are intrinsically difficult to adjudicate at law and as the body left to do so in most instances, the ABIO, regularly observes (discussed in detail later in this section when examining actual ABIO cases).

Turning to the particulars of each *EFT Code* provision dealing with consumer liability, clause 5.5(a) of the *EFT Code* provides a muddled, legalistic beginning as it sets out in much detail the complex multi-layered tests required to determine liability. However, for the specific instances or events in which the consumer is actually liable, clause 5.5(a) refers to yet another lengthy cross-clause contained elsewhere in the *EFT Code* (at clause 5.6).

Clause 5.5(a) states:

> Where the account institution can prove on the balance of probability that the user contributed to the losses through the user's fraud or the user's contravention of the requirements in sub-clause 5.6, the account holder is liable for the actual losses which occur before the account institution is notified that a device forming part of the access method has been misused, lost or stolen or that the security of the codes forming part of the access method has been breached.
>
> (Where an access method includes more than one code and the account institution proves that the user contravened the requirements of sub-clause 5.6 by voluntarily disclosing or by keeping a record of one or more codes but not all the codes in the access method, the account holder is liable under this paragraph only if the account institution also proves on the balance of probability that the user's contravention of sub-clause 5.6 was the dominant contributing cause of the losses).

As indicated, clause 5.5(a) is unable to be interpreted in its own right without considering what is required under the subsequent clause that it refers to: clause 5.6 of the *EFT Code*. That is, the five (5) instances or events where a consumer has contributed to the loss, if:

(a) the user voluntarily discloses one or more of the codes to anyone, including a family member or friend; or
(b) where the access method also utilises a device, the user indicates one or more of the codes on the outside of the device, or keeps a record of one or more of the codes (without making any reasonable attempt to protect the security of the code records) on the one article, or on several articles, carried with the device or liable to loss or theft simultaneously with the device; or
(c) where the access method comprises a code or codes without a device, the user keeps a record of all the codes (without making any reasonable attempt to protect the security of the code records) on the one article, or on several articles so that they are liable to loss or theft simultaneously; or
(d) where, after the adoption of this revised Code by the account institution, the account institution permits the user to select or change a code and, immediately before the user's selection or change of the code, specifically instructs the user not to select a numeric code which represents the user's birth date or an alphabetical code which is a recognisable part of the user's name and warns the user of the consequences of such a selection and the user selects such a numeric or alphabetical code; or
(e) the user acts with extreme carelessness in failing to protect the security of all the codes.

Where 5.6(d) applies, the onus will be on the account institution to prove on the balance of probabilities that it gave the specific instruction and warning to the user at the time specified and in a manner designed to focus the user's attention specifically on the instruction and consequences of breaching it. The user means the actual user, taking into account the capacity of the user to understand the warning.

For the purposes of this book, it is important to recall that the means of access and access devices and codes comprise only an EFT card, the secret code(s) being a PIN or PINs and through public terminals only, being an ATM or EFTPOS terminal.

Therefore, in order to reduce to plain terms and simplify the complicated requirements above, clause 5.5(a) taken together with the five (5) incidents or events under the related clause 5.6, for the purposes of this book, can be interpreted as meaning that the consumer has contributed to and is responsible for all losses resulting from unauthorised EFT transactions by:

1. Voluntarily disclosing the PIN to anyone, including a family member or friend; or
2. Indicating the PIN on or proximate to the EFT card or liable to loss or theft simultaneously with the EFT card; or
3. Keeping a record of the PIN (without making any reasonable attempt to disguise the PIN) with any article carried with the EFT card or liable to loss or theft simultaneously with the EFT card; or

4. Where the financial institution permits the consumer to select or change a PIN and, immediately before the consumer's selection or change of the PIN, specifically instructs the consumer not to select a numeric PIN which represents the consumer's birth date or an alphabetical PIN which is a recognisable part of the consumer's name and warns the consumer of the consequences of such a selection and the consumer still proceeds to select such a numeric or alphabetical PIN; or
5. Acting with extreme carelessness in failing to protect the security of the PIN or PINs.

It should be noted that following any one or more of these events being proven 'on the balance of probability', the consumer is liable for the actual losses which occur before the financial institution is notified that the EFT card has been misused, lost or stolen or that PIN security has been breached, except for:

i. that portion of the losses incurred on any one day which exceed the daily transaction limit or other periodic limit applicable to the EFT card or account(s); or
ii. that portion of the total losses incurred which exceed the balance of the consumer's EFT account(s) (including any prearranged credit); or
iii. all losses incurred on any accounts which the account institution and the account holder had not agreed could be accessed using the EFT access method.

It is also important to draw attention to the further complexity that is added to interpreting the already difficult, multi-layered clauses 5.5 and 5.6, and, hence, attempting to fairly and equitably apportion liability between financial institution and consumer, due to the following requirement inserted at the conclusion of clause 5.5:

> In determining whether an account institution has proved on the balance of probability that a user has contributed to losses under paragraph (a), all reasonable evidence must be considered, including all reasonable explanations for the transaction occurring.

The fact that the account has been accessed with the correct access method, while significant, will not of itself constitute proof on the balance of probability that the user has contributed to losses through the user's fraud or through the user contravening the requirements in sub-clause 5.6.

Whilst appearing to be a helpful guide for financial institutions, consumers and the ABIO where an alleged unauthorised EFT transaction is initiated with an EFT card and using the correct PIN at first attempt, it is submitted that this requirement does not go far enough in stating whether or not mere proof by the financial institution from its EFT computer system log records ('while significant') is sufficient 'proof on the balance of probability' that the EFT transaction was authorised by the consumer. It is presumed that it is not adequate, as otherwise, if the EFT transaction is to be regarded as 'authorised', then there would not have been any question as to loss or contribution to the loss.[290] Therefore, it is arguable that rather than assisting interpretation, this guidance serves only to add another layer of complexity and ambiguity to the *EFT Code's* requirements.

Before considering the difficult practical issues in interpreting these substantive provisions of the Australian *EFT Code*, along with undertaking a comparative analysis vis-à-vis the *US EFT Act's* requirements, it is important to first define and examine the complex multi-layered threshold tests contained in the above related clauses 5.5(a) and 5.6.

The first observation is that there is no definition or guidance provided in the *EFT Code* for the pivotal threshold test for the financial institution that it must '*prove on the balance of probability*' that a consumer has contributed to losses resulting from an unauthorised EFT transaction. As indicated in Chapter 1 (at Section 1.7: Definitions above), a legal definition for 'balance of probability' is:[291]

The weighing up and comparison of the likelihood of the existence of competing facts or conclusions. A fact is proved to be true on the balance of probabilities if its existence is more probable than not, or if it is established by a preponderance of probability or to the reasonable satisfaction of the tribunal of fact.

---

290 See, eg, Benjamin Geva, 'Consumer Protection in Electronic Funds Transfers' (Research Paper for the Office of Consumer Affairs, Industry Canada, 21 March 2002) 115.

291 Aronson and Hunter, Litigation: Evidence and Procedure, above n 43, 698-9, 716-23; and, see, J D Heydon, Cross on Evidence (7th Australian ed, 2004); Butterworths, Concise Australian Legal Dictionary, above n 43, 44, 60; and the Definitions provisions of the Evidence Act 1995 (Cth).

Note also that Chief Justice King in the South Australian case of SGIC v Laube (1984) 37 SASR 31 expressed the view that a 'mathematical probability' cannot amount to proof in a civil case because it relates only to 'a class of events' and courts must be convinced of the occurrence of the individual event within that class by information concerning that particular event. The question is not whether the likelihood is greater than 50 per cent, but whether the decision is based on information from a "reasonable search". What is a "reasonable search" will depend on the circumstances, the seriousness of the allegation, the inherent unlikelihood of a particular occurrence and the gravity of the consequences of a particular finding. A "reasonable search" was held, in that case, to include a search for any witness to the defendant's state of sobriety and the subsequent calling of those witnesses (if any). This seems to be relevant in considering 'balance of probability' as well as the additional tests of 'dominant contributing clause' and 'extreme carelessness'.

There is also the 'rule' promulgated in the High Court of Australia case of Jones v Dunkel (1959) 101 CLR 298, 505, which was then further explained in subsequent cases such as Brandi v Mingot (1976) 12 ALR 551 and Clayton Robard Management Ltd v Siu (1987) 6 ACLC 57. That is, if a party has 'particular knowledge' and doesn't produce or call evidence in support of it, there is a natural inference by the court that it would not have assisted their case. Accordingly, in the EFT context, where banks have knowledge or records or documents, but do not call evidence and/or produce them, then there is likely to be that adverse inference by the court in the customer's favour.

Curiously, though, after overlooking to provide any definition or guidance for the fundamental 'balance of probability' threshold test, the *EFT Code* does attempt to define two lesser, ancillary terms in the 'End notes' annexed to the *EFT Code,* however, even so, it should be noted that clause 20.3 states that such explanatory notes _do not_ form part of the *EFT Code*:

(i) '*Dominant contributing cause'* – the dominant contributing cause of the losses is the cause that is more than 50% responsible for the losses when assessed together with all other contributing causes; and
(ii) '*Extreme carelessness'* – means a degree of carelessness with the security of *the* codes which greatly exceeds what would normally be considered careless behaviour. For example, storing the user's username and password for Internet banking in a diary or personal organiser or computer (not locked with a PIN) under the heading 'Internet banking codes'.

The second-limb of the key clause 5.5 dealing with the liability for unauthorised EFT transactions is at clause 5.5(b), which deals specifically with another element: unreasonable delays by the consumer in notifying the financial institution of an unauthorised EFT transaction(s). Again, though, it must be said that no definition is provided in the *EFT Code* for what constitutes 'an unreasonable delay in notification' by the consumer. Compounding this problem is that this clause is particularly unwieldy, legalistic and also adopts the aforementioned, undefined threshold test of 'proof on the balance of probability'.
Clause 5.5(b) provides that:

Where the account institution can prove on the balance of probability that a user has contributed to losses resulting from unauthorised transactions by the user unreasonably delaying notification after becoming aware of the misuse, loss or theft of a device forming part of the access method, or that the security of all the codes forming part of the access method has been breached; the account holder is liable for the actual losses which occur between when the user became aware (or should reasonably have become aware in the case of a lost or stolen device) and when the account institution was actually notified.

Clause 5.5(b) concludes with the following proviso to also be taken into account in the event of a dispute surrounding an unreasonable delay in notifying the financial institution of an alleged unauthorised EFT transaction:

In determining whether a user has unreasonably delayed notification under paragraph 5.5(b), the effect on the user of any charges imposed by the account institution relating to the notification or the replacement of the access method must be taken into account.

Further analysis of this element, including an ABIO case example and comparison with the *US EFT Act*, is undertaken in the section titled: 'unreasonable delay in notification', below.

To add yet another twist to an already complicated array of requirements, clause 5.5 concludes with a USA-styled monetary tier for calculating liability where the above clauses 5.5(a) and (b) do not apply.

Clause 5.5(c) provides:

> Where a code was required to perform the unauthorised transactions and neither paragraph (a) nor (b) applies, the account holder is liable for the least of:
> i. $150 (or such lower figure as may be determined by the account institution); or
> ii. the balance of those account(s) (including any pre-arranged credit) from which value was transferred in the unauthorised transactions and which the account institution and the account holder have agreed may be accessed using the access method; or
> iii. the actual loss at the time the account institution is notified (where relevant) that the device has been misused, lost or stolen or that the security of the codes has been breached (excluding that portion of the losses incurred on any one day which exceed any applicable daily transaction or other periodic transaction limit(s)).

Presumably, this added provision is intended to be a kind of 'fall back' provision to cover instances where fault concerning a disputed, unauthorised EFT transaction is 'unclear'. That is, it is neither (i) clear that the consumer has not contributed to such losses where the consumer is expressly excluded from any liability (clause 5.4); or (ii) clear on the balance of probability that the consumer has in fact contributed to such losses by compromising the security of the EFT card and/or PIN under one or more of the instances described in clauses 5.5(a), (b) and 5.6. Thus, it is perhaps something of a last resort measure for the ABIO to embrace where the evidence regarding contribution is not decisive or hopelessly deadlocked after having been forced to stumble its way through all the difficult multi-layered threshold tests first.

By way of comparison with the position in the USA, on the question of a consumer's 'contribution to the loss', the only provision in the *US EFT Act* that places liability on the customer is that of the consumer's failure to 'check periodic statements' as a determining factor (as discussed above in the introduction to this section of the book). In contrast to the *US EFT Act*, the *EFT Code* does not allow a financial institution's terms or conditions of use to deem periodic statements accurate unless the customer notifies inaccuracies to the financial institution within a 'reasonable period' (yet, critically, as stated, the *EFT Code* does not have a prescriptive time limit. This issue is considered in further detail under 'unreasonable delay in notification' below).

An example of the practical application of this provision of the *US EFT Act* was in the USA case of *Kramer v Chase Manhattan Bank*,[292] where it was found that a bank should not be held responsible for losses caused by a customer's failure to safeguard his or her ATM card and identification code, but primarily due to the customer's failure to timely examine bank statements. Under the Australian *EFT Code*, a similar result would likely be reached, but on the basis of the consumer's contribution to the losses by compromising the security of the EFT card and PIN, rather than on the basis of delays in reporting the losses.

---

[292] N.A. 235 A.D.2d 371 (1997).

Ultimately, a similar finding was also reached by a USA appeals court in the controversial case of *Kruser v Bank of America*,[293] where the facts and finding were briefly as follows:

The Krusers maintained a joint EFT account with the Bank, and the Bank issued each of them an EFT card and separate personal identification numbers which would allow access to funds in their account from automatic teller machines. The Krusers also received with their cards a 'Disclosure Booklet' which provided to the Krusers a summary of consumer liability, the Bank's business hours, and the address and telephone number by which they could notify the Bank in the event they believed an unauthorised transfer had been made.

The Krusers believed Mr. Kruser's card had been destroyed in September 1986. The December 1986 account statement mailed to the Krusers by the bank reflected a US$20 unauthorised withdrawal of funds by someone using Mr. Kruser's card at an automatic teller machine. The Krusers reported this unauthorised transaction to the Bank when they discovered it in August or September 1987.

Mrs. Kruser underwent surgery in late December 1986 or early January 1987. She remained hospitalised for 11 days. She then spent a period of six or seven months recuperating at home.

During this time she reviewed the statements she and Mr. Kruser received from the bank.

In September 1987, the Krusers received bank statements for July and August 1987 which reflected 47 unauthorised withdrawals, totalling US$9,020, made from an automatic teller machine, again by someone using Mr. Kruser's card. They notified the bank of these withdrawals within a few days of receiving the statements. The Bank refused to credit the Krusers' account with the amount of the unauthorised withdrawals citing that the significant delay in notification of the initial US$20 loss excused the bank of liability under the *US EFT Act*.

The ultimate issue to be resolved was whether, as a matter of law, the failure to report the initial unauthorised US$20 withdrawal which appeared on the December 1986 statement barred the Krusers from recovery for the significant losses totalling US$9,020 incurred in July and August 1987.

The Court held that because Mrs. Kruser received and reviewed bank statements during her recuperation there were no extenuating circumstances where serious illness might have excused her failure to notice the initial unauthorised withdrawal pursuant to the applicable sections of the *US EFT Act*. She in fact did review the statements in question. There was also no evidence supplied by the Krusers in support of their contention Mrs. Kruser was also caring for her ill relative during the relevant time period. Moreover, nothing in the record reflected any extenuating circumstances which would have prevented Mr. Kruser from reviewing the bank statements either. The understanding he had with Mrs. Kruser that she would review the bank statements did not excuse him from his obligation to notify the bank of any unauthorised electronic transfers.

The Court therefore found that the Bank had established that the losses incurred in July and August 1987 as a result of the unauthorised electronic transfers by someone using Mr. Kruser's EFT card could have been prevented had the Krusers reported the unauthorised use of Mr. Kruser's card as reflected on the December 1986 statement. The Bank was entitled to judgment as a matter of law.

---

[293] 281 Cal Rptr 463 (Cal. App. 5th Dist. 1991).

A further example from the USA, where the bank was found liable for not acting following the consumer's notification of an unauthorised EFT transaction, was in the case of *Bisbey v DC National Bank*,[294] where the bank was in fact held liable under the *US EFT Act* for its failure 'to comply with provisions in the Act when addressing a lawful inquiry about possible mistaken fund transfers'. Similarly, in *Pickman v Citibank*,[295] the bank was also found liable, despite the consumer not reporting losses for 3 months (beyond the required notification period maximum of 60 days), but because the consumer successfully put the integrity and security of the bank's EFT computer system into question. The court decided the issue 'in favour of the human, rather than the machine' quoting 'to err is human'.[296]

The central theme across these cases from the USA is the sanctity of the tiered no-fault regime and the paramountcy of timely notification by the consumer above and beyond all else, including consumer negligence with the EFT card and/or PIN. As mentioned, the reverse is true of the *EFT Code*. This divergence in approach will be examined in detail shortly using recent actual cases from the ABIO.

Another variation from the *US EFT Act* is the *EFT Code's* inclusion (above) of the 'balance of the account (including any pre-arranged credit)' as a factor in assessing consumer liability. In addition to the prescriptive notification requirements in the *US EFT Act*, the *EFT Code's* inclusion of the 'account balance' factor in limiting consumer liability is the second substantive difference with the *US EFT Act*. Consumer liability may well be reduced under the *EFT Code* if the balance is less than either A$150 or the actual loss whereas in the USA it is a flat US$50 unless the loss was less.

But it is in the area of 'causation of loss,' that the *EFT Code's* coverage becomes vague and uncertain vis-a-vis the simple, strict *US EFT Act's* provision at §1693g outlined earlier. In particular, where financial institutions attempt to avoid liability for losses in respect of unauthorised EFT transactions on the basis of conduct by the customer, which although strictly in breach of the *EFT Code*, does not relate directly to the cause of the loss. For example, the PIN is kept with the card, but only the card is stolen and thus no causative link between a breach of the *EFT Code* and the loss (should the PIN not have been seen). Clause 5.6 (above) states that the consumer must have contributed to the loss on the balance of probability yet in the absence of any guidance or definition of what that means it is most unclear what is required to prove or disprove this.

In practice, the ABIO comments that this is the fundamental difficulty in applying the *EFT Code* to real cases.[297] In particular, interpreting the four (4) main elements of clauses 5.5 and 5.6 as follows:

1. Proving '<u>simultaneous loss or theft of the EFT card with the PIN</u>';
2. What constitutes '<u>reasonable disguise of the PIN?</u>'

---

294 253 App. DC 244, 793 F2d 315 (DC Cir, 1986).
295 443 NYS.2d 43 (Civ Ct City of NY, 1981).
296 Ibid.
297 See, eg, Australian Banking Industry Ombudsman, Annual Report, 2001/2002.

3. Where a consumer believes that s/he has not contributed to the loss despite the 'correct PIN being used at first attempt' in the disputed transaction – and the related issue of 'shouldering' (where a consumer is observed keying in the PIN at an earlier transaction); and
4. Whether or not there was an 'unreasonable delay in notification' by the consumer.

Each of these four (4) critical issues are examined in turn by reference to actual ABIO case examples, which demonstrate the complexity of not only interpretation, but of resolution. To illustrate the comparative 'difference' and 'similarities' with the position in the USA, the cases will also be 'solved' using the substantive provisions of the *US EFT Act*.

Simultaneous loss or theft of EFT card and PIN

As stated, the issue of fault or contribution by the EFT cardholder is irrelevant in the USA. In Australia, the situation is altogether different. As indicated above, a key and repeated requirement under the Australian *EFT Code* is that the EFT cardholder must not facilitate the *simultaneous* loss or theft of both the EFT card and the corresponding PIN. Whether the EFT cardholder has so facilitated simultaneous loss or theft of the EFT card and PIN is a matter of 'weighing the evidence', which, of course, requires application of the complex, multi-layered and undefined legal threshold tests referred to above (namely, 'proof on the balance of probability', 'significance', 'dominant contributing cause' and 'extreme carelessness'). This very point is borne out in the following two ABIO case examples.

(a) Card and PIN kept in a safe [298]

Mr and Mrs W each had a card and a PIN attached to each card. As they were going overseas, they wished to put their cards in a secure place. They put their EFT cards and their records of their PINs in a safe hidden in their home. When they returned from their holiday, they discovered that their home had been broken into, the safe found and valuables taken.

The thief had used their EFT cards and using the correct PINs from the records had made substantial withdrawals from both accounts.

Even though Mr and Mrs W had gone to some trouble to keep their cards secure in a safe, when the *EFT Code* (clauses 5.5 and 5.6) was applied to their case, it showed that they had kept the records of their PINs with their EFT cards in a place which meant they were liable to be stolen 'simultaneously.' In these circumstances, the bank could not be found liable for the losses suffered by Mr and Mrs W.

In stark contrast, in the USA, Mr and Mrs W would only be liable for between US$50 (if the loss is reported within 2 days) and US$500 (if the loss is reported within 60 days) depending upon when they reported the theft.

[298] Australian Banking Industry Ombudsman Limited, Annual Report, 1995/1996, 24.

(b) Card in wallet and PIN in drawer [299]

Mrs A put her record of her PIN, undisguised, in a drawer in her home. Mrs A kept her EFT card in her wallet which was in a backpack which she usually carried with her.

The question which arose in this case for the Ombudsman was: if Mrs A's PIN was in a drawer in her bedroom and the EFT card was in her backpack, were the card and the PIN liable to simultaneous loss or theft if Mrs A then left her backpack in the bedroom too?

In this case, it could not be concluded by the Ombudsman that the backpack was in the bedroom at the time of the theft and so could not be liable to loss or theft simultaneously with the PIN. The Bank therefore was ordered to bear the losses in full.

A further detailed discussion of this problematic 'nexus' issue is combined with that of the closely related issue of *'correct PIN at first attempt'* below.

Reasonable disguise of the PIN

As set out above, the 'reasonable disguise' requirement is also dealt with at length and in a complex, cross-provisional manner in clauses 5.5(a), 5.6(d), and, further requirements inserted at the conclusion of clause 5.6, of the *EFT Code*. Indeed, these 'further requirements' which purport to clarify what is a reasonable disguise are altogether imprecise, and, most curiously, even extend to requiring the financial institution to '*focus the user's attention*' and assess '*the capacity of the user to understand'*.

The following actual case example from the ABIO was adjudicated before the above revised arrangements, but provides an insight into what is considered 'reasonable' by the ABIO: [300]

Mr J had used the radio call signs: Alpha = 1, Bravo = 2 etc. to disguise his PIN. He had a record of several PINs written on a piece of paper. He identified each of his different cards using the signs 'Victor' for Visa card etc. All of his cards were stolen and accounts accessed by a thief. Was this a reasonable disguise?

The Ombudsman's view was that consumers should not use this kind of simple code as it is now known by thieves and was, therefore, not a 'reasonable disguise.'

The *US EFT Act* is silent on the issue of 'reasonable disguise' and would again presumably apply the timeliness of notice test to allocate liability. It appears that Mr J would only be liable for between US$50 and US$500 depending upon whether the loss was reported within 2 days or 60 days of Mr J becoming aware of the loss.

Although determined under the previous Australian *EFT Code*, the ABIO result is considered particularly harsh when the current, revised *EFT Code* only states that the consumer is liable where the financial institution specifically instructs the consumer not to select a numeric code which represents the <u>user's birth date</u> or an alphabetical code which is a recognisable part of the <u>user's name</u> and warns the user of the consequences of such a selection and the user still proceeds to select

---

299 Australian Banking Industry Ombudsman Limited, Annual Report, 1993/1994, 16.

300 Australian Banking Industry Ombudsman Limited, Annual Report, 1995/1996, 26.

such a numeric or alphabetical code. It is also submitted that these *de minimis* examples (derivatives of a consumer's birth date and name) do not go far enough if the ABIO is prepared to interpret this requirement to a much higher standard which then undermines the *EFT Code's* guidance and hence clarification for the consumer of what is and what is not acceptable.

In fact, in several ABIO Annual Reports, the ABIO has warned customers to be careful not to use a number which is the same as another number carried in their wallets. For instance, a driver's licence will include a date of birth, so if a wallet is lost and the consumer has used their birth date as the PIN, this information is considered readily available to a thief. Historically, the Ombudsman had urged customers to select their own PIN if they felt they would have difficulty remembering a PIN. However, in a recent report,[301] the ABIO discovered that self-select PINs were usually related to something too readily identifiable with the consumer.

In practice, many financial institutions have now taken steps to clarify the 'reasonable disguise' issue in their terms and conditions of use. The Commonwealth Bank has the most detailed approach. Its terms and conditions of use,[302] provide six (6) examples of where it does not consider a reasonable attempt has been made to disguise the PIN (ie, a PIN record in reverse order, a phone number where no other phone numbers are used, where a mere prefix is added, the PIN is contained within a series of numbers and is in some way highlighted, the PIN as a date where no other dates are recorded or as an easily understood code, eg. A=1, B=2 etc). Although legally uncertain in relation to the above *de minimis* requirements of the *EFT Code*, the Commonwealth Bank's approach does seem to be a reasonable and sensible one and it perhaps would be advisable for all financial institutions to adopt it in their terms and conditions.

While the wording is generally different between financial institutions, the procedures for the way consumers record their PINs appears to be strictly outlined in the terms and conditions of use. From the research of financial institutions' practice undertaken for this book, some go as far as to forbid the maintenance of <u>any</u> record. One such instance of this was cited by the ABIO: [303]

> The bank made it a condition of Mr P's use of his card that he was not permitted to keep a written record of his PIN.
>
> The Ombudsman determined that this term of the conditions of use 'elevated' Mr P's responsibilities under the *EFT Code* rather than clarifying them. The *EFT Code* said Mr P could not keep a record of his PIN with his card or in a place which might make it liable to be lost or stolen simultaneously with his card. It did not say that he could not keep a record of the PIN.
>
> The Ombudsman took the view that it was therefore implicit in the *EFT Code* that a record might be kept and it would not be reasonable to expect that a consumer would have no record at all of their PIN.

---

301 Australian Banking Industry Ombudsman Limited, Annual Report, 1998/1999, 28.

302 Commonwealth Bank, Transaction, Savings and Investments Accounts – Product Disclosure Statement (01/2006).

303 Australian Banking Industry Ombudsman Limited, Annual Report, 1995/1996, 23.

Following the above case, the ABIO also noted that financial institutions 'must stop short of elevating the responsibility imposed on the consumer by the *EFT Code*'.[304] In addition to this clear ABIO statement, such behaviour may also give rise to a breach of s 12ED of the *ASIC Act* (as discussed previously in terms of the 'warranty' requirement at clause 2 of the *EFT Code*), and possibly s 12EB of the *ASIC Act* which prohibits a supplier of financial services from excluding, restricting or modifying the statutory conditions and warranties.

Correct PIN at first attempt

The ABIO notes that there is much confusion where the disputed transaction is the result of the entry of the correct PIN at first attempt in a disputed, unauthorised EFT transaction.[305] The ABIO takes the approach that although it is not conclusive that the consumer contributed to the loss, it is a 'substantial factor' (the revised *EFT Code* states that it is a 'significant' factor) in determining whether a record of the PIN, which was not reasonably disguised, may have been kept with the card, so that both were liable to loss or theft simultaneously.

Unlike the *US EFT Act's* burden of proof being on the financial institution to show that the EFT was authorised, the ABIO's decision is based not merely on assigning a burden of proof, but on the 'weight of the information available', as the following two cases illustrate:

(a) In favour of the consumer [306]

Ms H had a joint EFT account with her fiancé. Ms H was shopping with a friend. She withdrew $40 from her account and remembered removing the card, the cash and the withdrawal slip from the ATM and thought she put all three items in her wallet.

Two days later her fiancé also withdrew $40 from the account and noticed that the balance was lower than expected. He contacted Ms H who checked her wallet and noticed her card was missing. She telephoned the bank who informed her that withdrawals totalling $1,100 had been made from her account.

The bank said that as the correct PIN had been used at first attempt, Ms H was responsible for the disputed withdrawals.

The Ombudsman determined that the 'weight of information' supported the conclusion that the withdrawals were not made by Ms H; that it could not be shown that a record of the PIN was lost or stolen 'simultaneously' with the card as the card was the only item lost. It appeared that the most likely scenario was that Ms H had been 'shouldered' at the ATM and had not voluntarily disclosed her PIN or kept a record of her PIN with the card, nor did she unreasonably delay notification of the loss to the bank.

Accordingly, the Ombudsman determined that Ms H had not contributed to the losses resulting from the unauthorised withdrawals and the bank should bear the loss.

---

[304] Ibid.

[305] Ibid 25.

[306] Ibid.

(b) In favour of the financial institution [307]

Mr B left his wallet containing his EFT card in his car, locked it and went for a short walk with his family. When he returned to his car, he found that it had been broken into and his wallet, cheque book, passport, driver's licence and a bundle of personal papers had been stolen.

Mr B drove to the nearest town and reported the theft to the bank. In his next account statement, he discovered that the thief had withdrawn $500 from his account. He disputed his liability for the unauthorised withdrawal. The bank maintained that Mr B was liable as the account was accessed at first attempt using the correct PIN. Therefore, Mr B must have a PIN record with the EFT card which was not reasonably disguised and the two were stolen simultaneously.

Mr B said that he had never used his EFT card electronically and had not kept a record of the PIN.

The bank's computer logs for the disputed withdrawal showed that the thief had about 40 minutes within which to break into the car, steal the card and papers, drive to the next town and then access Mr B's account using the correct PIN at first attempt. Mr B was not able to specifically confirm that he had destroyed the PIN record for his card.

The Ombudsman found in favour of the bank given the use of the correct PIN at first attempt, the speed with which the account had been correctly accessed at first attempt, the absence of any malfunction with the ATM used by the thief, and the fact that a number of miscellaneous papers had been stolen simultaneously with the card, the weight of the information available supported the view that there was probably a forgotten record of the PIN kept with the papers, which was therefore liable to simultaneous loss or theft with the card.

Again, the *US EFT Act* would apply the timing of notification to the bank test, which would have limited Mr B's liability to between US$50 (bank notified within 2 days of Mr B's discovery) and US$500 (notification within 60 days of discovery). Therefore, in the event of notification within 2 days, as seems to be the case, the result would likely have been significantly less than the actual loss Mr B suffered (A$500).

In the previous case where Ms H was found not to have contributed to the losses, under the *US EFT Act* there would not have been such a detailed and protracted assessment of contribution and evidence, she would still be liable, though, for US$50 for having notified the losses within 2 days of becoming aware of them as liability is the lesser of US$50 or the amount of the transaction (A$1,100) for unauthorised transactions occurring before notice (of loss or theft of an EFT card and/or PIN) to the institution.

The following ABIO case is an example of where liability was apportioned equally between the consumer and financial institution because fault was deemed by the ABIO to be 'unclear' and the ABIO adopted a sensible non-*EFT Code* test of 'reasonable alternative explanations'. This result still seems to be particularly severe on the consumer given that the ABIO could have called upon the 'fall back' provision under clause 5.5(c) where fault is unclear and imposed only a $150 liability on the consumer.

[307] Ibid 26.

(c) *Shared liability* [308]

Ms M's handbag was stolen from her place of work. A short time after the theft, the first of several unauthorised transactions was conducted on Ms M's account. Ms M wrote to the ABIO claiming that she was not liable for the unauthorised transactions totalling $2,000 (above the daily ATM transaction limit of $1,000) because she said that she had not used her card with a PIN and did not have a record of her PIN in the handbag. The bank had allocated all liability to Ms M on the basis that she must have kept a record of the PIN with the card as her account was accessed at first attempt.

The Ombudsman's investigations revealed that Ms M was not sure what had happened to the PIN record and that some of the disputed withdrawals were conducted over-the-counter at a branch (where no daily limits apply).

The Ombudsman resolved that the 'only reasonable explanation' was that the thief found a record of the PIN in her handbag and used this to access the account. The Ombudsman noted that the *EFT Code* refers only to daily limits for ATMs, not in-branch terminals. Therefore, the $1,000 ATM daily transaction limit was applied per the *EFT Code* and so the bank and Ms M each accepted liability of $1,000.

Another very recent ABIO case (below)[309] shows that despite the revised *EFT Code* seeking to place the burden of proof squarely on the financial institution in the event of a disputed, unauthorised EFT transaction, in practice the burden effectively remains at the foot of the consumer to disprove the '*significant*' evidential weight assigned under the *EFT Code* of the 'correct PIN being used at first attempt'. This contention is supported by the fact that even though the ABIO determined that the consumer had not performed the ATM transaction, nor authorised it, and, that the financial institution could not make out that the consumer contributed to the losses on the balance of probability, the consumer was still not 'cleared' of culpability (clause 5.4) and was therefore still required to contribute $150 under the 'unclear' provision at clause 5.5(c).

Mr S had an account which he operated with an EFT debit card. Mr S had recently sold his home. He was expecting the mortgagee of his former home to deposit the net proceeds of the sale to the account.

He later learnt that his account had been closed, a new account had been opened, and that the sale proceeds had been deposited to, and subsequently withdrawn from, the new account via ATM withdrawals. He said he did not close his account nor open the new account, was unaware of the deposit of the net proceeds to the account, and did not withdraw the sale proceeds.

The financial institution said it closed the original account because it was overdrawn. It said that Mr S had opened the new account and had produced photo identification when doing so. It said that Mr S must have performed the withdrawals totalling $23,000 (or must have compromised PIN security) since they were all performed with the correct PIN on the first attempt.

The ABIO investigation showed that: Mr S was the victim of a fraud which involved the opening of the new account, the depositing of part of the net proceeds of sale to the new account, and the withdrawal of the $23,000 in proceeds of sale from the new account. Furthermore, that Mr S was living in another state when the new account was opened and

---

308 Ibid.

309 Australian Banking Industry Ombudsman Limited, Annual Report, 2003/2004, 32.

could not have opened it. Moreover, Mr S did not receive the PIN or the card for the new account, which were given, and sent, to the person who opened the new account.

The ABIO Resolution: the case manager issued a Finding that concluded that Mr S had not performed the ATM withdrawals or authorised them and that the financial institution had not proved on the balance of probabilities that Mr S had contributed to the losses resulting from the unauthorised transactions by breaching the *EFT Code*.

It was recommended that Mr S's liability be limited to $150.

The financial institution accepted the Finding and reimbursed Mr S the remaining balance of the $23,000 which had been withdrawn from the account.

Tyree considers the ABIO 'weight of information available' test to be logically flawed and supports the USA approach.[310] Tyree also refers to the evidence of the correct PIN being used at first attempt as the 'one-shot rule'. [311]

On the question of 'contribution', these ABIO cases illustrate how simple the strict USA regime of liability works and just how subjective the meaning of the key terms of the Australian *EFT Code* are and how difficult it is to apportion loss.

To assist the ABIO's interpretation of clauses 5.5 and 5.6, other commentators have come up with inventive solutions.[312] For example, increase the consumer's liability to 20% of the daily transaction limit for the most difficult 'evidentiary stalemates' (eg, the correct PIN being used at first attempt in a disputed, unauthorised EFT transaction, and, the situation where a consumer may have been involuntarily observed keying in the PIN). This '20% of the daily transaction limit' solution might have been preferable in the ABIO 'glove box case' involving Mr B (cited above) where the ABIO found in favour of the bank despite acknowledging an evidentiary stalemate. The inquiries at several branches of financial institutions for the purposes of this book indicated that ATM daily limits are not more than $1,200.

The 'shouldering' examples earlier (ie, the case of Ms H when shopping and the litigated case from the USA of *Ognibene*) are an ever-increasing trend according to the ABIO in cases researched back to 1992/93. Whenever there is a chance that a consumer has been 'shouldered' while accessing an EFT terminal, the consumer has generally enjoyed the benefit of the ABIO's interpretation of clauses 5.5 and 5.6 of the *EFT Code* (as in the USA with *Ognibene*), but still not 'cleared' of responsibility and thus still remains liable for the $150 'fall-back' solution.

Indeed, the terms and conditions of use obtained from financial institutions for the purposes of this book clearly exhibit their concerns about 'shouldering' and their endeavours to minimise this: The ANZ Bank's user guide succinctly states that: 'When using a PIN, do not allow anyone to look over your shoulder'.[313] However, as already mentioned, this is merely a guide booklet only as ANZ did not have or supply actual EFT terms and conditions of use. The Commonwealth Bank goes further with an onerous provision: 'Do not let anyone watch

---

310 Tyree, above n 125, 335.

311 Ibid.

312 Sneddon, above n 73, 37.

313 ANZ Bank, Internet, Phone, ATM and EFTPOS Banking – Your Guide (10/2005).

you...check the location of mirrors, security cameras or any other means of observing your PIN entry, and then shield it from anyone at the terminal'.[314] This could arguably be seen as 'elevating' a consumer's responsibilities above that permitted under the EFT Code. Given this obvious concern, it is curious why financial institutions have at the same time been reluctant to implement ASIC's security recommendation [315] (relating to Australian Standard AS3769), which suggests a hood or other form of shielding be placed over the EFT terminal's keypad. It was observed as part of the research undertaken for this book that financial institutions are at least gradually replacing vertical ATM keypads (which are readily visible to others) with the much safer horizontal ATM keypads.

Unreasonable delay in notification

To recall, under the *EFT Code's* clause 5.5(b), should the consumer 'unreasonably delay notification of the loss,' which is not defined, the liability is as follows:

> The actual losses which occur between when the consumer became aware (or should reasonably have become aware in the case of a lost or stolen device) and when the financial institution was actually notified.

Unlike the *US EFT Act*, which contains a prescriptive 2/60 day time limit (detailed in the first part of this section of the book), the *EFT Code* leaves what is an 'unreasonable delay in notification' open to interpretation. The ABIO provides an example [316] of where this can be exceedingly complex to determine:

> Ms T disputed 13 transactions totalling $5,800 between 20th January and 3rd February. Ms T reported the loss of her card to the bank on the 3rd February, saying that her card was lost on the 16th January and that the last transaction she made herself was at a food store in Bondi (NSW) on 15th January.
>
> One question for the Ombudsman to determine was whether Ms T had unreasonably delayed notifying the bank of the loss of her card. Ms T said she had not become aware that she had lost the card until she went to deposit a cheque on 3rd February. The financial institution's EFT system computer logs showed that Ms T used her card 20 times in the 19 days between 28th December and 15th January and the Ombudsman took the view that the pattern of Ms T's use of her card indicated that it would have been usual for her to have used her card within 2 to 3 days of her last use on the 15th January.
>
> Ms T said she didn't use the card as she usually did because she was preoccupied with looking for a new flat. The Ombudsman determined that the weight of information available supported the conclusion that Ms T ought reasonably to have become aware of the loss of her card before 3rd February, and that she had therefore unreasonably delayed notification of the loss of her card and so contributed to her losses.

---

314 Commonwealth Bank, Transaction, Savings and Investments Accounts – Product Disclosure Statement (01/2006).

315 Australian Securities and Investments Commission, Report of Compliance with the Payment System Codes of Practice and the EFT Code of Conduct, 1999/2000 (2001) 63.

316 Australian Banking Industry Ombudsman Limited, Annual Report, 1995/1996, 27.

In this case, the position under the *US EFT Act* would require Ms T to have notified the loss or theft of her card within 2 days of discovery to limit her liability to US$50 or risk a greater liability of US$500 if reported within 60 days, and unlimited liability up to the actual losses of A$5,800 thereafter. Clearly, with Ms T immediately notifying her loss when she became aware of them, she would have been exposed to a capped amount of US$50 only. This is significantly below the actual loss of A$5,800 that Ms T suffered. However, in this instance the ABIO's 'weight of information available' test appears particularly well applied where the ABIO examined and took into account Ms T's actual pattern of EFT behaviour. However, the clear majority of the ABIO cases indicate that matters are not so easily determined under the complex *EFT Code* requirements.

It should also be pointed out that the *US EFT Act* provides a more favourable error resolution requirement (§ 1693f) that institutions provisionally re-credit the consumer's account after 10 days if the investigation has not been completed or otherwise exposed to treble damages. In Australia, the *EFT Code* requires no such procedure be followed. This is discussed further at Section 4.7 below.

Given the increasing incidence of disputed, unauthorised EFT transactions from ASIC data (discussed earlier), the weakness in the key clause 5 of the *EFT Code* is complex and protracted multi-layered provisions and its failure to explicitly define key threshold tests or at least provide some clear guidelines to be followed where the weight of information is equivocal. At present, the practical application of the *EFT Code* is extremely difficult as the ABIO regularly observes in its annual reports, yielding a range of uncertain outcomes.

Thus, the underlying question of how to apportion loss for unauthorised transactions is exceedingly difficult, short of adopting a 'cut and dried' US-style approach. Perhaps it ultimately depends upon personal opinions about the extent to which consumers need or deserve to be protected from third party fraud, faults on the part of financial institutions, and their own carelessness.

4.5 Liability for EFT system malfunctions

As mentioned earlier, under common law, there is a duty by a bank to honour a customer's cheque if funds are available to cover it (including a pre-arranged credit limit which has not been exceeded). In the event of a failure to do so, a bank may be liable for breach of contract by failing to comply with the customer's mandate.

An EFT command could be seen in the same light, with a financial institution bearing responsibility for any failure to provide funds. Prior to the *EFT Code's* implementation in December 1989, financial institutions had clauses in their terms and conditions of use excluding <u>any</u> liability for losses arising from any failure of their own EFT systems.[317] It is worth noting that such exclusion clauses would no

[317] Report of the Working Group, above 136, 23.

doubt now attract the attention of ASIC pursuant to the *ASIC Act* (s 12ED see below).

The Australian Consumers Association has also expressed concern about technical malfunctions of ATMs in particular. It has outlined cases where consumers have suffered losses in excess of their account balance due to electronic terminals being 'off-line' (ie, not being connected to a bank's central computer and consequently unable to verify a consumer's account details and balance), and also occasions when terminals advised 'insufficient funds' when this was not the case at all.[318]

While the reverse situation occurred in the unusual case of *Kennison v Daire,*[319] it illustrated the problems that can occur when an EFT terminal is 'off-line.' In this case, a person who had closed his bank account, but retained his EFT card, was able to withdraw $200 because the EFT terminal was not connected to the financial institution's central computer at the time he initiated the EFT transaction. The consumer was ultimately convicted of larceny.

Clause 6 of the *EFT Code* adopts a similar stance to the *US EFT Act*[320] in prescribing that institutions be responsible for losses caused by 'failure' in EFT machinery or computer software.[321] Clause 6.1 provides:

> Account institutions will be responsible to their users for loss caused by the failure of an institution system or institution equipment to complete a transaction accepted by an institution system or institution equipment in accordance with the user's instructions.

However, what constitutes 'failure' is not defined under the *EFT Code.* Does it, for example, include under-payments at an ATM? Or over-payments to retail merchants through EFTPOS? Failures resulting in wrong debits or credits? Failures resulting in authorised transfers not being made? And inadequate security permitting unauthorised access to an EFT system?

Also, the *EFT Code* does not explicitly apportion responsibility for losses arising from 'off-line' EFT transactions to financial institutions (other than within the 'equipment failure' provision). Generally, it is obvious when an electronic terminal is 'off-line' as it will have a 'Not in Use' or „Out of Service' message displayed on its screen. The wording of the *EFT Code's* clause 6.2 (below) indicates that financial institutions are not responsible where a consumer should have been aware that the system or equipment was unavailable for use or malfunctioning. However, the *EFT Code* specifically deems financial institutions liable for all losses caused by 'insiders' in clause 5.2(a):

> [T]hat is, fraud or negligence of employees of the financial institution or of merchants who are linked to the EFT system or of the agents and employees of such merchants.

---

318 Australian Consumers Association, EFT in Australia : Issues and Problems (1984) 4-5.

319 (1986) 160 CLR 129.

320 Electronic Funds Transfer Act, 15 USC § 1693 (1978) and Regulation E § 205 (1981).

321 Electronic Funds Transfer Code of Conduct (original, 1989) cl 6.1.

In addition to the *EFT Code*, a financial institution would be obliged to exercise due care and skill in managing its electronic terminals and equipment under s 12ED of the *ASIC Act*, which implies various conditions and warranties into a transaction including the 'supply of financial services'. It is suggested that the *EFT Code* should make specific reference to this mandatory statutory provision in the *ASIC Act* to give the *EFT Code's* requirements more potency and legal effect.

Clause 6.2 of the *EFT Code* also stipulates that institutions should not attempt to limit liability to direct losses only:

> The account institution is not to deny, implicitly or explicitly, a right to the user to make claims for consequential damage which may arise as a result of a malfunction of an institution system or institution equipment however caused, except, where the user should have been aware that the system or equipment was unavailable for use or malfunctioning, the account institution's responsibilities may be limited to the correction of any errors in the account, and the refund of any charges or fees imposed on the account holder as a result.

This provision deserves particular attention. It may well mean that institutions could be liable for amounts greatly in excess of the amount of the failed EFT transaction. Whether such a failure would mean an institution would be held liable if a consumer, by virtue of the failure, was unable to meet regular personal or even commercial commitments is not certain, but exemplifies the significance of such a blanketing clause. The original EFT Working Group fell way short of this in recommending that financial institutions should accept liability for direct losses only in their terms and conditions of use, but that the contract be 'silent on consequential losses'.[322]

By way of comparison, the *US EFT Act* makes an institution liable to a customer for all damages 'proximately caused' by failure to make an EFT in the correct amount or in a timely manner, except where (a) the consumer's account has insufficient funds; (b) the funds are subject to legal process or other encumbrance; (c) such a transfer would exceed an established credit limit; or (d) an electronic terminal has insufficient cash to complete the transaction.[323]

The USA case of *Evra Corporation Inc. v Swiss Banking Corporation*[324] established that a financial institution's liability was limited to 'direct loss' rather than 'consequential loss,' unless the financial institution was put on advance notice by the consumer of the circumstances which would give rise to the consequential loss. In *Evra,* the failure by a financial institution to carry out a consumer's relatively small EFT transaction caused the customer to default in respect of far greater commercial obligations.

Indeed, it could be argued that it would not be unreasonable for financial institutions to limit their liability in the area of 'consequential loss' provided that the consumer is given notice of the limitation. However, this might again be governed by s 12EB of the *ASIC Act* which could prohibit such a limitation of liability as well as s 12ED requiring financial institutions to provide their services

322 Second Report of the Working Group, above n 137, 18.

323 Electronic Funds Transfer Act, 15 USC § 1693 (1978) and Regulation E § 205 (1981).

324 673 F 2d 951 (1982).

with due care and skill (although the research undertaken for this book did not yield any Australian cases dealing with this issue).

In the absence of such protection, the customer would be left to choose whether to accept the systemic risks of an EFT transaction or choose some other payment method.

4.6 Countermand rights

Consumers have also been concerned by the absence of formal 'countermand' (stop payment) or reversal rights under EFT.[325] With a cheque, a customer can follow the bank's appropriate steps and issue a stop payment instruction to the bank. The bank is then under a duty to obey the countermand. This duty is the converse of a banker's duty to obey a customer's mandate in paying a cheque.[326]

In EFT, the consumer must negotiate several steps at an EFT terminal before the transaction is complete. Generally, the PIN is entered first, followed by the transaction type (withdrawal, deposit, balance enquiry, transfer etc.), then the account is selected and the amount. At any stage up to this point, a consumer can elect to terminate the EFT transaction by pressing the 'cancel' key. However, it is submitted that once the EFT transaction is completed (ie. the 'enter' button on an EFT terminal is pressed), reversal or stop payment is impossible to achieve. Because an EFT transaction is generally an 'on-line' and 'real time' cash-based chain of events, processing is immediate. It would be hard to envisage how any stop payment mechanism initiated by a consumer could ever be built into the EFT system. In an EFT transaction, the 'presentation', 'clearance' and 'payment' sequence is instantaneous and cash-based.

A customer's only right to countermand payment of an EFT transaction appears to be in the limited case of 'pre-authorised' EFTs (eg. monthly periodical debits). The wider reach of the *US EFT Act* formally confers this right. The *US EFT Act* provides[327] that a consumer may stop payment of a pre-authorised EFT transaction by notifying the financial institution orally or in writing at any time up to 3 business days before the scheduled date of the EFT.[328] The *US EFT Act* also provides for the procedures to be followed in pre-authorised EFT credits to a consumer's account, as well as notice of any variations in the amount of a pre-authorised EFT transaction.

---

[325] See, eg, White, above n 77.

[326] Weerasooria, above n 83, 181.

[327] Electronic Funds Transfer Act, 15 USC § 1693 (1978) and Regulation E, § 205 (1981).

[328] Ibid § 205.10(c).

4.7 Dispute resolution procedures

Prior to the advent of the original *EFT Code* (1989) and the *Code of Banking Practice* (1993), financial institutions' terms and conditions of use did not include an error and/or dispute resolution procedure.

From the analysis undertaken in Section 4.4 of this chapter (above), it could be argued that compared to paper-based transactions, EFT places consumers at a relative disadvantage in that there is often an 'evidentiary stalemate' following a disputed EFT transaction (as discussed at length earlier). For example, a consumer demonstrating to a bank that he or she has not given the bank a mandate to debit his or her account following successful unauthorised access by a third person who had not been voluntarily disclosed with the PIN. As also discussed earlier, in the case of a cheque it is arguable that it is for the bank to prove that a signature was forged; the written signature is at least available as evidence and its characteristics can then be examined in detail.

In a disputed EFT transaction, the computer and EFT system logs of a card issuer, together with EFT receipts issued at the terminal and regular periodic statements, assume importance. Clause 10 specifically requires that these be made available to the consumer.

The *EFT Code's* clause 10 generally contains a dispute resolution procedure similar in structure (though the time requirements differ) to that contained in §1693f of the *US EFT Act*.

Pursuant to clause 10, on notification of the complaint, the financial institution must conduct an investigation and notify details of its progress or the result within 21 days, but must complete its investigation within 45 days (unless there are 'exceptional circumstances,' but this is also not defined, save for a very limited non-binding explanatory note in the 'End notes' that 'exceptional circumstances may include delays caused by foreign account institutions or foreign merchants being involved in resolving the complaint').

Importantly, unlike the *US EFT Act*'s specific tiered notification requirements, there is also no time limit within which consumers must report their complaints. A dissatisfied EFT consumer may obtain copies of the information on which the financial institution relied (for example, EFT computer or system logs). This provision was taken from the *US EFT Act*.

Under the terms of the *EFT Code*, the onus here could arguably rest with the financial institution. If it cannot positively establish an error or cannot produce adequate EFT system records relating to a disputed EFT transaction, it cannot debit the consumer's account with the amount of the disputed EFT transaction. In addition, the *EFT Code's* clause 10 provides that where a financial institution, its employees or agents, fail to observe the allocation of liability and complaint investigation and resolution procedures as prescribed under the *EFT Code*, then the financial institution will be liable for the full amount of the disputed EFT transaction where such failure prejudiced the outcome of the complaint or resulted in an unreasonable delay in its resolution (again, the *EFT Code* is silent on what constitutes 'unreasonable').

Moreover, unlike the *US EFT Act*, the *EFT Code* does not go so far as requiring that the consumer's account be provisionally re-credited with the amount in dispute should the dispute not be resolved after just 10 days. Furthermore, the *US EFT Act* (at §1693f(e)) stipulates that if the consumer's account is not provisionally re-credited within the 10-day period or the financial institution did not make a good faith investigation of the alleged error, then the consumer shall be entitled to treble damages (although, it should be noted that the consumer would have to apply to court seeking this).

In Australia, in the event of a consumer still being dissatisfied following the financial institution's investigation into the disputed EFT transaction, then the matter may be reviewed through the ABIO, State consumer affairs agencies, small claims tribunals or the courts. In this respect, clause 10.9(c) requires that financial institutions provide written notice following the completion of an investigation that these external avenues of review are available to the consumer in the jurisdiction of the consumer. It should be noted, though, that the ABIO is not intended to be an avenue of appeal where a judgment has already been given on its merits before a competent court or tribunal. If proceedings are still brought before another court or review body, the dispute can also be considered by the ABIO so long as both the financial institution and consumer agree and consent in writing.

4.8 Conclusion

The comparative legal analysis using critical comparative law method in this chapter forms the first and perhaps most fundamental component of the multi-disciplinary analysis which continues in Chapter 5. It is suggested that this comparative legal analysis is both rewarding and revealing for it enables not only a more objective analysis of the divergent regulatory approaches of each nation, but the comparison brings to the fore the opportunities for some convergence or integration on either side, as much as it highlights the key differences.

The observations from the comparative legal analysis in this chapter will be reflected in many of the specific findings in Section 6.1 of Chapter 6, and, in turn, will inform several of the recommendations advanced in Section 6.2 when constructing an efficient framework for the regulation of EFT in Australia.

The remaining elements of the extended multi-disciplinary approach to analysing and evaluating EFT regulatory options will be discussed next in Chapter 5.

Chapter 5. Multi-disciplinary Analysis of EFT Regulation: Economic, Ethical and Other Considerations

Following the comparative legal analysis of the substantive provisions of the *EFT Code* and *US EFT Act* in Chapter 4 using the critical comparative law method, in this chapter a further in-depth analysis of EFT regulatory options is undertaken using other disciplinary criteria. Namely, by employing economic efficiency criteria, regulation cost-benefit considerations, examining the rationales for government regulation, exploring whether 'market failure' is prevalent in the EFT system, a consideration of administrative feasibility and social acceptability of regulatory options, and, finally, examining the role and utility of ethics in formulating financial rules.

This chapter is structured as follows: In Section 5.1, a framework for evaluating the economic efficiency of current EFT regulatory arrangements in Australia and the USA is presented using liability and loss allocation theories. In Section 5.2, a preliminary qualitative cost-benefit analysis is undertaken including looking at the effects of government regulation on EFT consumer utility and social welfare at large, on the one hand, and, on incentives to innovate and supply new products and technologies, on the other. The focus in Section 5.3 is on different regulatory costs and an analysis is conducted on the ways in which legislative (rather than self-regulatory) requirements might affect the cost of providing EFT products and services, including some limited empirical survey evidence. In Section 5.4, a framework is constructed to assist EFT regulators and industry participants to undertake a systematic evaluation of the relative economic costs and benefits of different EFT regulation initiatives. The need to take account of administrative feasibility and social acceptability of a particular regulatory option is discussed in Section 5.5. The role and utility of ethical principles in formulating EFT rules is considered in Section 5.6, and, finally, the conclusion is presented in Section 5.7.

5.1 Economic efficiency approach to liability and loss allocation

If an unauthorised transaction theoretically profits a third party and leaves a loss to be distributed between the financial institution and the consumer, then it is critical that an optimal EFT regulation model ought to contain economically efficient loss allocation rules. A stated objective of the revised current *EFT Code* was to establish a regime for allocating losses arising from unauthorised EFT transactions that distributes those losses between the financial institution and consumer, according to the circumstances of the loss.[329]

The research undertaken for this book revealed that there is no specific analytic criteria for efficient loss allocation for unauthorised EFT transactions in Australia from which specific regulatory rules (statutory or otherwise) may be derived and appraised. Because EFT regulation concerns not only technical legal considerations, but monetary considerations as well, an economic analysis intuitively could be useful. Of course, this search for economic tools to guide the form and substance of an improved EFT regulatory regime may not provide an absolute or yield an optimal outcome, rather, after the comparative legal analysis undertaken in Chapter 4, it is intended to provide another perspective, another gauge in the quest for better regulation. Ultimately, no single alternative will be ideal, and each may create some incentives which will work at cross-purposes with one another.

The quest for better loss allocation rules is particularly relevant because of the significant increase in the number of unauthorised EFT transactions and non-compliance by financial institutions with the *EFT Code*. Also, the *EFT Code* is overdue for review by ASIC (clause 24.1(a) of the revised *EFT Code* (effective 1 April 2002) stipulated that ASIC would undertake a review within 2 years).
Various criteria for evaluating laws and regulations have been proposed in the economics literature reviewed for this book. For the purposes of this book, it is suggested that Cooter and Rubin's [330] economic framework published in 1987 is of the most utility in the search for a more efficacious EFT regulatory regime.[331] Cooter and Rubin usefully distilled three (3) principles for an economic efficiency approach to liability and loss allocation rules: loss reduction, loss spreading and loss imposition. These may then each be expanded as follows:

1. Loss reduction – liability should be allocated to the party or parties that can reduce the incidence of losses at the lowest cost ('least cost avoider');
2. Loss spreading – liability should be allocated to the party or parties best able to spread the losses (in consumer EFT transactions this is almost always the financial institution); and
3. Loss imposition – liability allocation rules should be simple, clear and decisive so as to minimise the costs of interpreting and administering them.

---

[329] Australian Securities and Investments Commission, Discussion Paper, above n 15, 26.

[330] Cooter and Rubin, above n 52, 63.

[331] However, it is acknowledged that the Cooter and Rubin position on formulating regulatory regimes makes the assumption that participants are 'rational actors', whereas some of the literature on law and economics has perhaps moved on and is increasingly drawing on behavioural sciences and sociological perspectives to model actors in ways which recognise the complexity of human behaviour: See, eg, Deepak Lal, Unintended Consequences: The Impact of Factor Endowments, Culture, and Politics on Long-Run Economic Performance (1998) 9-11 (Eg, at 12-13, Lal deals with varying degrees of shame and guilt).

Under Principle 1, the objective is to assign losses to the 'lowest-cost avoider' of whatever causes the losses, and thereby minimise the chance of the loss occurring. For example, a driver running into the rear of a car in front of him is normally presumed to be at fault because he is generally in the position to avoid the accident at lower cost than is the driver in front.

In the EFT transaction context, both financial institutions and consumers can take action to reduce losses: the consumer by reasonably safeguarding the EFT access methods for accessing the EFT account and the financial institution by maintaining and improving the reliability and security of the EFT system and EFT access methods to reduce the scope for unauthorised transactions to occur.[332] Thus, an economically efficient loss allocation rule based on Principle 1 would therefore assign liability as follows:

- To the consumer where there has been a failure by the consumer to reasonably safeguard the access method (the precise terms of this liability may then take account of the nature, strengths and weaknesses of the access method approved by the financial institution). This ought to then encourage consumers to safeguard the access method; and
- In other cases, to the financial institution, to encourage it to improve the security of the access method and EFT system over time. [333]

The access method or authentication mechanism so far chosen by account institutions, the PIN and magnetic stripe card, is a relatively inferior access method. That is, it is inferior when compared with manual signature and with other electronic alternatives, such as a chip-card, biometrics and digital signatures.[334]

The initial choice to use the prevailing PIN/magnetic stripe card technology and the continuing choice to use it some 20 years on is driven, quite reasonably, by considerations of lower cost for the financial institution. But the financial institution's cost structure is also reduced to the extent it can 'externalise' the risk and cost of unauthorised transactions by shifting it onto consumers at large.

The historical perspective discussed earlier in Chapter 2 shows that, without regulation or regulatory persuasion, there is no direct economic incentive for financial institutions to internalise that risk and improve the security of the access method and EFT system.[335]

The lowest-cost avoider principle involves perhaps four (4) considerations to determine which party is in a better position to bear liability.[336]

First, and most obvious, the lowest-cost avoider must actually be able to take some action that will minimise losses. If the party selected cannot control its expo-

---

332 Australian Securities and Investments Commission, Discussion Paper, above n 15, 29.

333 Ibid.

334 Ibid.

335 Ibid.

336 These considerations are drawn from material generously supplied by the Federal Reserve Board of the USA.

sure, then the liability assignment amounts to no more than a search for the party or parties most able to pay.

Second, the costs of avoidance must be considered in relation to the value of the activity in which the potential 'victim' is involved. That is, if the lowest-cost avoider will only exercise care by either ceasing or drastically reducing a valued activity, then it may be preferable to either spread the losses or else find a somewhat more expensive avoider.

Third, assigning liability to the lowest-cost avoider must bring about 'internalisation of losses'. In other words, the costs must actually be borne by the lowest-cost avoider in order to induce that party to avoid the costs. This means that the party selected should not be able to cheaply avoid the losses by shifting them to another party.

Finally, even if it is not clear who the lowest-cost avoider is, one can assign losses to the party best able to determine the lowest-cost avoider and to contract with it.

In theory, then, assigning losses to the lowest-cost avoider should lead to minimum costs. That all said, the notion of a lowest-cost avoider approach may still have its flaws. It could be argued that the concept is of limited value because it assumes that only one party should be expected to exercise care. In other words, it compares the costs of avoidance of each party assuming that the others make no attempt at avoidance. Therefore, it would seem to exclude the possibility of intermediate liability assignments that might more effectively induce the optimal amount of avoidance from all parties concerned. However, the problem with this criticism is that, whilst an ideal rule might seek to get each party to contribute its share of avoidance, developing such a rule would require a great deal of information regarding relative costs of avoidance among the parties. That is, rather than identifying just the lowest-cost avoider, one would have to rank each party according to comparative advantage in avoidance and determine relative liabilities consistent with the ranking. Another problem is that assigning liabilities to more than one party would involve a more complex rule and thereby create more potential for costly litigation if a failure did occur.

Principle 2 concerns 'loss spreading', which seeks to minimise the costs to each party by spreading losses as widely as possible. Cooter and Rubin usefully articulate the distinction from loss reduction as: 'loss spreading presumes that a loss has already occurred and assigns liability to the party that can more effectively spread it, but the loss reduction principle assigns liability for the more complex purpose of affecting human behaviour'.[337]

Thus, according to Principles 1 and 2, rules governing unauthorised EFT transactions may be evaluated both on how effectively they spread losses and how effectively they could modify behaviour.

While loss spreading (Principle 2) is seemingly quite straightforward, it can be concluded that the lowest-cost avoider principle (Principle 1) requires a detailed process in determining which party best or better fits the description.

---

337 Cooter and Rubin, above n 52, 63.

Principle 3 (akin to that in the *US EFT Act*) is based on the implication that the rules for allocation of liability should be simple, clear and decisive to minimise the costs of administering them. As the EFT Working Group noted,[338] this Principle suggests that:

- a no-fault allocation system is better than one that requires the evaluation of fault; and
- if a fault-based system is used, the obligations on parties should be clear and specific so that a breach of those obligations can be easily determined with little cost.

This suggests that broad standards such as 'the consumer is to take all reasonable steps to safeguard the EFT card and PIN' are less appropriate than specific standards. They are less appropriate because broad standards involve significant judgment and argument as to their interpretation in particular cases.[339] This is expensive, time consuming and somewhat arbitrary.

Turning then to the *EFT Code* vis-à-vis the *US EFT Act*, some preliminary observations may be made. It would seem that the original *EFT Code* attempted something of a 'hybrid' between the first and second principles. That is, an intermediate approach to allocation of losses between loss reduction and loss spreading. It sought to assign liability to the financial institution as the 'least cost avoider' and the consumer as the 'least cost avoider' depending on the circumstances of the disputed EFT transaction. Therefore, it intended to share losses between the consumer and financial institution following a fault-based system whereby liability is allocated to the consumer when at fault in specified ways with the security of the PIN or has been unreasonably slow in notifying the financial institution of the loss. Any other loss was allocated to the financial institution (apart from the first $50).

The EFT Working Group commissioned by ASIC, when reviewing the original *EFT Code* in 1999, commented inter alia, that: the difficulty with a fault-based loss allocation model, at least concerning fault in regard to (EFT card and/or) PIN security, is the lack of direct evidence that either side can bring as to who performed the transaction and how they came to know the access method. This led to an evidential impasse, a temptation for financial institutions to make judgments in their own interests when faced with an absence of direct evidence and resulting cynicism on both sides. Independent dispute resolution bodies such as the ABIO were then put in the difficult position of effectively having to make judgments on the bona fides of a consumer and accepting on faith financial institution statements about the accuracy and infallibility of their EFT systems. The difficulties were compounded by the fact that the original *EFT Code* did not formally allocate the burden of proof in unauthorised EFT transaction disputes one way or the other. This meant that there was no easy way out of an evidential impasse.[340]

---

338 Australian Securities and Investments Commission, Discussion Paper, above n 15, 30.
339 Ibid.
340 Ibid.

The EFT Working Group resolved that the better approach for a revised *EFT Code* was to take into account Principle 3 (that liability allocation rules should be simple, clear and decisive so as to minimise the costs of administering them).[341] That is, to effectively apportion liability between the consumer and financial institution on a no-fault basis (thus eliminating time consuming, costly and contentious fault assessment). Liability would be apportioned to the financial institution unless the financial institution could affirmatively prove that the consumer was fraudulent or grossly negligent in specific respects. The intention behind this model was that the vast majority of cases would be dealt with at the no-fault apportionment level. The EFT Working Group contended that in only a small minority of cases would an institution be able to affirmatively prove gross negligence or fraud to the higher standard specified ('proof on the balance of probability'). This option therefore could have been expected to reduce the time and resources and contentiousness in many EFT unauthorised transaction disputes.

Such a model would also be expected to be efficient to administer. Therefore, when liability is to be allocated on the basis of fault, the obligations of the consumer should be specific and clear so that a breach of those obligations can be easily determined with little cost. Broad standards should therefore be avoided. The consumer's responsibilities would be stipulated as clearly and specifically as possible.[342]

Thus, the new *EFT Code* would be a model of liability apportionment with no fault for most cases and fault with a high onus on the financial institution in limited cases.

Following the comparative legal analysis of the Australian and USA regulations, which was undertaken in Chapter 4, it is suggested that the resulting *EFT Code* did not achieve the Principle 3-styled loss allocation rules it sought to implement.

Although the burden of proof issue is expressed to be on the financial institution in most instances, the problematic interpretation of the actual cumbersome provisions of the revised *EFT Code* continues to be its undoing. Many of the multi-layered threshold tests (intended to be binding), which then, in turn, refer also to expansive cross-provisions as well as the attached incomplete explanatory notes (intended to be non-binding), are not defined and are just as broad in nature as the sort of standards the new *EFT Code* sought to avoid.

Despite its intentions and no-fault pretences, it is submitted that the revised *EFT Code* thus remains something of a 'hybrid' allocation of losses between loss reduction, and, to a lesser degree, loss spreading principles. Thus, it essentially retains a fault-based set of liability rules providing incentive for efficient precaution by both parties at once, but as the ABIO continues to experience, determinations of fault or negligence are complex, and, hence so expensive, that the overall cost of imposing fault-based rules may well exceed the utilities gained in loss reduction or loss spreading.

---

341 Ibid 31.

342 Ibid.

Moreover, for a loss reduction approach to assigning liability to be effective, both parties need to be responsive to the liability rules so that the liability is apportioned to whichever party can more cheaply take precaution to prevent the loss, or divide liability according to each party's capacity for precaution. Plainly, this is not the case under the *EFT Code* in view of ASIC's latest report highlighting the dramatic rise in the incidence of reported unauthorised EFT transactions by consumers (in both absolute and proportional terms), as well as the significant rise in non-compliance by financial institutions with the *EFT Code's* requirements.[343]

In marked contrast, the *US EFT Act* adopts the third ('loss imposition') principle in its purest form by decreasing the law's level of ambiguity. As stated, under the *US EFT Act*, consumers are not liable at all for carelessness with the EFT card and/or PIN. Consumers are only liable, subject to tiered caps, for losses caused by delays in reporting lost or stolen devices (EFT cards and/or PINs), or failing to report unauthorised EFT transactions which appear on a periodic statement (see *US EFT Act* §1693g). The *US EFT Act* provides for a deductible, which keeps increasing as the delay in informing the financial institution of an unauthorised EFT transaction grows. According to the Federal Reserve,[344] this approach is very easy to administer and avoids all disputes about consumer carelessness with EFT cards and/or PINs, as well as tribunals of fact having to 'weigh the evidence' of the parties and other complex factual matters in expensive and protracted litigation.

A final observation on this economic efficiency approach, based on Cooter and Rubin's economic model, is that any attempt to achieve optimal efficiency in the EFT payment system ought to also have regard for the approaches to regulating other payment system instruments; in particular, the divergent loss allocation rules between consumer EFT products, credit cards and paper-based payment instruments such as cheques.

A review of the various payment system regulations in Australia and the USA reveals an array of disparate rules and standards of loss allocation, all of which are used in part by consumers as cash or cash equivalents. Therefore, any concerted attempt to achieve optimal efficiency in one instrument of the payments system would seem unrealistic if regulators continue to treat loss allocation rules for cheques and payment cards differently. It is clear that the Australian and USA laws concerning error, fraud and unauthorised use in payment systems varies among payment devices (eg, the marked contrast of EFT with cheques under the common law as discussed in Chapter 2). Perhaps, though, regulators, when designing payment system rules, did not anticipate new payment devices or methods such as EFT in their attempt to allocate risks optimally. However, another view might be that regulators regard different payment system instruments as presenting different levels of risk and function, hence requiring different classification and so justifies a variance in the rules due to the different precautions and loss risks of each.

---

[343] Australian Securities and Investments Commission, Report of Compliance with the EFT Code of Conduct, 2003/2004 (2005).

[344] See, eg, Board of Governors of the Federal Reserve, Report to Congress, above n 9.

For example, the loss allocation rules for credit cards do vary considerably from those for EFT debit cards. Credit card associations, such as Visa and MasterCard, operate a complex system of contractual rules and discretions for disputed credit card transactions.[345] This is generally referred to as the 'charge-back system' and is very favourable to consumers. Under these rules and discretions, if the holder of a credit card disputes a transaction on the ground that it was unauthorised, the issuer of the credit card involved may reverse the transaction immediately, upon notification by the consumer, so that the disputed amount is charged back against the retail merchant's account.

Therefore, the consumer then steps outside the loss allocation loop in the credit card system. But as between the credit card issuer and the merchant, which party bears the loss? In this regard, the loss allocation in EFT debit card transactions is different from credit cards. Credit card association rules generally allocate the loss to the issuer, on the basis that the issuer is better situated to adopt security measures than the merchant. Unlike credit card transactions, the consumer using a PIN-based EFT debit card may remain anonymous to the merchant as long as the consumer possesses the correct PIN.

Accordingly, on this analysis, imposing liability on the consumer for unauthorised EFT debit card transactions in most cases makes no sense. In general, the loss of cash is final only because cash can be spent anonymously, but this is not the case with credit cards that are used at the point of sale. In other words, the physical limitations of cash itself result in a misallocation of the costs of merchant misconduct and may even encourage such misconduct. Currency and coin, once received by a merchant, cannot be charged back to that merchant by a consumer if the merchant is engaged in fraud or does not agree to the return of defective merchandise, for example, while credit card payments can. It seems surprising then, yet true, to regard even the simplest face-to-face cash transaction as containing the seed of 'market failure'.

The use of payment cards makes it feasible in most cases to correct this misallocation through the intervention of the financial institutions that operate the payment system. Those institutions are capable of protecting themselves through security procedures. Since most EFT cards do, or should, require use of a PIN, it is suggested that the allocation of loss to the consumer should be limited to cases in which the PIN is negligently or culpably divulged by the consumer to the wrongdoer or in which the consumer's negligent or culpable conduct otherwise compromises the EFT security system implemented by the financial institution to protect against unauthorised use of the EFT card and/or PIN.

In the USA, where credit cards continue to predominate over EFT debit cards (although the margin is decreasing as discussed in Chapter 2),[346] and most con-

---

345 Australian Securities and Investments Commission, Discussion Paper, above n 15, 31-2.

346 Since 2000, EFT debit card payment volumes and cards in circulation have grown rapidly in the USA. From 2000 to 2003, use of EFT debit cards in the USA grew 23.5% per year compared with 6.7% for credit cards, totalling 15.6 billion EFT debit card transactions compared with 19 billion credit card transactions in 2003. EFT debit cards

sumers own both kinds of cards, these forms of discrimination against EFT debit consumers in favour of credit consumers are becoming increasingly controversial. In a recent article by Arnold S Rosenberg, a USA payments system academic,[347] it is argued that there is no clear rationale for distinguishing between credit cards and EFT debit cards on functional grounds:

> [T]hese payment devices serve similar functions. Checks and ATM cards are equivalents for the purpose of gaining access to the customer's account at the bank, and checks and credit cards are equivalents for the purpose of incurring obligations to pay third-party providers of goods and services. Efforts to allocate the risk of loss for use of these payment devices also would appear to share the same objectives…to allocate losses in a manner that induces each party involved in a payment transaction to take cost-effective precautions against loss.

Indeed, the similarity of function between all 3 non-cash payment devices (cheques, credit cards and EFT debit cards) is increasing as EFT debit cards are increasingly usable to pay for goods at the point of sale (EFTPOS). As the functions of credit cards and EFT debit cards converge (where, like EFT debit cards, credit cards are used primarily for convenience rather than revolving credit), it is submitted that arguments for treating EFT debit consumers like users of cash rather than like credit consumers become weaker.

5.2 Benefits and rationales for government regulation[348]

This section presents an analytical framework for examining the effects of government regulation on EFT consumer utility and social welfare at large, on the one hand, and, incentives to innovate and on the development and adoption of new products and technologies, on the other. That is, a preliminary regulation cost/benefit analysis. In particular, the rationales for and the effects of government regulation, with a particular emphasis on the regulation of emerging technologies such as consumer EFT services.[349] This section also includes a discussion of the relative benefits of EFT products and services to consumers and society at large. A corresponding regulation cost analysis is presented in Section 5.3 which follows.

The welfare of a society is greatly influenced by the ability of its economic system to foster growth in the production of goods and services. There are said to be three (3) fundamental sources of economic growth: (i) increases in human re-

in 2005 were used in about one-third of all in-store transactions in the USA, compared with 20% in 2001.

347 A S Rosenberg, Better than Cash ? Global Proliferation of Debit and Prepaid Cards and Consumer Protection Policy, above n 91.

348 This section draws both directly and extensively from the Board of Governors of the Federal Reserve, Report to Congress, above n 9, 7.

349 This section draws extensively from Case and Fair, above n 53, 295; and the Board of Governors of the Federal Reserve, Report to Congress, above n 9, 9-16.

sources; (ii) increases in capital resources; and (iii) technical progress. Indeed, Solow has observed that technical progress is an extremely important factor in influencing the rate of economic growth.[350]

Although, it should be said that many new products or technologies may be developed without a clear understanding of how they ultimately will be utilised by users and providers, nor the regulatory challenges posed.

In a market economy, society relies primarily on the forces of competition to induce market participants to behave in an economically efficient manner. This implies that firms efficiently produce the goods and services that consumers' desire and that prices reflect the costs of the resources employed in the production process. Yet, even when most of the important resource allocation decisions in an economy are made by the private sector, government intervention may be appropriate in some areas.

Hence, it can be confidently asserted that government intervention may be warranted when the unfettered operations of the private sector fail to achieve an economically efficient outcome, that is, in the presence of so-called 'market failure'. In an operating market such as EFT services, private agreements reached between parties may produce economically efficient results without the need for legal intervention. Intervention, therefore, becomes necessary when the market fails to produce these efficient results on its own. As discussed in Section 5.1 above, rules that are designed to achieve economic efficiency in payments law should therefore enforce agreements between private parties even when no market failure has occurred. When market failure exists, legal rules may improve upon private agreements if they are designed with the goal of minimising costs in mind.[351]

Economists have identified four (4) major sources of market failure:

(i) imperfect market structure,
(ii) the presence of public goods,
(iii) the existence of external costs and benefits, and
(iv) imperfect information.[352]

Imperfect market structure refers to a situation in which the number of sellers (or buyers) in a market is small enough that a single market participant can significantly influence the price at which a product is sold. In such a market, the forces of competition may be insufficient to drive prices and output to social welfare maximising levels.[353]

Public goods are goods or services that bestow collective benefits on society; they are, in a sense, consumed jointly by all members of society. Classic examples are national defence and public health.[354] A key characteristic of a public good is that, once it is produced, everyone is able to consume it regardless of whether or

---

350 See, eg, Solow, above n 55, 312-20.
351 Cooter and Rubin, above n 52, 68.
352 See, eg, Case and Fair, above n 53, 295.
353 Ibid.
354 Ibid.

not he or she pays for it. As a result, public goods may be either under-produced or not produced at all in a completely unregulated market economy.

External costs and benefits ('externalities')[355] arise when the production or consumption of a product generates costs or benefits that accrue to parties not directly involved in the production or consumption process. Pollution and highway congestion are classic examples of negative externalities; maintaining one's home and yard is an example of an activity that generates a positive externality. In the absence of government intervention, private parties typically do not have the incentive to produce or consume socially optimal quantities of externality-generating products.

The conclusion that competitive markets lead to socially desirable outcomes depends on, among other things, the assumption that all market participants have complete information about product characteristics and prices. In the absence of full information, market participants may undertake transactions that have unanticipated outcomes. In some cases, the government may find it appropriate to attempt to mitigate the problems associated with imperfect information by either providing information to market participants or requiring firms to provide such information.

Market failure often provides the motivation for government intervention, but government action alone cannot necessarily solve the problems associated with market failure.[356] When the market structure is imperfect, imposing a competitive market structure is not always possible or desirable. Regulation, which is often relied upon to improve the allocation of resources in imperfectly competitive markets (eg, natural monopolies), provides an imperfect substitute for competition.

Thus, government intervention may prohibit specific behaviours, require certain product characteristics, set or limit prices, or mandate disclosure of information. Government responses to market failures, while having the potential to improve market outcomes, may also have unforeseen and sometimes adverse consequences. Although it should be said that regulatory intervention may not always achieve the desired outcome. Moreover, even when market failure justifies a regulatory response, the costs as well as the benefits of the regulation must be considered.[357]

In markets such as for EFT services where information problems may inevitably arise, ensuring that all market participants are fully informed is not always possible, even with government intervention. For example, when products are particularly complex, it may be difficult to identify the most important information and to provide it in a format that consumers can readily utilise. Policymakers must also take care that any information they require firms to provide is not potentially

---

[355] Ibid; and see, eg, J C Fuhrer and J Sneddon-Little, 'Technology and Growth: An Overview' (1996) New England Economic Review 3.

[356] See, eg, L S Goodman, 'The Interface between Technology and Regulation in Banking' in A Saunders and L J White (eds), Technology and the Regulation of Financial Markets (1986) 181-6.

[357] Board of Governors of the Federal Reserve, Report to Congress, above n 9, 8-9.

misleading. Moreover, in requiring firms to provide information to consumers, policymakers must weigh the costs and benefits of such requirements.[358]

But for all this, the financial services sector has long been subject to government regulation. Regulation of financial institutions has been directed toward the achievement of 3 broad objectives: minimising the risks to the public associated with instability of financial markets and the failure of financial institutions, limiting the ability of financial institutions to exercise undue market power, and protecting consumers against unfair practices.

Turning to the effects of government regulation, market failure may create a legitimate need for government regulation, but policymakers must recognise that such action may influence the behaviour of individuals or firms in unintended and often unpredictable ways. For example, regulatory compliance inevitably generates costs, which may be partially or fully passed on to consumers. Additionally, government policies designed to address problems caused by market failure can affect the risks and returns associated with investment in developing new products and technologies. These effects can be particularly important when the product or technology being regulated is at an early stage of its development.[359]

So in regulating emerging technologies such as EFT, regulation at an early stage of product development may affect the direction or speed of product or technology development. A desire to minimise regulatory compliance costs may influence firms' choices among alternative research and development paths and ultimately have an important impact on the specific features of resulting products. For example, firms may design new products so as to take advantage of regulatory 'loopholes', thereby avoiding actual or anticipated regulatory costs. Alternatively, firms may decide not to offer products having certain characteristics because of burdensome regulatory requirements.

Imposing regulations on a product or technology that is still emerging may either speed up or slow down the development process. For example, government regulation has the potential to promote standardisation. In some situations, the establishment of 'industry standards' (whether government imposed or privately determined) can greatly facilitate both the development process and market acceptance of a new product.

Although there may be potential benefits associated with early regulation of an emerging technology, there are also substantial risks. Given the uncertainties inherent in the development of a new product or technology, assessing the relative magnitudes of the costs and benefits of early statutory regulation in any particular case is often difficult. Regulatory mistakes may arise because regulators cannot foresee developments which may be costly to correct. On balance, it would seem, above all else, prudent for government to proceed cautiously and to engage in

---

358 Ibid 11.

359 Ibid 12; and see Charles F Haywood, 'Regulation, Structure, and Technological Change in the Consumer Financial Services Industry' in ABT Associates Inc. (USA) Report No. 79-34, The Costs and Benefits of Public Regulation of Consumer Financial Services (1979) 69-124.

early statutory regulation only when the benefit-cost trade-off is particularly compelling.[360]

In the end, though, the EFT payment systems in Australia and the USA are characterised by a number of competing products that enable consumers and merchants to select the payment option that is best suited to meet their needs in carrying out any particular retail transaction. These products include currency, cheques, money orders, credit and EFT cards, various forms of electronic transfers, and, in very limited circumstances, stored-value cards. Most of these products are subject to some form of regulatory restriction, which affects their costs and availability (for example, in Australia, currency under the *Banking Act 1959* (Cth) and accompanying *Banking (Foreign Exchange) Regulations* and the *Currency Act 1965* (Cth), cheques under the *Cheques Act 1986* (Cth) and credit cards under the *Uniform Consumer Credit Code*). Regulation of any of these alternative products may affect all of them, by influencing the choices consumers and merchants make among the competing options.

Another policy aspect worthy of mention is that any asymmetric regulatory treatment of competing alternatives may confer competitive advantages (or disadvantages) on certain products.[361] Government regulatory policies may play an important role in determining how these products evolve and the extent to which they achieve market acceptance. In deciding whether and, if so, how to regulate EFT services, policymakers must carefully assess the potential effect of their decisions on the evolution of the payment system.[362] For choices made today may significantly influence the payment options available to market participants in the future.

Ultimately, though, the willingness of consumers to accept a new product or technology depends on the perceived benefits that the new EFT product or technology offers and the costs associated with it.[363] Market participants may evaluate these benefits and costs in relation to those of competing payment system alternatives (ie, cheques or credit cards). Regulation can affect the acceptance of a new technology or product by influencing the benefits or costs associated with its use or by requiring the provision of information that enhances the ability of market participants to understand these benefits and costs. For example, consumer protection regulations may influence EFT product characteristics in ways that make the product more or less attractive to consumers.[364] On the one hand, the presence of consumer protection regulations may promote consumer acceptance of a new technology or product by reducing the consumer's risk exposure and thereby increasing consumer confidence. On the other hand, though, excessive consumer protection regulations may deter product acceptance by unduly focusing consumers' attention on product risks or complexities or by requiring product characteris-

360 Board of Governors of the Federal Reserve, Report to Congress, above n 9, 14.
361 Ibid 14-15.
362 Haywood, above n 359, 69-124.
363 Board of Governors of the Federal Reserve, Report to Congress, above n 9, 16.
364 See, eg, Goodman, above n 356, 181-6.

tics that consumers do not value.[365] Even when a regulation is largely irrelevant, because it requires product characteristics or information that firms would provide voluntarily, it can raise producers' costs and hence the prices faced by consumers.[366]

Regulation can also affect retail merchant (ie, EFTPOS) acceptance of new products or technologies. In the case of EFT products, experience in the USA to date, suggests that widespread retail merchant acceptance may be more difficult to achieve than consumer acceptance.[367] If regulation imposes costly requirements on retail merchants offering this payment option, it may create a significant obstacle to the technology's ultimate success.

To the extent that the provision of information about a new product or technology facilitates market acceptance, private sector firms have an incentive to provide that information. Standardising both the format and the content of the information provided can substantially reduce the difficulty of comparing competing products. Government regulation is one mechanism for achieving such standardisation; however, other alternatives exist. The private sector can often agree upon standards that promote acceptance of a new product or technology; in some instances, government regulators can facilitate such private agreements by encouraging the standard-setting process.

5.3 Regulation cost analysis

Regulation gives rise to different types of costs. This section discusses the types of regulatory costs and analyses the ways in which legislative (rather than self-regulatory) requirements might affect the cost of providing EFT products and services.[368] The analysis draws on qualitative and some limited statistical evidence of compliance costs for the *US EFT Act* and statistical studies of regulatory cost functions in the USA. These results are then extrapolated for Australian conditions to assess the likely cost impact of more formal regulation of EFT in Australia.

5.3.1 Definitions

The cost of regulation consists of opportunity and operating costs that arise from activities or changes in activities that are required by government. Opportunity costs occur when a regulation causes the producer to forgo profitable activities.[369] They generally result from prohibitions of certain activities. For example, in bank-

---

365 Ibid.

366 Ibid.

367 Board of Governors of the Federal Reserve, Report to Congress, above n 9.

368 This section also draws from USA material generously supplied by the Federal Reserve Board of the USA and the Board of Governors of the Federal Reserve, Report to Congress, above n 9.

369 Board of Governors of the Federal Reserve, Report to Congress, above n 9, 45-50.

ing, retail branch restrictions may prevent banks from taking advantage of profitable lending opportunities outside their local areas and may also make them vulnerable to downturns in local business conditions. Another opportunity cost is the forgone interest from the prohibition of investing reserves in interest-bearing assets.[370]

Opportunity costs also arise when regulation increases costs to such an extent that they discourage the introduction of a new product.[371] Operating costs may arise from requirements that banks perform certain tasks. Regulatory requirements include frequent reporting to the government central bank, the Reserve Bank of Australia, as well as to the financial regulator, ASIC, consumer disclosures to the ACCC and standards for operating procedures. In each case, employee time, material, and equipment must be devoted to performing specific activities; and managerial efforts must be devoted to understanding requirements of the regulation, implementing required actions, and ensuring compliance with the formal regulation or sanctions may be forthcoming.

There are two types of operating costs: start-up and ongoing.[372] Start-up costs are the one-time costs of changing activities to conform to the requirements of a regulation. They may include legal expenses for interpreting the regulation, advising managers, and reviewing procedures and forms; managerial expenses for reviewing and revising procedures and forms, coordinating compliance activities, and designing internal audit programs; training expenses; costs for information systems and storage of records; expenses for programming and testing of software; and costs of designing new forms and destroying obsolete forms.[373]

Ongoing costs are the recurring costs of performing the activities required by a regulation. Ongoing costs include costs such as managerial expenses for monitoring employees' compliance and for coordinating compliance examinations with regulatory agencies; labour expenses for preparing reports and disclosure statements; expenses for resolving errors; and printing and postage for disclosures.

It should be noted, however, that the distinction between start-up and ongoing costs may not always be so clear. For example, if a regulation changes frequently, the process of monitoring and implementing changes in the regulation may in itself be an ongoing activity, and the cost of this activity may legitimately be considered an 'ongoing cost'. In some cases, the cost of implementing frequent changes may be substantial and possibly greater than other recurring costs.[374] Moreover, the distinction between start-up and ongoing costs also may not be clear when the regulatory requirements for product innovations are considered. New products and changes in features of existing products may not fit clearly into regulatory definitions, making it necessary for managers to make efforts to learn the

370 Ibid.

371 Ibid.

372 Ibid; and see Schroeder, above n 67.

373 Ibid.

374 Formal rulemaking is not the only way that regulatory requirements may change. In some instances, the Reserve Bank of Australia or the Australian Securities and Investments Commission interpretations or court decisions can also change regulatory requirements.

appropriate regulatory treatment of the product or feature. Moreover, managers' time and the possible delay in introducing innovations may be considered an ongoing cost in a dynamic market.

Some regulations require institutions to perform activities that they would not do in the absence of regulation. Take, for example, the *Financial Transaction Reports Act 1988* (Cth) ('FTRA'), which requires banks to file with the government authority, the Australian Transaction Reports and Analysis Centre ('AUSTRAC') reports of large cash transactions (greater than AUD$10,000), certain currency transactions, an international funds transfers above AUD$10,000 and other 'suspect' transactions.[375] This was considered to be particularly onerous on financial institutions and is an example of the type of regulation that forced these institutions to perform activities they would not otherwise have done. Other regulations govern activities that financial institutions would have performed in any case even in the absence of formal regulation. For example, the uniform legislation under the *Consumer Credit Code 1996* (Cth), which requires quite rigorous disclosures of credit account terms containing certain information at certain times.[376] Many banks may provide disclosures without being required to do so, and, indeed, it is possible that most banks already provided disclosure statements before the law was enacted (although banks may not have provided all of the information exactly as required by the law).

The total cost of a regulation is the cost of performing all of the activities that that regulation requires. The incremental cost of a regulation is the cost of activities that are performed only because the law mandates them.[377] Activities that are mandated by the law, but would be performed in the ordinary course of business are part of the total cost of a regulation, but not part of the incremental cost. Because total cost includes costs that banks would have incurred anyway, incremental cost is considered to be a more relevant measure of the economic cost of a regulation than total cost.[378]

In some cases, total cost and incremental cost may be the same, but in other cases they may differ. In the case of the FTRA, for example, the total cost of performing the activities required by the regulation is probably about equal to the incremental cost. In the case of the *Consumer Credit Code*, however, since most banks provided disclosure statements without the regulation, the incremental cost is likely to be less than the total cost.

The need to identify required activities that would be performed in the absence of regulation makes measurement of incremental regulatory costs difficult. Over time, many such activities may come to be viewed as part of routine banking business, especially if they are a relatively small part of a necessary or unregulated activity, and, thus may be overlooked when identifying regulatory activities. More-

[375] See, eg, A L Tyree, Banking Law in Australia (5th ed, 2005) 408-10.

[376] Ibid.

[377] Note that the benchmark for determining the incremental cost of a regulation may not be an unregulated regime.

[378] Board of Governors of the Federal Reserve, Report to Congress, above n 9, 45.

over, regulation may force an institution to perform an activity in a different, more costly way than it would otherwise choose. This added cost is a component of incremental cost, but it may be easy to overlook and difficult to measure.[379]

5.3.2 Compliance and evidence of costs of regulation

Experience with the *US EFT Act* provides a logical starting point for assessing the possible costs of applying legislative consumer protection regulations to EFT in Australia. In particular, this sub-section examines comments received from interested parties in the USA in the process of the formal rulemaking (ie, across 1978-79), as well as a survey of compliance costs conducted by the Federal Reserve Board in 1981, 2 years after the *US EFT Act* was implemented. In addition, the survey provides quantitative estimates for the cost of compliance with the regulation. This sub-section also discusses the sources of incremental compliance costs associated with the *US EFT Act*. It is suggested that many of these costs are generic to any financial regulation, whilst others occur because of specific *US EFT Act* requirements.

Start-up costs

Many requirements under the *US EFT Act* mandate compliance actions that financial institutions ought to be taking under the existing *EFT Code* and otherwise in the normal course of business.[380] For example, even before the *EFT Code* and *US EFT Act*, financial institutions typically provided periodic statements on request containing a list of electronic and other transactions. They provided receipts for many transactions, in some cases had procedures for resolving errors, and some may have informed customers about account terms and changes in terms through written disclosures. Deposit account providers also provided customers with certain protection against unauthorised use in the case of cheques by providing, under common law, that consumers are not liable for cheques they have not signed.[381] Despite the similarities between some existing practices and the requirements of regulation through legislation, the USA experience is that all financial institutions incurred some degree of start-up costs.[382] In the USA, the Federal Reserve observes that even financial institutions that performed all of the required activities probably did not perform them exactly as specified in the rigorous *US EFT Act*.[383]

To bring the financial institutions' policies and procedures into compliance with the *US EFT Act*,[384] managers first had to spend significant time learning the

379 Ibid.

380 This section draws from USA material generously supplied by the Federal Reserve Board of the USA and the Board of Governors of the Federal Reserve, Report to Congress, above n 9.

381 Board of Governors of the Federal Reserve, Report to Congress, above 9, 45.

382 Ibid.

383 Ibid.

384 Ibid 45-6.

requirements of the new formal regulation. Indeed, managers had to review existing policies, procedures, forms and manuals and modify them to comply with the regulation; coordinate employees' compliance activities throughout the institution including across the nation and overseas; and design an audit program to ensure compliance. Specialist legal services and teams were required to interpret the regulation and provide guidance to financial institutions' staff. Employees had to undertake detailed training in order to carry out the strict new procedures, which were designed to implement the requirements of the statutory regulation.

Financial institutions also incurred expenses for design and editing of forms and disclosure statements, modification or disposal of old forms, and printing an initial inventory of new forms and disclosure documents. Data processing systems had to be changed to retain, process, and report the information required by the statutory regulation at times specified in the *US EFT Act*. These changes may have included programming, purchases of new EFT software, testing, purchases of EFT terminals and other specialist hardware, installation of equipment and construction of premises for equipment.

Ongoing costs

Incremental costs, measuring only costs that are incurred because of regulation, are considered to be more appropriate than total costs as a basis for measuring regulatory costs.[385] Since many of the requirements of the new statutory regulation involved modifications or an expansion of existing activities rather than the performance of new activities, not all activities required by the *US EFT Act* would have given rise to significant incremental costs.[386] Sending periodic statements, for example, would generally not be a new cost, but invariably would have generated an incremental cost because of the more regular reporting the *US EFT Act* requires (ie, monthly or quarterly). Furthermore, additional paper, computer usage, and postage might be incremental costs if, say, location and other information required to identify individual EFT transactions were not reported in the absence of statutory regulation. Similarly, employees' time spent answering consumer enquiries and resolving alleged errors would not all be incremental costs.[387] The *US EFT Act* may have stimulated some additional enquiries or claims of errors. The cost of responding to these additional enquiries and claims of errors is appropriately classified as an incremental cost, even though determining the additional cost due to the regulation may be difficult.[388]

---

[385] This section draws from USA material generously supplied by the Federal Reserve Board of the USA and the Board of Governors of the Federal Reserve, Report to Congress, above n 9.

[386] Board of Governors of the Federal Reserve, Report to Congress, above n 9, 47-8.

[387] Ibid 47.

[388] Ibid.

The salary and overhead expenses for a compliance officer or department is an incremental cost. The time that the compliance officers or department devotes to compliance with the *US EFT Act* is part of its ongoing cost.

However, internal auditing of compliance with regulations; coordination of the compliance reviews with supervisory agencies; monitoring changes in the regulation, interpretations, and court decisions; and modifying compliance procedures are all recurring costs that are incurred solely because of regulation. Legal services for review of any additional complaints; interpretation of changes in the regulation, interpretations, and court decisions; and expenses of litigation are incremental costs.

As mentioned, only part of the employees' time spent responding to enquiries and resolving alleged errors would be incremental. Time spent documenting compliance with regulatory requirements would be an incremental cost. Training expenses for maintaining employee skills and informing employees of new regulatory requirements would also be incremental costs.

Some financial institutions may not have made all of the required disclosures in the absence of the statutory regulation (eg, initial disclosure of terms and conditions of use, annual notices of error-resolution procedures, changes in terms and conditions of use or notices for preauthorised EFT transactions) and may have incurred incremental ongoing costs for printing or purchasing of disclosures and additional postage expense for mailing these disclosures. Some financial institutions may have incurred telephone expenses for error-resolution activities and preauthorised EFT transaction enquiries beyond those that they would have incurred without the statutory regulation. Additional losses due to the *US EFT Act's* limitations of consumers' liability for unauthorised or disputed unauthorised EFT transactions and civil damages due to violations of the *US EFT Act's* strict requirements both for unauthorised transfers, errors and consequential damage resulting from these as well as EFT system malfunctions would also be ongoing or prolonged incremental costs due to statutory regulation.[389]

Survey evidence – USA

Unfortunately, there is a paucity of cost/benefit analysis of EFT regulation for either self-regulation, statutory regulation or hybrid forms of the two. The most recent survey information available on the cost and activity impact of statutory regulation is somewhat dated. In 1981, the Federal Reserve conducted a mail survey to gather information about compliance costs for several consumer protection regulations.[390] The *US EFT Act*, which became effective in 1979, was one of the regulations included in the survey. Sixty-seven financial institutions that agreed to participate in the survey responded to the questionnaire. Specifically, these 67 institutions across the USA were asked to estimate their start-up costs for implementing the *US EFT Act* and their incremental ongoing expenses of the regulation in 1980, the full year following the *Act's* implementation. The Federal Reserve question-

[389] Ibid 48.

[390] Ibid.

naire specified cost categories for reporting the data, defined incremental cost, provided guidance on the way to estimate costs, identified the major requirements of the regulation and also listed possible activities to satisfy the new regulatory requirements. These questionnaire design features helped guide responses, stimulate respondent memory and ensure uniform responses.[391]

These survey responses were subsequently reviewed and tabled by Schroeder,[392] who indicated that start-up costs for the *US EFT Act* were, on average, US10 cents per EFT transaction and annual ongoing incremental costs approximated US11 cents per EFT transaction. Refer to Table 5.1 below.

At this point, it is important to note that following enquiries of representatives of all the major Australian retail banks, as well as of their peak industry body, the Australian Bankers' Association, there appears to be no available transaction cost data for compliance with electronic banking regulation in Australia. Accordingly, following a detailed review of the survey evidence from the USA, an attempt will be made to extrapolate that data to foreshadow the possible cost and activity impact of a statutory regulation regime in Australia.

Table 5.1. Average cost per EFT transaction for compliance with the *US EFT Act*, by type of cost and deposit-size of bank, 1980[393]

US Cents per EFT Transaction				
Size of Bank by Deposits (US$ Millions)				
Type of Cost	Less than 500	500–2,999	3,000 or more	All Banks
Start-up	11	12	6	10
Ongoing	17	8	4	11

In 1980, approximately 1.3 billion EFT transactions occurred in the USA, implying start-up costs of US$130 million and ongoing incremental costs of US$140 million per year.[394]

Both Schroeder and Zimmer[395] concluded that the Federal Reserve survey responses suggest that the cost of complying with the *US EFT Act* may have been a significant component of the total cost of EFT transactions.[396]

391 Ibid.

392 Schroeder, above n 67, 143.

393 Ibid. Note: Statistics in this table are weighted averages of data reported by Schroeder. The weights are based on aggregate deposits at all commercial banks in 1980.

394 Schroeder, above n 67, 143.

395 L F Zimmer, 'ATM Acceptance Grows, Builds Customer Base for Other EFT Services' (1981) Magazine of Bank Administration 31.

396 Ibid.

To put this figure in perspective and to show that it is more likely than not quite realistic, a contemporary study in 1981 by accountants, Peat Marwick Mitchell, estimated a direct cost to financial institutions of US7 cents per transaction for making direct electronic deposits of social security payments into customer accounts.[397] Thus, statutory regulation of financial institutions in the USA may have more than doubled the cost of this transaction to about 18 cents per EFT deposit given those hitherto 'unregulated' social security deposits would be caught by the *US EFT Act's* regulatory provisions. Interestingly, the same study estimated a direct cost of 24 cents for depositing social security checks with a human teller and 59 cents for depositing social security checks by mail.

Other types of electronic transactions may have had different costs, but it seems reasonable to conclude that compliance with the *US EFT Act* accounted for a substantial share of the cost of making electronic transactions.

Table 5.1 also shows that large banks reported somewhat lower start-up and ongoing incremental compliance costs for the *US EFT Act* than did smaller banks. These results are consistent with the existence of economies of scale. Indeed, if there are economies of scale, then the ongoing costs of compliance for the regulation could be expected to be lower today (because of the much greater number of electronic transactions) than they were in 1980.[398]

The Federal Reserve survey responses indicate that the time that managers spent learning the requirements of the statutory regulation and modifying procedures to comply with them contributed substantially to the start-up cost for implementing the requirements of the *US EFT Act*. Managerial expenses accounted for more than one-third of total start-up costs overall and nearly one-half of total start-up costs at smaller banks with less than US$500 million in deposits (see Tables 5.2 and 5.3 below). The cost of modifying data processing systems accounted for another third of total start-up costs overall.

---

397 Peat, Marwick, Mitchell & Company and Electronic Banking Inc., The Costs and Benefits of Participation in the Treasury's Direct Deposit Program, prepared for the Bank Administration Institute, National Association of Mutual Savings Banks, United States League of Savings Associations, and United States Department of the Treasury (1981) 7.

398 Note: In some activities, cost reductions are achieved over time simply because of learning. See, eg, K Arrow, 'Economic Welfare and the Allocation of Research for Invention' in R Nelson (ed), The Rate and Direction of Inventive Activity: Economic and Social Factors (1961). Note: Also, there is no evidence as to whether learning causes cost reductions in regulatory compliance. If there are cost reductions from this source, ongoing incremental costs of compliance for the US EFT Act and Regulation E would be lower today than they were in 1980.

Table 5.2. Distribution of start-up costs for compliance with the *US EFT Act* across categories of start-up cost, by deposit-size of bank, 1980[399]

Percent %				
Size of Bank by Deposits (US$ Millions)				
Type of Cost	Less than 500	500–2,999	3,000 or more	All Banks
Start-up				
Management	43	28	26	36
Training	16	7	8	12
Data processing	19	50	47	33
Equipment	6	4	2	4
Disclosures	10	8	14	10
Other	5	3	4	4
TOTAL [400]	100	100	100	100

Table 5.3. Distribution of ongoing incremental costs for compliance with the *US EFT Act* across categories of ongoing incremental cost, by deposit-size of bank, 1980[401]

Percent %				
Size of Bank by Deposits (US$ Millions)				
Type of Cost	Less than 500	500–2,999	3,000 or more	All Banks
Ongoing				
Management	28	28	16	26
Labour	46	32	36	43
Training	4	4	6	4
Equipment	6	1	10	5
Disclosures	9	16	8	10
Postage	6	18	18	10
Other	2	1	8	3
TOTAL [402]	100	100	100	100

In contrast to start-up costs, ongoing incremental costs detailed above in Table 5.3 included substantial expenses for non-supervisory labour. Overall, 43 percent of ongoing incremental costs to comply with the *US EFT Act* were for non-supervisory employees, who perform routine activities such as preparing and distributing disclosure statements/terms and conditions of use, explaining disclosed information to customers and resolving errors and disputes. The managerial and

[399] Schroeder, above n 67, 143.
[400] Components may not sum to 100 per cent due to rounding.
[401] Schroeder, above n 67, 143.
[402] Note Components may not sum to 100 per cent due to rounding.

legal expenses were a smaller share of ongoing incremental costs than for start-up costs, accounting for 26 percent of the ongoing incremental costs for the *US EFT Act*. The small, but nonetheless significant share of management and legal expenses arose from the need to monitor employees' compliance; coordinate compliance reviews with regulators; handle customer disputes that non-supervisory employees were unable to resolve; and learn regulatory changes, regulator interpretations and court decisions that affected compliance.

Survey evidence – extrapolated for Australia

Whilst acknowledging upfront the limitations of the USA data for Australia in terms of its age, different banking system and different ingredient economic costs, an extrapolation may still be of some utility in foreshadowing the likely impact of any statutory regulation (or a hybrid with self-regulation) for EFT in Australia.

Using data sourced directly from the economic research division of the Reserve Bank of Australia ('RBA') specifically for this book, it is possible to extrapolate the USA cents per EFT transaction in 1980 to Australian cents per EFT transaction in 2005. The two (2) necessary types of data required to facilitate this extrapolation are: (i) the relevant 1979/80 and 1980/81 average currency exchange rates to enable a conversion from American Dollars ('USD') to Australian Dollars ('AUD') effective 1980; and (ii) all the consumer price index ('CPI') quarterly movements since 1980 in order to adjust the converted AUD cost figures effective 1980 under (i) above to a 2005 base (where the quarter to 12/2005 represents the last CPI movement measured).

1. The relevant 1979/80 and 1980/81 average currency exchange rates from the RBA are 1.1148 USD per AUD and 1.1610 USD per AUD.[403] Taking the average of these two financial years, a computed currency conversion rate of 1.1379 is achieved. This currency conversion rate of 1.1379 can then be applied to the USD per EFT transaction cost figures as at 1980 in Table 5.1 above to arrive at an AUD per EFT transaction cost figure for each item as at 1980. That is, the 'start-up' and 'incremental ongoing' cost figures of USD$0.10 and USD$0.11 per EFT transaction, respectively, become AUD$0.0879 and AUD$0.0967 per EFT transaction, respectively.
2. Adjusting the resulting 1980 AUD per EFT transaction cost figures for the subsequent 25 years necessitates 100 quarterly CPI adjustments each of which will not be detailed here.[404] Suffice to state that a basket of goods and services for CPI purposes that cost AUD$0.0879 and AUD$0.0967 respectively in 1980 would have cost AUD$0.28 and AUD$0.30 respectively in 2005 (repre-

[403] Reserve Bank of Australia, Australian Economic Statistics 1949-50 to 1996-97: Occasional Paper No 8 (2006) <http://www.rba.gov.au/Statistics/op8_index.html> at 13 February 2006.

[404] Reserve Bank of Australia, Quarterly Statistical Release: Measures of Consumer Price Inflation (25January 2006) <http://www.rba.gov.au/Statistics/measures_of_cpi.html> at 13 February 2006.

senting a total change in cost of 215% over the 25 years between 1980 and 2005 at an average annual CPI rate of 4.7%pa).

The resulting AUD per EFT transaction costs for both start-up and incremental ongoing costs are set out in Table 5.4 below:

Table 5.4. Estimated average cost per EFT transaction for compliance with statutory EFT regulation by type of cost, 2005[405]

	Australian Cents per EFT Transaction
Type of Cost	All Financial institutions
Start-up	28
Ongoing	30

The most recent ASIC data on the number of EFT transactions in Australia was for the year to 31 March 2004, where 2.53 billion EFT transactions occurred in Australia. Based on the extrapolated cost figures of AUD$0.28 and AUD$0.30 respectively above, this implies an estimated start-up costs figure of AUD$708 million and an estimated ongoing incremental costs figure of AUD$758 million per year.

To be of any utility, these significant cost estimates must be qualified by two important considerations. First, the underlying data sourced from the USA is based on a survey of some 67 financial institutions of varying sizes whereas in Australia, there are 185 institutions that subscribe to the existing *EFT Code* and include not only banks, but smaller building societies and credit unions as well. The USA survey evidence clearly showed that costs are significantly higher for smaller institutions than for larger ones who can spread the costs over more activities and a much larger customer base. Second, the estimated AUD cost figure for start-up costs of AUD$708 million is predicated on EFT providers not having any regulatory compliance systems and infrastructure in place at the time statutory regulation is introduced. This, of course, is not the case in Australia as all subscribers at least have some compliance systems and procedures in place.[406]

Accordingly, the more relevant cost estimate is that for ongoing incremental costs post-regulation of AUD$0.30 per EFT transaction per annum, which equates to a total EFT industry cost of AUD$758 million per annum.

---

405 Ibid. Note: Statistics in this table are weighted averages of data reported by Schroeder, above n 67. The weights are based on aggregate deposits at all commercial banks in 1980.

406 Refer to any of the Australian Securities and Investments Commission, Reports of Compliance (Annual).

Economies of scale

As discussed above under Section 5.2, the existence of economies of scale in regulatory compliance costs is entirely possible.

Schroeder observed that costs may exhibit economies of scale because of 'indivisibilities' in regulatory compliance.[407] Several compliance activities discussed above seem to have this characteristic. For example, the EFT computer system hardware and software required to process EFT transactions, generate required EFT disclosures and compliance reporting generally cannot be divided. The financial institution buys the entire package, which it can then use to produce any number of disclosures across all its retail banking products and services. If the cost is fixed, then it could be expected that, for example, the average cost of disclosures will decrease as the number of disclosures increases. Another example of indivisibility might be the time needed to learn the requirements of the EFT regulation. Bank officers cannot afford to learn only part of the EFT regulation's requirements, nor can employees be partly trained. Thus, a finding of economies of scale for statutory or revised regulation seems entirely reasonable.

5.4 A framework for the systematic evaluation of EFT regulation costs and benefits

Although it is considered beyond both the scope of this book to address in detail an econometric or mathematical modelling of costs and benefits of EFT regulation initiatives, it is nevertheless of some utility to proffer a simplified framework for such an analysis.

5.4.1 Purpose

In the absence of any particular cost-benefit analysis criteria as applied to EFT regulation, such a framework may assist the systematic evaluation of the relative costs and benefits of different EFT regulation initiatives so as to provide for more informed decisions on impacts and resource allocation among the different policy options advanced in this book. Potential evaluators may include each of those regulators with responsibility for the various aspects of the EFT system, as well as those with access to current, meaningful industry-wide banking industry and/or EFT cost-benefit data. Those identified may include: the ABIO, the RBA, ASIC, the ACCC, consumer advocacy groups, the Australian Bankers' Association, or, at the ultimate level, the Australian federal government Department of Treasury.

Indeed, potential evaluators may use this framework as a reference document for devising a methodology for analysing EFT regulation costs and benefits. The framework is intended to be something of a step-by-step guide to undertaking both

[407] Schroeder, above n 67, 143.

a cost-benefit and cost-effectiveness analysis, from identifying some of the types of data to collect through to reporting the results of the analysis.

It should also be stated that this framework is designed to facilitate an evaluation of how cost-effective an intervention has been, as much as for a forward-looking economic appraisal.

Given the broad range of regulatory interventions possible as detailed in this chapter, specifically, and throughout this book, generally, this framework cannot cover all of the cost-benefit issues that will invariably arise for each policy option. Rather, the intention is for this framework to set out principles and methods that could possibly apply to many if not all regulatory interventions.

By systematically recording and comparing the cost of inputs with both the outputs and outcomes of a regulatory intervention, the analysis permits a determination of the economic efficiency of regulatory interventions. This will facilitate both more informed decisions on resource allocation between different policy options to be made and perhaps enable the following key questions to be answered:[408]

- What is the true (opportunity) cost of an intervention?
- Does the outcome(s) achieved justify the investment of resources?
- Is this the most efficient way of realising the desired outcome(s) or could the same outcome(s) be achieved at a lower cost through an alternative course of action?

The cost-effectiveness analysis should therefore hope to inform decisions on how to allocate scarce resources both within and between regulatory initiatives in order to achieve the most efficient regulation of EFT. It will also make this decision process more transparent by organising information on inputs, outputs, impacts and outcomes (all defined below) in a single comparative framework.

This framework should not, of course, be regarded as providing the final or absolute answer since it cannot hope to incorporate all outcomes (nor inputs in most cases) arising from a particular regulatory intervention. There are also likely to be a host of reasons for allocating resources in a particular way which fall outside the analysis. Nevertheless, it does provide a useful tool for assessing the use of scarce resources and comparing the relative cost-effectiveness of different interventions on a common basis.

5.4.2 Key definitions and practical examples

For the purposes of the evaluation of the various EFT regulatory options or interventions, the following key definitions and practical examples in Figure 5.1 are necessary.

---

[408] See, eg, B Welsh, D Farrington and L Sherman, Costs and Benefits of Preventing Crime (2001) 184.

Inputs are defined as any additional human, physical and financial resources that are used to undertake a particular EFT regulatory option. For example, in a regulatory intervention that mandates precise rules for the issuance of EFT cards and PINs by financial institutions as a measure to reduce the possibility of lost or stolen EFT cards and PINs as well as the incidence of unauthorised EFT transactions occurring at the initial issuance stage, inputs might include the computer software, hardware, materials and labour employed by financial institutions to establish the new EFT card and PIN issuance process and procedures.

Outputs are defined narrowly as the direct products of the process of implementation. They can arise only during the implementation period. Following the above example then, the new EFT card and PIN issuance processes and procedures installed are outputs and the dedicated computer system usage and number of staff and customers impacted may each be output measures.

Impacts on risk factors are defined as the effects of outputs that disrupt the causes of lost or stolen EFT cards and PINs and the incidence of unauthorised EFT transactions. Measuring such impacts is therefore a way of monitoring the process through which the regulatory intervention is expected to reduce lost EFT cards and PINs and the incidence of unauthorised EFT transactions at the initial issuance stage. In the above example, this could be a reduction in the number of lost or stolen EFT cards and PINs, thereby reducing the opportunity for unauthorised EFT transactions occurring at the initial issuance stage.

Outcomes are defined as the consequences of the intervention. These can arise both *during* and *after* the implementation period. Key outcomes should relate to the stated objectives of the regulatory intervention. In the above example, the reduction in the number of lost or stolen EFT cards and PINs and/or the resultant number of unauthorised EFT transactions attributable to the installation of dedicated computer systems, staff and customer disclosure practices may be the primary outcomes. But there are likely to be wider outcomes such as a change in the public's confidence in using EFT a payment option in preference to other payment system options such as cheques or credit cards. These wider outcomes may or may not be measurable and could be negative as well as positive.

Costs are defined as the monetary value of the inputs (defined above).

Benefits are defined as the value of outcomes to society that are attributed to the regulatory intervention and are expressed in monetary terms. Any calculated negative outcomes attributed to the EFT regulatory intervention may be referred to as *disbenefits*.

Figure 5.1 Definitions[409]

[409] These definitions have been adapted from M Hough and N Tilley, Auditing Crime and Disorder (1998) 91. However, they are only for the purpose of EFT regulatory intervention. They have been constructed to allow evidence to be gathered not only on the final consequences of an EFT regulatory intervention, but also on the mechanism through which an EFT regulatory intervention is assumed to achieve stated objectives.

5.4.3 Techniques for analysing costs and benefits of EFT regulation[410]

There are several ways in which inputs and outcomes can be analysed. The two (2) main techniques that will be used for EFT regulatory intervention options will be cost-effectiveness analysis ('CEA') and cost-benefit analysis ('CBA').

Cost-effectiveness analysis

CEA compares alternative cost streams to produce broadly similar outputs or outcomes. As argued in Section 5.1, the most efficient, least-cost alternative to produce the defined outcome (or set of outcomes) is the most desirable option, subject to account being taken of wider outcomes that cannot be incorporated in such an analysis.

For the purposes of EFT regulatory initiatives (and based on the example above), a CEA will estimate the costs of achieving defined outcomes, typically measured in terms of a reduction in the incidence of lost or stolen EFT cards and PINs and/or an accompanying reduction in the incidence of unauthorised EFT transactions. Hence, a CEA ought to indicate whether EFT regulatory interventions (and/or a combination(s) of regulatory interventions) have been more, or less, costly in achieving such a reduction than existing measures and/or alternative regulatory interventions.

Using the definitions in Figure 5.1 above, cost-effectiveness may be articulated in terms of the *input cost per unit of output or outcome* achieved. For example, it may be of utility to know the cost per EFT customer of implementing a precise EFT card and PIN issuance system (cost per output) or the cost per unauthorised EFT transaction prevented (cost per outcome). In order to derive a measure of cost-effectiveness, therefore, it would be useful to know the level of inputs used to implement an intervention, the cost of these inputs and the nature and level of outputs and outcomes.

However defined, though, outcomes will need to be *quantified* (ie, measured numerically) to enable a CEA to be undertaken. Accordingly, outcomes that relate directly to the stated objectives of the EFT regulatory intervention must be quantified.

410 The following analysis draws in part from Islam and Mak, above n 50.

Table 5.5. A stylised example of cost-effectiveness analysis (CEA)[411]

Assume there are two (2) EFT regulatory intervention options, EFT1 and EFT2, and let:		
Cost EFT1	=	AUD$120,000
Cost EFT2	=	AUD$100,000
Outcome EFT1	=	prevents 100 lost or stolen EFT cards or PINs
Outcome EFT2	=	prevents 60 lost or stolen EFT cards or PINs
Therefore: The average cost per prevented lost or stolen EFT card or PIN through EFT1 is AUD$1,200 (AUD$120,000/100) and the average cost of preventing one lost or stolen EFT card or PIN through EFT2 is AUD$1,667 (AUD$100,000/60). Per prevented lost or stolen EFT card or PIN, therefore, EFT1 is more cost-effective than EFT2.		

In order to compare the cost-effectiveness of alternative EFT regulatory interventions, they must share common outputs or outcomes and be measured on a common basis. Examples might include the number of (defined) lost or stolen EFT cards or PINs prevented, the unit reduction in probability of a lost or stolen EFT card or PIN occurring or the number of EFT consumers or financial institution staff the subject of the regulatory intervention.

Cost-benefit analysis

Cost-benefit analysis ('CBA') takes cost-effectiveness analysis a stage further by attaching monetary values to the outcomes of an EFT regulatory intervention. Once both the costs of inputs and the value of outcomes (benefits) are expressed in monetary terms a direct comparison may be made.

The result is articulated in terms of either a *benefit/cost ratio*, where the value of outcomes (benefits) is divided by input costs, or the *net economic benefit*, which is simply the sum of the value of benefits less the sum of input costs. The decision rule for a given project is to maximise the benefit/cost ratio or the net economic benefit or minimise the net economic cost, taking into account those outcomes that are not included in the calculation.

Following the above example for consistency between CEA and CBA methods, for many EFT regulatory interventions, outcomes should then be quantified in terms of a reduction in the number of lost or stolen EFT cards and PINs and/or the incidence of unauthorised EFT transactions occurring at the initial issuance stage.

[411] This simplistic example does not take into account the variance of estimates or the relative magnitude of the two EFT regulatory interventions: EFT1 and EFT2. Before it can be confidently asserted that one EFT regulatory intervention is more cost-effective than another, there would need to be a determination of whether the difference between the two calculated results is statistically significant. Also, the example does not examine marginal costs. Marginal costs describe the additional cost of increasing outcome by an additional unit. In this example, this is the cost of inputs required to prevent one more lost or stolen EFT card or PIN.

Since unauthorised EFT transactions undoubtedly have costs to society at large, including the two relatively innocent parties (the financial institution and consumer) and potentially affected parties such as all financial institutions and consumers across the EFT industry, the ABIO and the legal system generally, the value of an EFT regulatory intervention ought to be measured by the avoidance of costs (savings) to society of those unauthorised EFT transactions that *would otherwise have taken place.*

In order to calculate the savings to society resulting from an EFT regulatory intervention, it is suggested, therefore, that there is a need to know how many such unauthorised EFT transactions have been prevented as a result of the regulatory intervention, and how much these (prevented) unauthorised EFT transactions would have otherwise cost.

Table 5.6. A stylised example of cost-benefit analysis (CBA)

Using the example in Table 5.5 above (ie, that there are two (2) EFT regulatory intervention options, EFT$_1$ and EFT$_2$) and assuming that the average cost to society of a single unauthorised EFT transaction is AUD1,500 then for regulatory intervention EFT$_1$:	
Input cost EFT$_1$	AUD$120,000
Outcome quantity	100 unauthorised EFT transactions prevented
Outcome value (benefit)	100 x AUD$1,500 = AUD$150,000
Therefore:	
Benefit/cost ratio	AUD$150,000/AUD$120,000 = 1.25:1
Net economic benefit	AUD$150,000–AUD$120,000= AUD$30,000
For EFT$_1$ benefits outweigh its costs by AUD$30,000.	
The same calculation for EFT regulatory intervention option, EFT$_2$, yields the following results:	
Input cost EFT$_1$	AUD$100,000
Outcome quantity	60 unauthorised EFT transactions prevented
Outcome value (benefit)	60 x AUD$1,500 = AUD$90,000
Benefit/cost ratio	AUD$90,000/AUD$100,000 = 0.9:1
Net economic benefit	AUD$90,000–AUD$100,000= (AUD$10,000)
For EFT$_2$ costs outweigh its benefits and there is a net cost of AUD$10,000.	

It could reasonably be assumed that not all unauthorised EFT transactions may have the same level or types of costs to society. Accordingly, in a CEA, the simple quantification of unauthorised EFT transactions prevented at the initial issuance stage possibly ignores the difference in the quality of all outcomes achieved. Therefore, by attaching monetary values to different types of unauthorised EFT transactions, CBA may be able to measure this outcome quality. This is done by estimating, as accurately and convincingly as possible, the average cost to society of different types of unauthorised EFT transactions. Thus, the total value of benefits as a result of a particular EFT regulatory intervention option can then be estimated by multiplying the number of unauthorised EFT transactions prevented by the average cost of an unauthorised EFT transaction.

The CBA may then help to determine to what extent different EFT regulatory intervention options will be successful in reducing the cost of particular unauthorised EFT transactions to society, and, moreover, help to identify which EFT regulatory intervention options, or combinations of EFT regulatory intervention options, yield the greatest net economic benefit.

However, in contrast to CEA, different outcome measures do not preclude a comparison under CBA, to the extent that variables can be expressed in common (monetary) terms. For example, the net economic benefit of a particular EFT regulatory initiative could be compared with that of a different initiative, even though they may not share the same resource inputs, outputs or outcomes. In addition, multiple outcomes arising from a particular EFT regulatory intervention option will all be expressed in monetary terms and their relative quality will be reflected in their valuation. In reality, CBA cannot capture all of the costs and benefits to society of a particular EFT regulatory intervention option. Ultimately, then, this ought to make it all the more desirable to base the CBA on common outcome measures as far as is practicable.

Suggested steps for this framework of analysis

For a cost-effectiveness analysis (CEA), the following steps should serve as a useful framework:

i. Define the intervention, its objectives and the mechanism through which inputs have led to impacts and outcomes;
ii. Identify inputs;
iii. Identify outputs and outcomes;
iv. Quantify inputs;
v. Quantify attributable impacts and outcomes;
vi. Value inputs (costs); and
vii. Compare input costs with outputs and outcomes.

In a cost-benefit analysis (CBA), two (2) additional steps should be added to the above CEA framework:

viii. Value outcomes (benefits); and
ix. Compare costs with benefits.

A mathematical model for cost-benefit analysis

A cost-benefit analysis ('CBA') of a particular regulation or law may also be undertaken by applying more traditional econometric or mathematical evaluation methods. Economic evaluation has been defined as 'a process of analysing a number of plans or projects with a view to searching out their comparative advantages and disadvantages and the act of setting down the findings of such analysis in a logical framework'.[412]

From all the available traditional alternatives, the discounted cost-benefit method developed by Islam and Mak will be adapted in this study,[413] given the suitability of this method for designing optimal EFT regulation in Australia. The net present value is considered to be of utility as an adaptable basis for decision-making about the *financial* impact and/or desirability of a particular rule or law.

Accordingly, adapting the mathematical model advanced most recently by Islam and Mak[414] (and before that, Conyers and Hills),[415] computing a CBA for a particular regulation or law involves the following steps:

1. Definition of the particular regulatory option or law;
2. Identification and measurement of costs and benefits from a;
3. Valuation of costs as well as benefits into some monetary units;
4. Discounting the costs and benefits of the law to net present values (NPVs);
5. Presenting the results of analysis in a format; and
6. Making recommendations.

The formula for the NPV is as follows:[416]

$$NPV = \frac{NB_0}{(1+r)^0} + \frac{NB_1}{(1+r)^1} + \dots\dots\dots + \frac{NB_n}{(1+r)^n} \qquad 5.1$$

Which, in turn, is then calculated as follows:[417]

$$NPV = \frac{B_0 - C_0}{(1+r)^0} + \frac{B_1 - C_1}{(1+r)^1} + \dots\dots\dots + \frac{B_n - C_n}{(1+r)^n} = \sum_{t=0}^{n} \frac{B^t - C_t}{(1+r)^t} \qquad 5.2$$

Where:
NPV = the net benefits of a law (benefit-cost);
r = discount rate;
n = number of years;
t = year t
B = benefits from the law; and
C = costs of implementation of the law.
Thus, the cost-benefit ratio may be calculated as follows:[418]

---

412 See, eg, N Lichfield et al., Evaluation in the Planning Process (1975).

413 Islam and Mak, above n 50.

414 Ibid.

415 See, eg, D Conyers and P Hills, An Introduction to Development Planning in the Third World (1984).

416 Islam and Mak, above n 50.

417 Ibid.

$$C - B\,ratio = \frac{\sum_{t=0}^{n} \frac{B_t}{(1+r)^t}}{\sum_{t=0}^{n} \frac{Ct}{(1+r)^t}} \qquad 5.3$$

Using the above two (2) mathematical formulae, the decision rules for determining the desirability of a law are the following: (i) If the NPV of a particular law is positive (>0), then adopt that particular law; (ii) if the C-B ratio is greater than 1 (>1), then adopt that particular law; but subject to: (iii) reject the particular law if conditions (i) and/or (ii) do not hold true.

As stated, the above criteria, of course, computes an outcome expressed only in financial terms. However, for a comprehensive cost-benefit evaluation of the desirability of a particular regulatory option or law, a social cost benefit analysis ('SCBA') might be of more utility.

There are five (5) major areas to be considered in undertaking an SCBA after having computed the financial CBA (above), as follows:[419]

1. Identification and inclusion of indirect, external and intangible costs of laws;
2. Benefits of a law;
3. Valuation and inclusion of social benefits and costs of laws;
4. Shadow pricing of benefits and costs in addition to market prices;
5. The use of a social discount rate as against the market interest rate; and
6. Incorporation of public policy objectives.

By following the principles and methods discussed above, a social welfare function of the following form can be developed; that is, a social and economic evaluation and value judgement framework incorporating costs and benefits of a particular regulatory option or law:

$$SWF_t = W_t\left(NB_t\{L_t\}\right) \qquad 5.4$$

Where:
W_t = welfare
t = time

[418] Ibid.
[419] Ibid.

$$NB_t = \frac{[(B_t\{L_t\}) - (C_t\{L_t\})]}{(1+r)^t} \qquad 5.5$$

B_t = benefits of the law
C_t = costs of the law
r = discount rate
L_t = the law

The result is a social or welfaristic function, which can be derived from the preferences of society and provides the guidelines for social and/or justice choices. According to Islam, it can contain information about social value judgement, scientific information and expert opinion relating to social benefits and costs, social time preference, extra-welfaristic judgements, efficient and inter-temporal valuation of inputs and outputs.[420]

Recognising the confines of this study, this social or welfaristic mathematical function or model is intended to provide a basic foundation only and should also be explored in conjunction with the administrative feasibility and social acceptability framework that is advanced next in Section 5.5.

5.5 Administrative feasibility and social acceptability

In addition to, and conjugated with, the above methods, it is also considered meritorious to search for an efficient or optimal regulatory framework for EFT regulation in Australia that is administratively feasible and socially acceptable.

For the institutional participants (ie, the regulators and the EFT product and service providers), having a well-defined acceptable level of compliance with any new regulatory framework ought to provide a simple and administratively efficient model for supervising and complying with it. Thus, it should be possible for regulators and EFT providers, alike, to identify an acceptable level of risk and have these reflected in the new legal rules in order that value issues could be resolved at the time that standards are set, allowing a bank's or regulatory agency's technical staff to monitor compliance mechanically, without having to make case-specific economic, political and ethical decisions. For the public users of EFT products and services, a clearly enunciated acceptable level of risk reflected in any new legal rules would provide a concise focus for evaluating how well its welfare is being protected, saving the public from having to understand the underlying details of the technical processes and legal provisions giving rise to and addressing those risks.[421]

---

420 S M N Islam, Applied Welfare Economics (2001); and S M N Islam, Optimal Growth Economics (2001).

421 See, eg, Fischhoff, Acceptable Risk, above 251.

It is submitted that the acceptability of risk to regulators, institutions and the public is a relative concept and involves consideration of different factors.[422] Considerations in these judgements may include: the certainty and severity of the risk; the reversibility of the economic effect; the knowledge or familiarity of the risk; whether the risk is voluntarily accepted or involuntarily imposed; whether individuals are compensated for their exposure to the risk; the advantages of the activity; and the risks and advantages for any alternatives.

To regulate a new technology like EFT in a logically defensible way, one must consider all its consequences. That is, as discussed earlier in this chapter, both risks and benefits. Moreover, to regulate in an ethically defensible way (as explored in more detail in the next section, Section 5.8), one must consider its impact on individuals, as well as on society as a whole.

The acceptability of a particular risk regulation depends on many factors. In their everyday lives, people do not accept or reject the inherent risks in one payment method or another in isolation. Rather, they make choices among several courses of actions, whose consequences may include different perceived or real degrees of risk. If people accept a particular course of action, like using EFTPOS rather than cash at a supermarket, despite knowing about risks of the EFT card and PIN being compromised in front of the many other shoppers at the checkout, then those risks might be termed acceptable in the context of the consequences of carrying around a large quantity of cash. Therefore, risks and utilities need not be acceptable in any absolute sense. Those same individuals might choose to use cash if it brought a compensating benefit. Or, they might choose a less risky course of action (eg, paying for goods by cheque), if that could be done at reasonable cost. A level of risk and utility that is acceptable for one activity might seem unacceptably high or acceptably low in other contexts or for other individuals. Indeed, it could be argued that the level of risk may be different for different individuals even in the same context. In ordinary discourse, it is so easy to lose the essential context of decisions that the term 'acceptable' might even best be avoided.

In this light, an efficient regulatory option governing EFT products and services should be acceptable to an individual if it creates an acceptable balance of personal risks and benefits. If a regulatory option is acceptable for each member of society, then it ought to be satisfactory to society as a whole. One might call the risks of the regulatory option 'societally acceptable' (considering its benefits), just as one might call its benefits 'societally acceptable' (considering its risks).[423] A focus on societally acceptable regulation is therefore meritorious. This is the definition being advocated in this book: a regulatory option is societally feasible and acceptable if its benefits outweigh its risks for every member of society.[424]

---

422 Ibid.

423 Ibid.

424 There is no reason why these 'benefits' should be restricted to economic consequences or even non-economic ones for which putative economic equivalents exist. People could in principle, be compensated by peace of mind, feelings of satisfaction, or reduction of other risks. See, eg, B Fischhoff and L Cox, Conceptual Framework for Benefit Assessment in Benefits Assessment: The State of the Art (1985).

The ethical core of this proposal may be seen most sharply by contrasting it with the utilitarianism of approaches that look at the total benefits accruing to a society from a regulation, when judging the acceptability of its risks. A rough method for doing so is to perform a cost-benefit analysis, summarising economic measures of a particular regulatory option's total benefits and total costs (including the risks that it imposes). A central ethical assumption of many such analyses is that one should look at the overall balance of consequences for society, while ignoring the balance actually experienced by individuals. Under this assumption, one would not care if a particular regulatory option made society as a whole better off, at the price of making some of its members miserable. Nor would one care if a few people received very large net benefits, while many others had small net losses; or, if many people had small net benefits, while imposing large net losses on a few.[425]

Of course, a regulatory option must also be assessed in light of the available legal or administrative mechanisms required to administer it; whether it is possible to integrate existing infrastructure, staff and systems to supervise and comply with new regulatory procedures. Indeed, factors contributing to the increase in non-compliance with the existing *EFT Code* and a corresponding increase in the incidence of unauthorised EFT transactions are multiple as well as inter-related. Thus, any strategy aimed at addressing these corollary problems needs to be holistic and include a wide range of policy, legal, institutional and technical options in order to:

- Simplify and rationalise the policy and legal framework;
- Build capacity for easier compliance and enforcement; and
- Improve data and stakeholder knowledge about the EFT system and its regulation in general.

It follows, then, that a strategic approach should carefully balance measures to discourage non-compliance, such as stricter controls and penalties, with activities that encourage positive, confident behaviour by consumers and the public at large, such as incentives and simplified regulations. Measures aimed at increasing control alone are seldom successful where the economic attractiveness of non-compliance or illegal behaviour remains. In these cases, non-complying or illegal operators will always find a way to circumvent controls.

In consequence, there is a pressing need to develop a comprehensive and coherent strategy to tackle the problems in consultation with all stakeholders. Any strategy to tackle non-compliance and illegality should be based on an open, highly inclusive, multi-stakeholder process, based on effective participation of all interested parties. Although this may slow down the process, there is no doubt that a participatory approach is the best, if not the only way to produce a strategy capable of delivering long-term improvements in compliance, enforcement and public confidence and acceptance. Refer to Figure 5.2 below.

---

[425] Fischhoff, Acceptable Risk, above n 251.

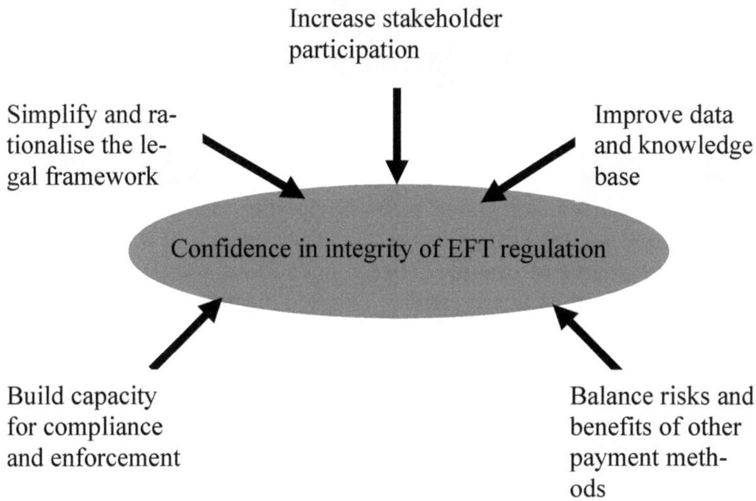

Figure 5.2 Elements of a strategy to promote administrative feasibility and social acceptance of EFT regulation

Accordingly, an analytical procedure is advanced in this study to attempt to meet these constraints in determining the acceptability of EFT regulation: an efficient or optimal regulatory model that is consistent with institutional capacity and infrastructure and also compatible with public utility and values. Embedded in an acceptable EFT regulatory framework, the suggested procedure would offer some chance of making the regulation of EFT in Australia more predictable and satisfying.

In a study such as this, it is considered near to impossible to work out all the details; the proposed EFT regulatory framework should be judged at the most basic level by whether the concept makes sense and whether its implementation seems workable. It should be appraised in absolute terms: How well could it ever work? What degree of closure would it provide? It should also be considered relatively (recognising the opportunities competing approaches have had to be proven or discredited): How does it compare to what we have?

Therefore, the proposed EFT regulatory framework advanced in this book will attempt to implement the non-utilitarian principle that a regulation must provide acceptable consequences for everyone affected by it. Pursuing it as far as possible should produce a better regulatory process than current approaches; ones focused on limited legal or economic principles (or no clearly explicit principles at all).

It follows then that if the proposed EFT regulatory framework is attractive, then one might undertake the task of working out its details. That would involve some daunting challenges; for example, estimating with some certainty the magnitude of the risks addressed by the regulation, on the one hand, and eliciting the public's willingness to trade off diverse costs and benefits, on the other.

It is submitted that such obstacles are a sign of strength rather than weakness. They are inherent in analytically defining institutionally and publicly acceptable risk regulation and revealed most clearly by an approach that attempts to address them head on.

Perhaps one final proviso is that the proposed EFT regulatory framework may not withstand all challenges; it may still be somewhat of an incomplete path to optimal regulatory reform, even if all its methodological problems were solved by employing this expanded, integrated multi-disciplinary approach. Therefore, an analytical principle for evaluating the acceptability of any new EFT regulation may still be a new source of struggle between institutions and the public, possibly involving disputes about its interpretation, lobbying, hearings, demonstrations and negotiations. An analytical approach to acceptability can only hope to forestall some conflicts, by identifying the most legal, economic and socially unacceptable solutions, and focus others, by concentrating attention on critical unresolved issues. For the public quite legitimately care as much about how decisions are made as what decisions are made.

5.6 Ethical considerations

Another discipline, which also provides some utility in examining appropriate regulation for the EFT system, is that of ethics in financial markets and services.[426] Financial markets and services may be judged by government, consumers and society at large against considerations of ethics: that embraces notions of fairness, equity, honesty and good faith. These considerations may not necessarily accord with the sort of economic efficiency principles discussed in Section 5.1. Ethics in finance is principally concerned with duty. That is, for the purposes of this book, the mutual duty between the EFT card-issuing institution and the EFT consumer. Financial ethical considerations thus ought to include, at a minimum, principles for the mutual obligations, fairness in financial transactions and exchanges, fiduciary duties and the welfare of society as a whole.[427]

Many of these ethical issues could be said to have been addressed, in part at least, by law and industry regulation in Australia. Financial laws range from long established common law banker-customer principles and contract law to federal statutory regulations administered by ASIC and the ACCC to enforce them. Then there are industry codes of conduct such as the *EFT Code* and Code of Banking Practice where industry agrees to set its own rules and enforce them when violations occur. The role of ethics, then, in such a highly regulated, disparate environment may be problematical or at the very least obscured or even overlooked altogether. It could be said that merely obeying or conforming to the relevant rules is sufficient to satisfy ethical obligations (eg, 'if it's legal, then it's morally

426 See, generally, H Shefrin and M Statman, 'Ethics, Fairness and Efficiency in Financial Markets' (1993) Financial Analysts Journal 21.

427 See, eg, Boatright, above n 252.

okay').[428] However, it could equally be contended that ethical principles already are at the core of much of the financial regulation that exists.

Thus, it is perhaps possible to view the EFT rules governing fraud, unauthorised transactions and liability for system failure and transaction errors as an attempt, in part at least, to enforce ethical standards as much as economic efficiency. Regulatory reform and issues not yet settled by law or self-regulation ought to be debated, in part, as matters of ethics. It follows, then, that EFT regulation, whether it be by government or industry, might be viewed as a rather ineffective and uncertain guide and so a commitment to high ethical standards, and not merely legal compliance, is essential.[429]

Several recent financial scandals and corporate collapses in both Australia and the USA not only undermine the public's confidence in ethics in financial markets and institutions,[430] but fuel a popular image of the financial world as one of greed.[431] In Australia, the HIH Insurance collapse and the alleged 'kickbacks' paid by the Australian Wheat Board to the Saddam Hussein regime for wheat contracts in Iraq are examples. Indeed, a 1996 USA poll revealed that a majority of respondents agreed with the claim that most people on Wall Street 'would be willing to break the law if they believed they could make a lot of money and get away with it'.[432]

These illustrations of egregious wrongdoing command our attention, but possibly give a misleading picture of the level of ethics in finance. People in finance engage in a vast array of activities involving the handling of financial assets of different parties.[433] Boatright contends that not only does the welfare of everyone depend on the care and use of these financial assets, but millions of transactions take place each day with a high level of integrity and ethical behaviour. However, there are ample opportunities in finance for some people to gain at the expense of others.[434]

Boatright also usefully advances the proposition that the ethics of an industry, an occupation or a profession is best understood not by examining the worst conduct of its members, but by attending to the conduct that is commonly expected and generally found.[435] It follows, then, that to derive some insight into ethical behaviour there should be just as much, if not more, focus on the number of authorised, undisputed EFT transactions than on the number of disputed, unauthorised EFT transactions. If there were 2,529,550,988 EFT transactions in Australia in the year to 31 March 2004 and there were 161,389 consumer complaints regarding

428 Ibid; and see, eg, Shefrin and Statman, above n 426.

429 Boatright, above n 252, viii.

430 See, eg, J L Badaracco and A P Webb, 'Business Ethics: A View from the Trenches' (1995) 37 California Management Review 8.

431 See, eg, Shefrin and Statman, above n 426, 21; and R E Frederick and W M Hoffman, 'The Individual Investor in Securities Markets: An Ethical Analysis' (1990) Journal of Business Ethics 579.

432 Boatright, above n 252, 2-3.

433 Shefrin and Statman, above n 426, 21.

434 Boatright, above n 252, 4.

435 Ibid 3-4.

EFT system malfunctions, unauthorised EFT transactions and other EFT errors, then logically there were 2,529,389,599 undisputed, authorised EFT transactions.[436] That is, if there was 63 disputed EFT transactions per million, then it follows that there were 999,937 undisputed EFT transactions per million. This is an overwhelming affirmation that the vast majority of financial transactions were carried out with integrity by both financial institution and consumer in accordance with the parties' expectations, instructions and agreed procedures.[437]

Turning, then, to the need for ethics in the EFT system, it could be said that financial transactions typically take place in both regulated and unregulated markets and presuppose certain moral rules and expectations of moral behaviour. The most basic of these is a prohibition against fraud and manipulation, but, more generally, the rules and expectations for financial markets are concerned with equity and fairness, which is often expressed, according to Boatright, as a 'level playing field'.[438] That is, the playing field can become 'tilted' by many factors, including unequal information, bargaining power, asymmetric regulation and resources between different financial products and services. In the EFT system, before anything else, the parties engage in a financial contract according to the terms and conditions of EFT use, thereby entering into short, medium or long term relations. These contractual relations typically involve the assumption of fiduciary trust duties or obligations as between the financial institution and consumer. The retail merchant in an EFTPOS transaction, for example, is another intermediary party to the contract. EFT transactions may be subject to unethical conduct because of opportunistic behaviour by fiduciaries, agents or customers. Furthermore, EFT transactions may have third-party effects such as the social impact of financial activity and so calls into question the responsibilities of financial decision makers to balance the competing ethical and moral interests of various groups.[439]

Although it is suggested that ethics represents, or ought to represent, a core consideration in formulating legal rules, it still begs the questions: can ethics be properly compelled and enforced by legal rules? Is legislating for ethical behaviour of itself enough and is it the appropriate response? To articulate these conundrums, Boatright usefully refers to a former USA Securities Exchange Commis-

---

[436] Australian Securities and Investments Commission, Report of Compliance with the EFT Code of Conduct, 2003/2004 (2005) 21-4.

[437] Note: However, it must be recognised that many Australian EFT consumers may not complain, and some because they do not know they can or because they cannot as a result of a lack of access, adequate information or resources. Also, it should be acknowledged that there must be some degree of self-regulation within the banking industry in the USA as well, or otherwise it would be reasonable to conclude that banking regulation in the USA would be markedly different in terms of the manner and extent in which it is regulated given what appears to be a regime, at face-value and through litigated cases at least, that is particularly onerous on the banks and quite consumer–friendly.

[438] Boatright, above n 252, 5.

[439] Ibid.

sion chairman who observed: 'It is not an adequate ethical standard to aspire to get through the day without being indicted'.[440]

Yet, perhaps formal legal rules may be too crude an instrument to regulate ethical behaviour, because, as mentioned, ethics comprises several guiding principles rather than being reduced to precise substantive rules.[441] Accordingly, from a purely 'teleological' viewpoint, perhaps softer, guiding rules and standards, such as those possible under a self-regulating industry code of conduct, are preferable after all if it can rise above hard legal rules and embrace virtuous notions like fairness, equity, honesty and good faith in all financial dealings, even if ethical principles may then be broken without legal consequences. Indeed, Boatright advances the belief that because of the variety of financial relationships and activities, parties need to obey the 'spirit' as well as the 'letter' of the rules as it would be 'perverse to encourage people in finance to do anything that they want until the law tells them otherwise'.[442] Consider, again, the *EFT Code* and the EFT terms and conditions of use drafted by institutions (both discussed in detail in Chapter 4), which together seek to specify the conduct required of each party and the remedies for non-compliance. However, as was highlighted in Chapter 4, contractual relations in the EFT system are, in many areas, multi-layered, vague, ambiguous, undefined, incomplete or otherwise problematic to interpret. The result, then, is that under current arrangements, there is uncertainty and disagreement about what constitutes ethical (as well as legal) conduct in the EFT system in Australia.

Ultimately, though, if the prime objective of EFT regulation is to achieve economic efficiency (as was argued in Section 5.1), then it ought to follow that financial markets may only be truly 'efficient' when its participants have confidence in the fairness and equity of those markets.[443] Perhaps, then, efficiency and ethics are not necessarily mutually exclusive objectives in pursuing an improved EFT regulatory regime. Fairness and equity might even have an 'economic value' if they can be seen as an ingredient of efficiency by increasing confident participation in the EFT system and promoting social welfare through striving for maximum output with minimum input and generating economies of scale.[444]

---

[440] Ibid 7.

[441] See, eg, C D Stone, Where the Law Ends: The Social Control of Corporate Behaviour (1975).

[442] Boatright, above n 252, 8.

[443] Ibid 31.

[444] Note: However, it should be acknowledged that this preferred conclusion could possibly be argued in the opposite depending on whether a teleological approach or a utilitarian approach to notions of 'ethics' and 'justice' is adopted. That is, there is indeed an underlying conflict or tension between economics and utilitarian ethics and ethical systems (eg, a Kantian approach) where one permits people to be used as a means to an end (greatest good for the greatest number/efficiency) and the other categorically forbids ever using a person as a means to an end.

5.7 Conclusion

The quest for better loss allocation rules in constructing an efficient or optimal regulatory framework is enhanced by employing criteria from other disciplines, which until now have not formed part of the EFT regulatory debate.

This chapter adapted an economic efficiency model for loss allocation rules in Section 5.1 and applied it to the current regulatory arrangements in both Australia and the USA and highlighted several shortcomings. However, its ultimate utility will be in informing the specific recommendations in Chapter 6 for an improved regulatory framework. The progressive cost-benefit analysis undertaken in Sections 5.2, 5.3 and 5.4 also yielded some unique findings: from an extrapolation of actual EFT survey evidence from the USA for Australian conditions through to constructing a framework for a systematic evaluation of EFT regulation costs and benefits. In Sections 5.5 and 5.6, other useful, hitherto unexplored criteria were discussed: an application of ethical principles and considerations to financial regulation, together with an assessment and strategy to take account of the administrative feasibility and social acceptability of any new regulatory arrangements.

Chapter 6. An Efficient or Optimal Regulatory Framework

Following the comparative law, economic, ethical, administrative, social and other criteria analysed in Chapters 4 and 5, the findings below in Section 6.1 are made from this research book to provide the theoretical foundation or framework to design and formulate an improved EFT regulatory regime in Australia.

These findings will then, in turn, inform the specific recommendations advanced in Section 6.2 for a more efficacious regime of regulation of the EFT system in Australia. The findings and recommendations for law reform are structured in point form as follows:

6.1 Findings

From the research and analysis undertaken for this book, the principal findings are as follows.

1. EFT debit as a payment method continues to expand rapidly by comparison with credit cards and traditional paper-based forms of payment.
2. Previous literature on EFT regulation is limited and fragmented. Research and commentary on EFT regulation to date has largely been domestic-focused and prepared in isolation by the respective institutional stakeholders involved. Until now, there has only been some limited legal analysis, but this is dated and does not take account of the revised regulatory arrangements in the form of the updated *EFT Code*, nor does it reflect the adverse trend in compliance and illegality. In addition, no multi-disciplinary analysis has yet been undertaken in the field employing such criteria as comparative law, conflict of laws, economics of law, regulation theory, ethical considerations, administrative feasibility and social acceptability.
3. Compliance with the *EFT Code* by financial institutions continues to deteriorate as ASIC again highlights its 'concerns' in the latest 2005 compliance report.[445]

[445] Australian Securities and Investments Commission, Report of Compliance with the EFT Code of Conduct, 2003/2004 (2005) 21-4.

4. The incidence of reported unauthorised EFT transactions has risen markedly in recent years from 14 per million transactions in 1995 to 41 per million in 2002,[446] and, anecdotally at least, is now 63 per million in the latest reporting year to 31 March 2004.[447]
5. It is conceivable that the self-regulating *EFT Code* is, in fact, underpinned by the statutory force of the revised *ASIC Act* of 2001 which now governs financial products and services. However, the *EFT Code* does not indicate how its provisions relate to legislation. Therefore, there is an inherent danger that consumers may be misled into believing that the terms of the code are simply advisory and remain unaware or confused about their legal rights. As a general rule, codes of practice such as the *EFT Code* do not explicitly relate their provisions to legislative provisions.
6. The 'critical comparative law' methodology adopted in this book reflects the belief that for this problem only similar yet divergent EFT regulation systems can benefit from each others' experience. That is, having identified a common core problem shared by Australia and the USA, the preferred comparative law approach is something of a hybrid one: to not only identify the differences in their regulatory responses, but to observe the possibilities for some convergence. It is submitted that convergence and divergence are not necessarily mutually exclusive concepts. Thus, common elements are sought ('integrative comparative law') just as much as differences stressed ('contrastive comparative law'). Further, it becomes apparent that because a legal rule operates well in one legal system does not necessarily mean that it will operate equally well in another. Also of particular interest is the inherent tension between formal and informal regulatory approaches to a common core problem.
7. Consumers at present do not benefit from adequate disclosure of the terms and conditions of use before obtaining EFT products and/or services. In practice, not all financial institutions have copies of their terms and conditions of use available for perusal prior to signing an EFT account application form ahead of obtaining EFT access. Not only are there variations between financial institutions on the matter of when terms and conditions of use are made available (if at all), financial institutions also have a varied approach to when the consumer is deemed to have accepted the terms and conditions of use, which would seem to be unacceptable and challenges the integrity of the EFT system in Australia.
8. Under clause 2 of the *EFT Code*, financial institutions must warrant that their terms and conditions of use comply or reflect its requirements. Although the *EFT Code* does not of itself have the force of statute law, as advanced earlier in Chapter 2, this warranty may give rise to civil and criminal liability under the *ASIC Act*, exposing a financial institution to a substantial fine if its terms and conditions do not comply with the *EFT Code's* requirements.

---

[446] Australian Securities and Investments Commission, Compliance with the Payments System Codes of Practice and the EFT Code of Conduct, 2001/2002 (2003) 50-60.

[447] Australian Securities and Investments Commission, Report of Compliance with the EFT Code of Conduct, 2003/2004 (2005) 21-5.

9. The *Ognibene v Citibank* (1981) case from the USA illustrates that handing over an EFT card is not like giving a third party a pre-signed, blank cheque. Giving a fraudulent party a pre-signed, blank cheque would be a breach of customer's duty to take reasonable care given that the cheque carries the customer's mandate to the bank to debit his/her account.
10. Compared to paper-based transactions, EFT places consumers at a relative disadvantage in that there is often an 'evidentiary stalemate' following a disputed EFT transaction. For example, a consumer demonstrating to a bank that he or she has not given the bank a mandate to debit his or her account following successful unauthorised access by a third person who had not been voluntarily disclosed with the PIN. Whereas in the case of a cheque, it is arguable that it is for the bank to prove that a signature was forged; the written signature is at least available as evidence and its characteristics can then be examined in detail.
11. The issuance and delivery method of EFT cards and PINs is not uniform across financial institutions in either Australia or the USA. Indeed, the limited survey sample (discussed in Section 4.3 of Chapter 4) of the procedures surrounding the issue of EFT cards and PINs also revealed a surprising variety of procedural methods and processes across those financial institutions.
12. The *EFT Code* does not compel financial institutions to obtain written acknowledgments, identification or confirmation of receipt for either or both the EFT card or PIN. By way of comparison, and a major shortcoming of the *US EFT Act*, is that it does not require *any* detailed procedures be followed in delivering EFT cards or PINs.
13. Given the evidential value to a consumer, neither the *EFT Code* nor the *US EFT Act* provisions expressly require that transaction receipts issued at EFT terminals include a receipt number. Making this a specific requirement would enhance the validity of the receipt, and thus the position of the consumer in a dispute, as the receipt number could be checked against the transaction number on a periodic statement and would also be of utility to the financial institution by facilitating a reconciliation of transaction numbers with those on the financial institution's daily EFT transaction reports and logs.
14. The true evidential effect at law of transaction receipts remains unclear and whether it is admissible in evidence as unequivocal proof of an EFT transaction needs to be clarified.
15. The *US EFT Act* requires that consumers inspect and verify transaction receipts and all entries on the periodic account statement. The *EFT Code*, however, does not go so far. Clause 4.4 merely provides that financial institutions may only *suggest* to consumers that all entries on statements be checked, but with no reference to EFT terminal transaction receipts. Therefore, there is no obligation on the consumer to inspect and authenticate the entries on the periodic account statement.
16. For unauthorised EFT transactions, in the USA, the underlying principle is that a consumer is only liable for authorised EFT transactions as well as for a limited amount of any unauthorised EFT transactions, up to the time of notification to the financial institution.

17. The *EFT Code* also, in small part, adopts a tiered approach in determining liability, but in a comparatively cumbersome, legalistic and protracted form. Such a legalistic and unwieldy approach does not necessarily guarantee certainty and clarity.
18. Markedly different definitions of an 'unauthorised EFT transaction' in the *EFT Code* (vague and imprecise) vis-à-vis the *US EFT Act* (comprehensive).
19. In determining liability for unauthorised EFT transactions, the consumer is excluded from liability under clauses 5.2, 5.3 and 5.4 of the *EFT Code where it is clear* that the user has not contributed to such losses. However, the *EFT Code* is silent on who has the burden of establishing this as between the financial institution and consumer and nor does it assist by providing any guidance, process or criteria for how such a conclusion can be drawn for the information of the consumer.
20. The multi-layered threshold tests required under clauses 5.5 and 5.6 of the *EFT Code* are intrinsically difficult to adjudicate at law and as the body left to do so in most instances, the ABIO, regularly comments, they result in complex, protracted and difficult practical issues in interpreting these substantive cross-provisions of the *EFT Code.*
21. There is no definition or guidance provided in the *EFT Code* for the pivotal threshold test for the financial institution that it must '*prove on the balance of probability*' that a consumer has contributed to losses resulting from an unauthorised EFT transaction.
22. Curiously, though, after overlooking to provide any definition or guidance for the fundamental 'balance of probability' threshold test, the *EFT Code* does attempt to define two lesser, ancillary terms (the 'dominant contributing cause' and 'extreme carelessness') in the 'End notes' annexed to the *EFT Code.* However, even so, it should be noted that clause 20.3 states that such explanatory notes *do not* form part of the *EFT Code.*
23. No definition is provided in clause 5.5(b) of the *EFT Code* for what constitutes 'an unreasonable delay in notification' by the consumer. Compounding this problem is that this clause is particularly unwieldy, legalistic and also adopts the aforementioned, undefined threshold test of 'proof on the balance of probability'.
24. Where an alleged unauthorised EFT transaction is initiated with an EFT card and using the *correct PIN at first attempt*, clause 5.5 of the *EFT Code* expressly states that this of itself is 'significant', but it does not go far enough in stating whether or not mere proof by the financial institution from its EFT computer system log records ('while significant') is sufficient 'proof on the balance of probability' that the EFT transaction was authorised by the consumer. Therefore, it is arguable that rather than assisting interpretation, this guidance serves only to add another layer of complexity and ambiguity to the *EFT Code's* requirements.
25. Where it is *unclear* as to whether the consumer has or has not contributed to losses, clause 5.5(c) sets out yet another formula for calculating liability with a USA-styled monetary tier. Where it is unclear, the consumer is liable for the lesser of A$150, the balance of the account or the amount of the actual losses.

It is suggested that this added provision is intended to be a kind of 'fall back' provision with 'unclear' presumably being when it is neither (i) clear that the consumer has not contributed to such losses where the consumer is expressly excluded from any liability (clause 5.4); or (ii) clear on the balance of probability that the consumer has in fact contributed to such losses by compromising the security of the EFT card and/or PIN under one or more of the instances described in clauses 5.5(a), (b) and 5.6. Thus, it is perhaps something of a 'life line' to the ABIO where the evidence regarding contribution is not decisive or hopelessly deadlocked after having been forced to negotiate its way through all the difficult multi-layered threshold tests first.

26. Cases used to illustrate the application of the *EFT Code* and *US EFT Act* yield a range of uncertain outcomes. In interpreting the *EFT Code*, the ABIO cases could be decided in at least 4 possible ways: (i) clear the consumer has contributed, (ii) clear the consumer has not contributed, (iii) unclear whether the consumer has contributed and (iv) shared liability between the consumer and financial institution in other instances.
27. Despite the revised *EFT Code* seeking to place the burden of proof squarely on the financial institution in the event of a disputed, unauthorised EFT transaction, in practice the burden effectively remains at the foot of the consumer to disprove the '*significant*' evidential weight assigned under the *EFT Code* of the 'correct PIN being used at first attempt'. The result is unsatisfactory. In some cases, the ABIO has determined that the consumer had not performed the ATM transaction, nor authorised it, and, that the financial institution could not establish that the consumer contributed to the losses on the balance of probability, yet the consumer was still not 'cleared' of culpability (clause 5.4) and was therefore required to contribute A$150 under the 'unclear' provision at clause 5.5(c).
28. The central theme across the litigated cases from the USA is the sanctity of the tiered no-fault regime and the paramountcy of timely notification by the consumer above and beyond all else, including consumer negligence with the EFT card and/or PIN. As mentioned, the reverse is true of the *EFT Code*.
29. The ABIO, as well as at least one of the 6 major banks surveyed, take a much broader approach than the EFT Code's narrow *de minimis* standard examples of what does not constitute a reasonable disguise of the PIN (ie, derivatives of a consumer's birth date and name).
30. Clause 6 of the *EFT Code* adopts a similar stance to the *US EFT Act* in prescribing that institutions be responsible for losses caused by 'failure' in EFT machinery or computer software. However, what constitutes 'failure' is not defined under the *EFT Code*. Does it, for example, include under-payments at an ATM? Or over-payments to retail merchants through EFTPOS? Failures resulting in wrong debits or credits? Failures resulting in authorised transfers not being made? And inadequate security permitting unauthorised access to an EFT system?
31. Also, the *EFT Code* does not explicitly apportion responsibility for losses arising from 'off-line' EFT transactions to financial institutions (other than within the 'equipment failure' provision).

32. In addition to the *EFT Code*, a financial institution may, in fact, be obliged to exercise due care and skill in managing its electronic terminals and equipment under s 12ED of the *ASIC Act*, which implies various conditions and warranties into a transaction including the 'supply of financial services'.
33. Clause 6.2 of the *EFT Code* seems to suggest that financial institutions may be liable for indirect or consequential losses as well; perhaps for amounts greatly in excess of the amount of the failed EFT transaction. Whether such a failure would mean an institution would be held liable if a consumer, by virtue of the failure, was unable to meet regular personal or even commercial commitments is not certain, but exemplifies the significance of such a blanketing clause.
34. Consumers are concerned by the absence of formal 'countermand' (stop payment) or reversal rights under EFT. With a cheque, a customer can follow the bank's appropriate steps and issue a stop payment instruction to the bank. The bank is then under a duty to obey the countermand. This duty is the converse of a banker's duty to obey a customer's mandate in paying a cheque.
35. The dispute resolution procedures in the *EFT Code* and *US EFT Act* appear similar, but work quite differently in practice. Importantly, unlike the *US EFT Act's* specific tiered notification requirements, there is no time limit under the *EFT Code* within which consumers must report their complaints.
36. Moreover, unlike the *US EFT Act*, the *EFT Code* does not go so far as requiring that the consumer's account be provisionally re-credited with the amount in dispute should the dispute not be resolved after just 10 days. Furthermore, the *US EFT Act* (at §1693f(e)) has the remarkable stipulation that if the consumer's account is not provisionally re-credited within the 10-day period, or the financial institution did not make a good faith investigation of the alleged error, then the consumer shall be entitled to *treble* damages.
37. The research undertaken for this book revealed that there is no specific analytic criteria for efficient loss allocation for unauthorised EFT transactions in Australia from which specific regulatory rules (statutory or otherwise) may be derived and appraised. Because EFT regulation concerns not only technical legal considerations, but monetary considerations as well, an economic analysis intuitively could be useful.
38. Various criteria for evaluating laws and regulations have been proposed in the economics literature reviewed for this book. For the purposes of this book, it is suggested that the economic framework presented by both Posner[448] and Cooter and Rubin[449] is of the most utility in the search for a more efficacious EFT regulatory regime. In particular, Cooter and Rubin usefully distilled three (3) principles for an economic efficiency approach to liability and loss allocation rules: loss reduction, loss spreading and loss imposition.
39. Despite the revised *EFT Code's* intention to adopt a no-fault regime along the lines of the *US EFT Act* and Principle 3, it is submitted that the revised *EFT Code* still remains something of a 'hybrid' allocation of losses between the

448 See, eg, Posner, above n 218.
449 Cooter and Rubin, above n 52, 63.

first 2 Principles: loss reduction, and, to a lesser degree, loss spreading principles. Thus, it essentially retains a fault-based set of liability rules providing incentive for efficient precaution by both parties at once. Such intermediate liability assignments might have the potential to more effectively induce the optimal amount of avoidance from all parties concerned, however, the problem with this is that, whilst an ideal rule might seek to get each party to contribute its share of avoidance, such a rule requires a great deal of information regarding relative costs of avoidance among the parties. That is, rather than identifying just the lowest-cost avoider, one has to rank each party according to comparative advantage in avoidance and determine relative liabilities consistent with the ranking. Another problem is that assigning liabilities to more than one party involves a more complex rule and thereby creates more potential for costly and protracted evidential disputes and litigation.

40. A further observation on the economic efficiency approach is that any attempt to achieve optimal efficiency in the EFT payment system ought to also have regard for the approaches to regulating other payment system instruments; in particular, the divergent loss allocation rules between consumer EFT products, credit cards and paper-based payment instruments such as cheques should be noted. A review of the various payment system regulations in Australia and the USA reveals an array of disparate rules and standards of loss allocation, all of which are used in part by consumers as cash or cash equivalents. Therefore, any concerted attempt to achieve optimal efficiency in one instrument of the payments system would seem unrealistic if regulators continue to treat loss allocation rules for cheques and payment cards differently. Indeed, the similarity of function between all 3 payment devices (cheques, credit cards and EFT debit cards) is increasing as EFT debit cards are increasingly usable to pay for goods at the point of sale (EFTPOS). As the functions of credit cards and EFT debit cards converge (where, like EFT debit cards, credit cards are used primarily for convenience rather than revolving credit), it is submitted that arguments for treating EFT debit consumers like users of cash rather than like credit consumers become weaker.

41. In a market economy, society relies primarily on the forces of competition to induce market participants to behave in an economically efficient manner. This implies that firms efficiently produce the goods and services that consumer's desire and that prices reflect the costs of the resources employed in the production process. Yet, even when most of the important resource allocation decisions in an economy are made by the private sector, government intervention may be appropriate in some areas. Hence, government intervention may be warranted when the unfettered operations of the private sector fail to achieve an economically efficient outcome, that is, in the presence of so-called 'market failure'. In an operating market such as that for EFT products and services, private agreements reached between parties may produce economically efficient results without the need for legal intervention. Intervention, therefore, becomes necessary when the market fails to produce these efficient results on its own. As discussed in Section 5.1 above, rules that are designed to achieve economic efficiency in payments law should therefore en-

force agreements between private parties even when no market failure has occurred. When market failure exists, legal rules may improve upon private agreements if they are designed with the goal of minimising costs in mind.

42. Any asymmetric regulatory treatment of competing alternatives may confer competitive advantages (or disadvantages) on certain products. Government regulatory policies may play an important role in determining how these products evolve and the extent to which they achieve market acceptance. In deciding whether and, if so, how to regulate EFT services, policymakers must carefully assess the potential effect of their decisions on the evolution of the payment system. For choices made today may significantly influence the payment options available to market participants in the future. Ultimately, though, the willingness of consumers to accept a new product or technology depends on the perceived benefits that the new EFT product or technology offers and the costs associated with it. Market participants may evaluate these benefits and costs in relation to those of competing payment system alternatives (ie, cheques or credit cards). Regulation can affect the acceptance of a new technology or product by influencing the benefits or costs associated with its use or by requiring the provision of information that enhances the ability of market participants to understand these benefits and costs.
43. The cost of regulation consists of opportunity and operating costs that arise from activities or changes in activities that are required by government. Opportunity costs occur when a regulation causes the producer to forgo profitable activities. They generally result from prohibitions of certain activities. There are two types of operating costs: start-up and ongoing. Start-up costs are the one-time costs of changing activities to conform to the requirements of a regulation. Ongoing costs are the recurring costs of performing the activities required by a regulation.
44. Experience with the *US EFT Act* provides a logical starting point for assessing the possible costs of applying some degree of legislative consumer protection regulations to EFT in Australia. Extrapolating 1981 survey evidence and some limited quantitative data gathered in the USA post-implementation of the *US EFT Act* for Australian conditions in 2005 must be heavily qualified, but nevertheless may have some indicative merit. Given 2.53 billion EFT transactions occurred in Australia in the year to 31 March 2004, based on the extrapolated cost figures of AUD$0.28 and AUD$0.30 respectively, this implies an estimated start-up costs figure of AUD$708 million and an estimated ongoing incremental costs figure of AUD$758 million per year.
45. In the absence of any particular cost-benefit analysis criteria as applied to EFT regulation, proffering a framework for the systematic evaluation of the relative costs and benefits of different EFT regulation initiatives should serve to provide a more informed basis for decisions on impacts and resource allocation among the different policy options advanced in this book. Potential evaluators may include each of those regulators with responsibility for the various aspects of the EFT system, as well as those with access to current, meaningful industry-wide banking industry and/or EFT cost-benefit data. Those identified may include: the ABIO, the RBA, ASIC, the ACCC, con-

sumer advocate groups, the Australian Bankers' Association, or, at the ultimate level, the Australian federal government Department of Treasury. Indeed, potential evaluators may use this framework as a reference document for devising a methodology for analysing EFT regulation costs and benefits. The framework is intended to be something of a step-by-step guide to undertaking both a cost-benefit and cost-effectiveness analysis, from identifying some of the types of data to collect through to reporting the results of the analysis. It should also be stated that this framework is designed to facilitate an evaluation of how cost-effective an intervention has been, as much as for a forward-looking economic appraisal.

46. An efficient or optimal regulatory framework for EFT regulation in Australia should also be administratively feasible and socially acceptable. For the institutional participants (ie, the regulators, the EFT product and service providers and industry bodies), having a well-defined acceptable level of compliance with any new regulatory framework ought to provide a simple and administratively efficient model for supervising and complying with it. For the public users of EFT products and services, a clearly enunciated acceptable level of risk reflected in any new legal rules would provide a concise focus for evaluating how well its welfare is being protected, saving the public from having to understand the underlying details of the technical processes and legal provisions giving rise to and addressing those risks.
47. Salient principles from the discipline of financial ethics should form part of an improved EFT regulatory framework. Formal legal rules may be too crude an instrument to regulate ethical behaviour, because ethics comprises several guiding principles rather than being reduced to precise substantive rules. Accordingly, from an ethical viewpoint, perhaps softer, guiding rules and standards, such as those possible under a self-regulating industry code of conduct, are preferable if it can rise above hard legal rules and embrace virtuous notions like fairness, equity, honesty and good faith in all financial dealings.
48. If the prime objective of EFT regulation is to achieve economic efficiency, then it ought to follow that financial markets may only be truly 'efficient' when its participants have confidence in the fairness and equity of those markets. Perhaps, then, efficiency and ethics are not necessarily mutually exclusive objectives in pursuing an improved EFT regulatory regime. Fairness and equity might even have an 'economic value' if they can be seen as an ingredient of efficiency by increasing confident participation in the EFT system, promoting social welfare and generating economies of scale.

These findings will generally inform the specific recommendations advanced next in Section 6.2 in constructing an efficient framework for the regulation of EFT in Australia.

6.2 Specific recommendations

Acknowledging the limitations and fragmented approaches to discussing and evaluating EFT regulation in the previous literature, the expanded, integrated multi-disciplinary criteria and analysis developed in this professional business doctoral dissertation enables a rather more comprehensive set of recommendations to be advanced for an improved regulatory framework for EFT in Australia.

It is submitted that such recommendations are particularly timely and relevant ahead of the overdue review of the revised Australian *EFT Code* by ASIC, which is expected to be undertaken across 2006-2007.[450]

i. In the context of assessing self-regulation generally, it is suggested that sector-by-sector self-regulation, such as for the *EFT Code's* self-regulatory industry standards, should form the basis of 'default rules' only. This is perhaps the course of most utility with recourse to the force of 'mandatory rules' to remedy conduct that would be illegal or actionable

ii. Because it is argued in this book that the *EFT Code* is, in fact, underpinned by the statutory force of the revised *ASIC Act 2001* (Cth), the relationship between the provisions of the self-regulating *EFT Code* and formal legislation should be clarified by explicit reference to the *ASIC Act 2001* (Cth) in clause 2 of the *EFT Code*, which presently only requires that EFT financial institutions must warrant that their terms and conditions of use comply with or reflect the requirements of the *EFT Code*;

iii. ASIC should *mandate* that all EFT product and service providers subscribe to the *EFT Code* and not merely *encourage* it as at present;

iv. The *EFT Code* should include a far more comprehensive definition of terms section in addition to its interpretation section in clause 1.5. Section 1693a of the *US EFT Act* provides a useful benchmark for a comprehensive definition of terms;

v. In view of the wide variance in EFT financial institution practices, EFT financial institutions should conform to a uniform EFT card and PIN issuance and delivery procedure. This should also include a requirement that EFT financial institutions be compelled to obtain written acknowledgements, verify consumer identification and confirmation of receipt for both the EFT card and PIN. At the least, a consumer ought to be given the choice of the delivery method (eg, between registered post or collection at a branch of the financial institution) and then the method and its attendant risks are clearly agreed and assigned as between the financial institution and consumer;

vi. Prospective consumers ought to be given adequate disclosure of the terms and conditions of use *prior* to obtaining EFT products and/or services. This

[450] This was advised by a representative from the Australian Securities and Investments Commission, 26 April 2006. The EFT Code is overdue for review by its regulator, ASIC (Note: clause 24.1(a) of the revised EFT Code (effective 1 April 2002) stipulated that ASIC would undertake a review within 2 years).

recommendation has regard for the observation that currently there are variations between financial institutions on when these are made available. Of particular concern is that not all financial institutions have copies of their terms and conditions of use available for perusal prior to signing an EFT account application form ahead of obtaining EFT access.

vii. The *EFT Code* should also strive to ensure uniformity as to when the consumer is deemed to have accepted the terms and conditions of use;

viii. In addition to the *EFT Code's* general language requirement in clause 2.1 that the terms and conditions of use be 'clear and unambiguous', the substantive content of financial institutions' terms and conditions of use should at least be made to contain consistent and plain wording, perhaps in accordance with a pro-forma annexed to the *EFT Code* itself;

ix. The *EFT Code* should include a requirement that some personal explanation of the terms and conditions of use be available at the request of the consumer;

x. EFT transaction receipts issued from an EFT terminal should include a clear, highlighted reference number peculiar to each EFT transaction which would enhance the validity of the receipt and also facilitate ready reconciliation with entries on a periodical statement. This measure would assist both the financial institution and consumer in the event of a subsequent dispute;

xi. Periodical statements issued on EFT accounts should be issued more frequently in accordance with the preferable provision in the *US EFT Act* at §1693d(c), which requires that statements on EFT accounts be issued to the consumer on a monthly basis if an EFT transaction has occurred in that month, but at least on a quarterly basis where no EFT transaction has occurred. This would be of utility to the consumer given the weight that many financial institutions place in their terms and conditions of use on the need for the consumer to retain and reconcile EFT transaction receipts and periodic statements;

xii. To be incorporated as part of Recommendation (iv), it is critical for the integrity and operation of the *EFT Code* that it should more clearly and concisely define its own key terms and threshold tests. Namely, for the pivotal clause 5 liability provisions, what constitutes an 'unauthorised EFT transaction', establishing 'proof on the balance of probability', an 'unreasonable delay in notification', and exactly what degree of evidential weight should be given to, and what exactly is meant by, the term 'while significant' in adjudicating disputes where an EFT transaction has allegedly been initiated using the 'correct PIN at first attempt' (including who exactly carries the burden of proof on this point: is it for the financial institution to establish something more or, as is more likely, is it for the consumer to disprove?);

xiii. The *EFT Code's* narrow *de minimis* standard examples of what does not constitute a reasonable disguise of the consumer's PIN (ie, derivatives of a consumer's birth date and name) should be expanded in line with the ABIO's far broader interpretation and higher standard of what is an unreasonable disguise of the PIN. This will provide more certainty and guidance, as well as clarification for the consumer of what is and what is not acceptable.

xiv. Undefined, vague and imprecise terms in clause 6 of the *EFT Code* dealing with liability for EFT technical or system malfunctions also need to be incorporated in a more comprehensive definitions section. In particular, what constitutes 'failure' given clause 6.1 provides that institutions are responsible for losses caused by 'failure' in EFT systems or EFT equipment. Does it, for example, include under-payments at an ATM? Does it, for example, include over-payments to retail merchants through EFTPOS? Does it, for example, include failures resulting in wrong debits or credits? Does it, for example, include failures resulting in authorised transfers not being made? Finally, does it, for example, include inadequate security permitting unauthorised access to an EFT system?;

xv. The *EFT Code* should also clearly ascribe responsibility for losses arising from 'off-line' EFT transactions to the financial institutions;

xvi. Clause 6.2 provides that financial institutions are not to deny the right for consumers to claim indirect or consequential losses arising from EFT system or equipment malfunctions. Clause 6.2 does need to state clearly the extent of liability to the financial institution or at the least provide some guidelines for determining its extent, or even provide a cap or tiered regime. For example, would an institution be held fully liable if a consumer, by virtue of the EFT system or equipment failure, was unable to meet regular personal or even much larger commercial commitments?;

xvii. EFT financial institutions should be compelled under the *EFT Code* to implement security modifications to their EFT equipment and EFT terminals (pursuant to Australian Standard AS3769) within a reasonable timeframe or otherwise be refrained from placing undue onus in their terms and conditions of use that consumers are to both check the security of the EFT terminals and equipment as well as survey those around them and shield the input of the PIN;

xviii. In respect of dispute resolution procedures, the *EFT Code* should incorporate the requirement under §1693f(c) of the *US EFT Act* that the consumer's account be provisionally re-credited with the amount of the EFT transaction in dispute should the dispute not be resolved within the current 45 day period assigned under the *EFT Code*;

xix. The *EFT Code* should also stipulate that financial institutions inform consumers in writing of the progress of the investigation after 45 days;

xx. The imminent review of the *EFT Code* by ASIC would be enhanced by incorporating aspects of the innovative multi-disciplinary analytic criteria discussed in this study. In particular, the economic efficiency and liability/loss allocation framework adapted from Posner, Cooter and Rubin. This is particularly relevant given that the analysis in this study reveals that the existing *EFT Code* essentially remains a fault-based regulatory regime despite its no-fault objective and pretences. ASIC needs to be clear in its economic objectives and align the substantive allocation of fault and burden of proof accordingly. If the current actual 'hybrid' loss-reduction and loss-sharing approach is to remain, then ASIC ought to acknowledge that such an approach requires a detailed investigation of the relative costs of avoidance among the parties. That is, rather than identifying just the lowest-cost avoider as the financial institution in most instances, ASIC should rank each party according to comparative advantage in avoidance and determine relative liabilities consistent with that ranking. Otherwise, the present situation of assigning liabilities to more than one party, according to vaguely-constructed liability rules, will continue to involve complex rules and costly and protracted evidential disputes and potential litigation;

xxi. The ASIC review should also have regard for the inherent asymmetry and bias in approaches to regulating other payment system instruments in Australia and internationally. In particular, the divergent loss allocation rules between consumer EFT products, credit cards and paper-based payment instruments such as cheques should be noted. A quest for optimal efficiency in regulating EFT, as just one instrument in the payments system, must acknowledge and be informed by different and asymmetric loss allocation rules and regulatory treatment of other competing payment methods.

xxii. The ASIC review would benefit from undertaking a contemporary survey of EFT product and service providers along the lines of the 1981 survey conducted by the Federal Reserve Board of the USA on start-up and ongoing compliance costs of EFT regulation. The extrapolation for Australian conditions in this study provides some general guidance, and, broadly indicates that full application of *US EFT Act*-styled statutory regulation in Australia would likely give rise to prohibitive start-up and ongoing incremental costs. It should be said, though, that the extrapolation contains too many qualifications to be relied upon in its own right;

xxiii. The step-by-step basic framework advanced in this study should be of utility to ASIC as a reference document for devising a methodology for analysing EFT regulation costs and benefits, both existing regulation as well as different regulatory options for the future;

xxiv. The model proposed in this study for assessing the administrative feasibility and social desirability of EFT regulatory options should also be explored by ASIC as part of its review; and

xxv. Finally, all aspects of the impending ASIC review should be viewed in light of the salient financial ethical principles advanced in this study.

Chapter 7. Summary and Conclusions

7.1 Summary of the issues, approach and findings

This book provides a new integrated multi-disciplinary analysis of EFT regulation in Australia in an attempt to identify the efficacy of current EFT regulatory arrangements as well as to appraise the merits of different EFT regulatory options to attain a more optimal and efficient regulatory regime for the future. The multi-disciplinary approach is *a general one* and this approach can be *adopted in legal rule formulation* of efficient laws in all legal issues in all countries irrespective of their political, economic and business organization.

The core issue addressed in this book is the fair allocation of liability between the consumer and financial institution in the event of a disputed or unauthorised EFT transaction. In response to this central concern, the tension between 'soft' self-regulatory measures and 'hard' or more formal legislative measures is considered along with the adequacy of the pre-existing common law principles governing traditional paper-based payment instruments.

The purpose of this study is considered especially apposite in view of ASIC's imminent comprehensive review of the self-regulating Australian *EFT Code* and both the increasing incidence of reported unauthorised EFT transactions and in non-compliance by EFT financial institutions with the *EFT Code*. It is also an important study because of the rapid recent growth in EFT transaction volume and the continued expansion of EFT products and services compared to other payment instruments, which are in a correspondingly deep decline. Moreover, there has been no previous study or review of the current *EFT Code*, which was revised in 2002.

In the EFT payments system, consumers are exposed to risks quite different from those in traditional payments instruments. These include flaws in the various methods employed by financial institutions for the distribution of EFT cards and PINs, problems adducing unequivocal evidence in the event of unauthorised use of the instrument and systemic errors and technical malfunctions in processing EFT transactions. Furthermore, the distinct nature of electronic authentication using an electronic device and secret code makes the general common law principles dealing with handwritten signature authentication in the case of paper instruments (eg, by analogy with a forged cheque) particularly unhelpful.

The two (2) EFT regulations the subject of this study are the Australian *EFT Code* and the *US EFT Act*. The latter was chosen for comparative purposes as it is a rare example of a legislative response to the above common core issues and risks, which the EFT system in the USA shares with Australia. Quite apart from its higher degree of formality and enforceability, the *US EFT Act* is also of utility as a comparison for its markedly different substantive provisions in seeking to reduce uncertainties for both consumers and financial institutions regarding liabilities related to EFT payments. Notwithstanding these notable divergences, like the Australian *EFT Code*, the *US EFT Act* also seeks to provide protection against unauthorised or erroneous EFT transactions that access consumer accounts, by setting guidelines to allocate liability for unauthorised EFT transactions as well as imposing documentation and record-keeping requirements to assist consumers in detecting and remedying disputed problems. The regulations also require that providers of EFT services disclose certain information regarding the terms and conditions of these services and inform customers of any changes in terms.

However, it is in the substantive analysis of the *EFT Code* and the difficulty in interpreting its requirements in practice that the real problematic issues arise in Australia. Unlike the *US EFT Act*, for example, which has a relatively simple and administratively convenient approach to apportioning fault, the *EFT Code* essentially shares the burden of proof between the EFT financial institution and the consumer in most instances. The consequence of the *EFT Code's* ambiguous, undefined and multi-layered legal tests and guidelines for determining the allocation of liability to either consumer or financial institution is that it leaves the ABIO, as the independent and preferred adjudicator of disputes, with the difficult and arbitrary task of hearing contrasting arguments and weighing the inconclusive evidence led by both sides before then seeking to reach a fair and equitable finding on the 'balance of probabilities'. Indeed, the practical application of the *EFT Code* is extremely difficult and confusing, as the ABIO regularly observes in its annual reports and is almost always evident in its actual case examples.

Paradoxically, the task undertaken in this book to research and analyse these difficult and complex regulatory issues is both helped and hindered by another important issue: the lack of literature on consumer EFT regulation. Helped, because it represents a unique opportunity to embark upon such a study afresh, and, hindered, because little benefit can be derived from previous studies and hence there are no foundations upon which to build or progress the debate, the research and the analysis. Indeed, as the central bank in the USA, the Federal Reserve, recently observed: 'the determinants and repercussions of EFT debit use have largely escaped academic scrutiny'.[451]

Accordingly, the significant gaps in this area provide a rare occasion to explore these contemporary and contentious issues using adapted multi-disciplinary techniques, including comparative law method, economic criteria and regulation theory methods, as well as ethical, social and administrative considerations.

In the present study, all of these methods are adapted in an integrated way. In this sense, the multi-disciplinary research and analytic approach adapted in this study is intended to not only drive the debate on an appropriate EFT regulatory framework forward, but also enable the construction of a framework and some actual pragmatic criteria on which to assess different EFT regulatory options.

---

[451] Federal Reserve Bank of New York, above n 3.

The comparative law method adopted reflects the belief that, for this problem, similar yet divergent consumer EFT regulation systems can benefit from each others' experience. That is, having identified a 'common core problem' shared by Australia and the USA, the preferred comparative law approach is described as the 'critical comparative law' approach; one that not only seeks to identify the regulatory differences, but observes the possibilities for some convergence. Thus, common elements are sought ('integrative comparative law') just as much as differences stressed ('contrastive comparative law'). In fact, this instructive critical comparative law process informed the majority of the twenty-five (25) specific recommendations in Section 6.2 of Chapter 6 above.

The second methods, economic analysis of law and regulation theory, are concerned with whether the application of formal legislative regulation (ie, USA-style regulatory provisions) to EFT in Australia is meritorious. Beginning with an examination of the economics of liability allocation and the economic rationales for government regulation, an analytical framework for evaluating the effects of regulation is assembled.

Other, often overlooked, criteria are also incorporated into this multi-disciplinary approach to financial regulation. Specifically, the application of ethical principles and considerations, as well as an assessment and strategy to take account of the administrative feasibility and social acceptability of different EFT regulatory options.

A limited survey sample is also undertaken in this study using the 'structured interview' data collection method. Considerable benefit can be derived from assembling and interpreting data from one of the major stakeholder groups, the EFT financial institutions themselves (ie, the 6 Australian banks, which between them account for some 91% of all EFT transaction volume).

After having articulated and discussed the problematic EFT issues (principally, in Chapters 1 and 2), the multi-disciplinary methods and criteria employed in this study (presented in Chapter 3) facilitated a broad, in depth analysis of these issues (in Chapters 4 and 5), which then, in turn, produced the series of 48 important findings (presented in Section 6.1 of Chapter 6) and 25 specific recommendations (presented in Section 6.2 of Chapter 6).

7.2 Limitations and further areas for research

As discussed in Section 1.7 of the introductory Chapter 1, when articulating the scope of the present study, the recently revised *EFT Code* extended its coverage from ATM and EFTPOS applications alone to Internet banking, telephone banking, stored-value cards and credit cards (to the extent that they are used for EFT purposes).

However, in the absence of any meaningful data on either the use or the incidence of unauthorised transactions under these extended uses, this book focuses on EFT debit cards deployed in ATMs and EFTPOS terminals using a PIN as the authentication means, where the vast majority of EFT transactions and problematic legal issues arise.

In evaluating the different regulatory approaches taken in the USA and Australia to the treatment of liability in the event of a disputed, unauthorised consumer EFT transaction, this book limited its comparative coverage to the *US EFT Act*, which arguably provides the most striking and informative benchmark comparison given the USA is not only a common law country like Australia, but that the USA responded to the same common core EFT problems and risk issues with the most markedly different response of those surveyed for the purpose of this book.

Given the burgeoning consumer preference for EFT usage within the payments system, it would be of great utility for the subject area to have a broader, more global approach to research and analysis taking in the regulatory approaches adopted in other jurisdictions. For example, a comparative legal analysis of the Australian *EFT Code* with that of the EFT regulation in European (civil law) countries (eg, Denmark and Switzerland), Asia (eg, the hybrid common law-civil law legal system of Malaysia) and other common law countries (eg, Canada, the United Kingdom and Ireland).

Another scope issue is territorial reach. As EFT products and services continue to expand, and be used, across the globe, further research into jurisdictional conflict of laws and recourse for disputed or unauthorised EFT transactions or foreign EFT computer system malfunctions would be a meritorious task to be undertaken.

Acknowledging and respecting the confines of this book, it is considered beyond both the scope and purview of this book to address in detail an econometric or mathematical modelling of costs and benefits of EFT regulation initiatives. Nevertheless, future research and studies could benefit from using the economic framework and mathematical model put forward in Section 5.4 of Chapter 5 of this book to undertake a systematic evaluation of the relative cost-effectiveness and cost-benefits of different EFT regulation initiatives. Potential evaluators who could use this economic model and step-by-step guide may include each of those regulators with responsibility for the various aspects of the EFT system, as well as those with access to current, meaningful industry-wide banking industry and/or EFT cost-benefit data. Those identified may include: the ABIO, the RBA, ASIC, the ACCC, consumer advocacy groups, the Australian Bankers' Association, or, at the ultimate level, the Australian federal government Department of Treasury. The framework is designed to facilitate an evaluation of how cost-effective an intervention has been, as much as for a forward-looking economic appraisal. The intention behind this framework is that it may facilitate more informed decisions on both EFT risk regulation and resource allocation between the different EFT regulatory and policy options advanced in this book.

7.3 Conclusions

From all the research material and international data garnered for this book, the assignment of fault clearly plays a pivotal role in the formation of EFT rules generally, and, more particularly, in the allocation of liability for losses in different jurisdictions.

In assessing the treatment of *fault* in the current regulatory arrangements in Australia, and determining what ought to be the desired or more optimal rule, the following observations can be made. First, a rule or regulatory option based on fault is hopelessly complicated, particularly in determining the consumer's contribution or negligence, its degree, as well as the causal link between that contribution or negligence and the actual loss. Second, a rule or regulatory option which allocates some portion of the loss to the consumer, even where the consumer is not at all at fault, is plainly unfair. Finally, there is also the issue of providing financial institutions with sufficient incentives and motivation to enhance the security and integrity of the EFT system, which, arguably, a fault based rule does not do.

In terms of economic efficiency theory, the existing Australian *EFT Code* attempts to implement the loss allocation rule of assigning liability to the least cost avoider. Therefore, it shares losses between the user and the financial institution. It follows a fault-based system where liability is allocated to the user when the user has been at fault in specified ways with the security of the PIN or has been unreasonably slow in notifying the institution of the loss.

The difficulty with Australia's fault-based loss allocation model is the lack of direct evidence that either side can bring as to who performed the transaction and how they came to know the access method (PIN). An evidentiary stalemate invariably arises and an independent dispute resolution body like the ABIO is put in the difficult position of having to make judgments on unclear facts. These problems are compounded by the undefined, complex, multi-layered threshold tests required under *EFT Code*, which confuses the purported allocation of a burden of proof on the EFT financial institution. In the absence of definitions and guidelines, these threshold tests require interpretation by reference to the principles of the common law. As stated throughout this book, the importation of traditional paper-based tests, rules and principles from the common law sit uneasily with EFT generally and electronic authentication particularly.

In marked contrast, fault concepts are virtually eliminated under the statutory scheme in the USA. The *US EFT Act* takes into account the economic principle that liability allocation rules be simple, clear and decisive so as to minimise the costs of administering them. The *US EFT Act* effectively apportions liability between the user and institution on a no-fault basis, thus eliminating contentious and time-consuming fault assessment. Under the USA model, users are not liable at all for carelessness or negligence with the secret code (PIN). They are only liable for losses caused by delays in reporting lost or stolen EFT cards, or failing to report unauthorised transactions which appear on a periodic statement.

It is submitted that in view of the increasing incidence of non-compliance by financial institutions, and, both the absolute and proportional increase in the number of disputed, unauthorised EFT transactions in Australia, the *EFT Code* should take steps to clarify the assignment of a burden of proof in all instances, or at least provide clear, unambiguous definitions for all the threshold legal tests as well as simple-language guidelines to be followed in the event of an 'evidentiary stalemate'. To enhance enforceability, financial institution compliance and also to increase consumer awareness of all avenues of legal redress, it is critical that the *EFT Code* is amended to make explicit reference to the relevant provisions and statutory force of the *ASIC Act*.

From this extensive multi-disciplinary study, it is anticipated that the broader field of electronic commerce regulation will benefit from the extended methodology and analysis. For consumer electronic banking regulation in particular, the expectation now is that all 25 specific recommendations will be addressed or at least given due consideration in the upcoming comprehensive review of the Australian *EFT Code* by the financial services regulator, ASIC. This would enhance the efficacy and enforceability of the revised *EFT Code* to keep in step with the burgeoning consumer preference for EFT use in the age of modern banking technology.

Appendix

Limited Survey Sample – Structured Interview Data Collection Method Conducted : Friday, 10 February 2006			
BANK	Do you have a copy of your Bank's EFT terms and conditions of use available?	Do you have someone at this branch of your Bank that can personally explain the EFT terms and conditions of use to me?	Does your Bank have a formal procedure for issuing EFT cards and PINs?
ANZ Bank	Yes *	No	Unsure
Bendigo Bank	Yes ∞	Unsure	Yes
Commonwealth Bank	Yes	No	Yes
National Australia Bank	Yes #	Unsure	Yes
St George Bank	Yes	Unsure	Unsure
Westpac Bank	Yes	No	Unsure

* ANZ Bank provided what its EFT Representative Officer stated was that Bank's comprehensive EFT Terms and Conditions of Use. In fact, it was a brief and general customer guide booklet on how to use the Bank's electronic banking products and services with no terms and conditions of use contained therein.

∞ Bendigo Bank provided a Terms and Conditions of Use booklet for 'Bendigo Phone & e-Banking', which that Bank's EFT Representative Officer said were 'virtually identical' to those for EFT banking products and services.

NAB provided a Terms and Conditions of Use booklet for 'Internet Banking' only, which that Bank's EFT Representative Officer said covered all electronic banking products and services.

Bibliography

1. American Bar Association Task Force on E-commerce and Alternative Dispute Resolution <www.law.washington.edu/ABA-eADR> at 17 November 2004.

2. ANZ Bank, *Internet, Phone, ATM and EFTPOS Banking – Your Guide* (10/2005).

3. Aronson, M, and Hunter, J, *Litigation: Evidence and Procedure* (6th ed, 1998).

4. Arrow, K, 'Economic Welfare and the Allocation of Research for Invention' in R. Nelson (ed), *The Rate and Direction of Inventive Activity: Economic and Social Factors* (1961).

5. Australian Banking Industry Ombudsman Limited, *Annual Report, 1992-1993.*

6. Australian Banking Industry Ombudsman Limited, *Annual Report, 1993-1994.*

7. Australian Banking Industry Ombudsman Limited, *Annual Report, 1994-1995.*

8. Australian Banking Industry Ombudsman Limited, *Annual Report, 1995-1996.*

9. Australian Banking Industry Ombudsman Limited, *Annual Report, 1996-1997.*

10. Australian Banking Industry Ombudsman Limited, *Annual Report, 1997-1998.*

11. Australian Banking Industry Ombudsman Limited, *Annual Report, 1998-1999.*

12. Australian Banking Industry Ombudsman Limited, *Annual Report, 1999-2000.*

13. Australian Banking Industry Ombudsman Limited, *Annual Report, 2000-2001.*

14. Australian Banking Industry Ombudsman Limited, *Annual Report, 2001-2002.*

15. Australian Banking Industry Ombudsman Limited, *Annual Report, 2002-2003.*

16. Australian Competition and Consumer Commission, *Summaries of the Trade Practices Act and the Prices Surveillance Act* (1995).

17. Australian Consumers Association, *EFT in Australia: Issues and Problems* (1984).

18. Australian Payments System Council, *Annual Report 1994/95.*

19. Australian Science and Technology Council, *Towards a Cashless Society* (May, 1986).

20. Australian Securities and Investments Commission, *Discussion Paper on an Expanded EFT Code of Conduct* (July, 1999).

21. Australian Securities and Investments Commission, *Annual Report: 1998/1999.*

22. Australian Securities and Investments Commission, *Annual Report: 1999/2000.*

23. Australian Securities and Investments Commission, *Annual Report: 2000/2001.*

24. Australian Securities and Investments Commission, *Annual Report: 2001/2002.*

25. Australian Securities and Investments Commission, *Annual Report: 2002/2003.*

26. Australian Securities and Investments Commission, *Annual Report: 2003/2004.*

27. Australian Securities and Investments Commission, *Compliance with the Payments System Codes of Practice and the EFT Code of Conduct* (2003).

28. Australian Securities and Investments Commission, *Discussion Paper on an Expanded EFT Code of Conduct* (1999).

29. Australian Securities and Investments Commission, *Report of Compliance with the Payments System Codes of Practice and the EFT Code of Conduct, 1999/2000* (2001).

30. Australian Securities and Investments Commission, *Report of Compliance with the Payments System Codes of Practice and the EFT Code of Conduct, 2001/2002* (2003).

31. Australian Securities and Investments Commission, *Report of Compliance with the EFT Code of Conduct, 2003/2004* (2005).

32. Australian Securities and Investments Commission, *Second Draft Paper on an Expanded EFT Code of Conduct and Commentary* (2000).

33. Australian Securities and Investments Commission official website <www.asic.gov.au> at 16 February 2006.

34. Badaracco, J L, and Webb, A P, 'Business Ethics: A View from the Trenches' (1995) 37 *California Management Review* 8.

35. Banking and Financial Services Ombudsman, Annual Report, 2003-2004.

36. Bendigo Bank, *Bendigo Phone Banking & Bendigo e-Banking Terms and Conditions* (02/2004).

37. Board of Governors of the Federal Reserve System, *Report to Congress on the Application of the Electronic Funds Transfer Act to Electronic Stored-Value Products* (1997).

38. Boatright, J R, *Ethics in Finance* (1999).

39. Boyle, J M, 'A Survey of the Mortgage Banking Industry Concerning the Costs and Benefits of Regulation' (Report for the USA Federal Trade Commission, 1982).

40. Braithwaite, John, and Grabosky, Peter N, *Of Manners Gentle: Enforcement Strategies of Australian Business Regulatory Agencies* (1986).

41. Bussani, M, 'Current Trends in European Comparative Law: The Common Core Approach' (1998) 21 *Hastings International & Comparative Law Review* 785.

42. Butterworths, *Concise Australian Legal Dictionary* (2nd ed, 2000).

43. Case, K E, and Fair, R C, *Principles of Economics* (1989).

44. Chandler, K M M, Crown, E M, and Brown, S A, *Consumer Information and Effects on Knowledge and Choice* (1991).

45. Collis, J, and Hussey, R, *Business Research – A Practical Guide for Undergraduate and Postgraduate Students* (2nd ed, 2003).

46. Committee of Inquiry into the Australian Financial System (J K Campbell, Chairman), *Final Report* (1981).

47. Commonwealth Attorney General's Department Electronic Commerce Expert Group, *Electronic Commerce: Building the Legal Framework* (April, 1998) <http://law.gov.au/aghome/advisory/eceg/ecegreport.html> at 24 September 2004.

48. Commonwealth Bank, *Transaction, Savings and Investments Accounts – Product Disclosure Statement* (01/2006).

49. Conyers, D, and Hills, P, *An Introduction to Development Planning in the Third World* (1984).

50. Cooter, R D, and Rubin, E L, 'A Theory of Loss Allocation for Consumer Payments' (1987) 66 *Texas Law Review* 63.

51. Eatwell, J, Milgate, M, and Newman, P (eds), *The New Palgrave – A Dictionary of Economics* (1991).

52. Elliehausen, G, 'The Cost of Banking Regulation: A Review of the Evidence' (Working Paper for the Board of Governors of the Federal Reserve System (1997).

53. European Commission's Recommendation: *Boosting Customers' Confidence in Electronic Means of Payment in the Single Market* (1997) COM (97) 353.

54. Federal Bureau of Consumer Affairs (Australia), *A Cashless Society? Electronic Banking and the Consumer* (1995).

55. Federal Reserve Bank of New York, *Why Use Debit Instead of Credit? Consumer Choice in a Trillion Dollar Market* (2004) <http://www.newyorkfed.org/research/economists/zinman/2842_debit_or_credit.pdf> at 7 October 2004.

56. Fein, M L, 'Regulating Cyberspace' (1995) 71 *Bank Management* 8.

57. Fischhoff, B, *Acceptable Risk: A Conceptual Proposal* (2005) <http://www.piercelaw.edu/risk/vol5/winter/Fischhof.htm> at 7 March 2006.

58. Fischhoff, B, and Cox, L, 'Conceptual Framework for Benefit Assessment' in *Benefits Assessment: The State of the Art* (1985).

59. Frederick, R E, and Hoffman, W M, 'The Individual Investor in Securities Markets: An Ethical Analysis' (1990) *Journal of Business Ethics* 579.

60. Friedman, David D, *Economic Analysis of Law* (1987) The New Palgrave: A Dictionary of Economic Theory and Doctrine <http://www.daviddfriedman.com/Law_and_Econ_S97E/Palgrave_L_E.html> at 12 March 2006.

61. Friedman, Lawrence M, 'Some Thoughts on Comparative Legal Culture' in Clark, David S (ed), *Comparative and Private International Law* (1990) 52-5.

62. Fuhrer, J C, and Sneddon-Little, J, 'Technology and Growth: An Overview' (1996) *New England Economic Review* 3.

63. Galanter, Marc, 'Why the Haves Come Out Ahead: Speculations on the Limits of Social Change' (1974) 9 *Law and Society Review* 95.

64. Gamertsfelder, Leif, 'The Commonwealth Electronic Transactions Bill 1999: Ailments and Antidotes' (1999) 1 *The Journal of Information Law and Technology* 1.

65. Geva, B, *Bank Collections and Payment Transactions* (2001).

66. Geva, B, 'Consumer Protection in Electronic Funds Transfers' (Research Paper for the Office of Consumer Affairs, Industry Canada, 21 March 2002).

67. Goetz, C J, *Cases and Materials on Law and Economics* (1984).

68. Goldsmith, J L, 'Against Cyberanarchy' (1998) 65 *University of Chicago Law Review* 1199.

69. Goodman, L S, 'The Interface between Technology and Regulation in Banking' in Saunders, A, and White, L J (eds), *Technology and the Regulation of Financial Markets* (1986).

70. Gutteridge, H C, *Comparative Law: An Introduction to the Comparative Method of Legal Study and Research* (2nd ed, 1949) 1.

71. Haywood, Charles F, 'Regulation, Structure, and Technical Change in the Financial Services Industry' in Haywood, Charles F, 'Regulation, Structure, and Technological Change in the Consumer Financial Services Industry' in ABT Associates Inc. (USA) Report No. 79-34, *The Costs and Benefits of Public Regulation of Consumer Financial Services* (1979).

72. Heydon, J D, *Cross on Evidence* (7th Australian ed, 2004).

73. Hirsch, W Z, *Law and Economics – An Introductory Analysis* (2nd ed, 1988).

74. Hough, M, and Tilley, N, *Auditing Crime and Disorder* (1998).

75. Huxley, Andrew, 'Golden Yoke, Silken Text' (1997) 106 *Yale Law Journal* 1885, 1924-5.

76. *Internet Law and Policy Forum* <http://www.ilpf.org> at 20 September 2004.

77. *Internet Law and Policy Forum,* 'Bringing Law, Policy and Business and Technology Together' from the web site at <http://www.ilpf.org/groups/bib4_15.htm> at 20 September 2004.

78. Islam, S M N, *Applied Welfare Economics* (2001).

79. Islam, S M N, *Optimal Growth Economics* (2001).

80. Islam, S M N, and Mak, C S Y, *Normative Health Economics – A New Pragmatic Approach to Cost Benefit Analysis, Mathematical Modelling and Applications* (2006).

81. Johnson, D, and Post, D, 'Law and Borders: The Rise of Law in Cyberspace' (1996) 48 *Stanford Law Review* 1367.

82. Kennickell, A B, and Kwast, M L, 'Who Uses Electronic Banking? Preliminary Results from the 1995 Survey of Consumer Finances' (Unpublished manuscript, presented at the Annual Meetings of the Financial Management Association, New Orleans, Louisiana, USA, October 1996).

83. Kloot, L, 'Some Legal Aspects of Electronic Funds Transfer' (1990) 1 *Accounting Research Journal* 28.

84. Kolodziej, A, 'Customer-Banker Liability in Electronic Banking' (1986) 7 *The Company Lawyer* 1.

85. Lal, Deepak, *Unintended Consequences: The Impact of Factor Endowments, Culture, and Politics on Long- Run Economic Performance* (1998) 9-11

86. Lichfield, N, et al., *Evaluation in the Planning Process* (1975).

87. Mann, R, 'Credit Cards and Debit Cards in the United States and Japan' (2002) 55 *Vanderbilt Law Review* 656.

88. Markesinis, Basil, 'Comparative Law – A Subject in Search of an Audience' (1990) 53 *Modern Law Review* 1, 21.

89. Martin Group Review of the Australian Financial System (S Martin, Chairman) (December, 1983).

90. Mattei, Ugo, *Comparative Law and Economics* (1997).

91. Ministry of Consumer Affairs (Victoria), *Electronic Funds Transfer Systems – How is the Consumer Faring?* (1989).

92. Moccia, L, 'Historical Overview on the Origins and Attitudes of Comparative Law' in De Witte, B, and Forder, C (eds), *The Common Law of Europe and the Future of Legal Education* (1992).

93. National Australia Bank, *EFT Terms and Conditions of Use* (1997).

94. National Australia Bank, *National Internet Banking – Product Disclosure Statement Including Terms and Conditions* (10/2005).

95. National Commission on Electronic Fund Transfers, *EFT in the United States – Final Report of the National Commission on Electronic Fund Transfers* (October, 1977).

96. Oborn, M J, 'Procedures Adopted by Australian Banks for the Resolution of Customer Complaints and the Role of the Australian Banking Industry Ombudsman' (1992) 3 *Journal of Banking and Finance Law and Practice* 268.

97. Orucu, E, 'Critical Comparative Law: Considering Paradoxes for Legal Systems in Transition' (2000) 4 *European Journal of Comparative Law* 1.

98. Peat, Marwick, Mitchell & Company and Electronic Banking Inc., *The Costs and Benefits of Participation in the Treasury's Direct Deposit Program*, prepared for the Bank Administration Institute, National Association of Mutual Savings Banks, United States League of Savings Associations, and United States Department of the Treasury (1981).

99. Pengilley, W, 'Misleading or Deceptive Conduct and Financial Institutions' (1989) 1 *Bond Law Review* 157.

100. Perritt, H, 'Jurisdiction in Cyberspace' (1996) 41 *Villanova Law Review* 1.

101. Perritt, H, 'Cyberspace Self-Government: Town Hall Democracy or Rediscovered Royalism?' (1997) 12 *Berkeley Technology Law Journal* 413.

102. Posner, R A, *Economic Analysis of Law* (3rd ed, 1986).

103. Procter, L, 'Reforming the Australian Payments System: The State of Play' (1993) 107 *The Australian Banker* 135.

104. *Report by the Treasury and the Trade Practices Commission on the Operation of the EFT Code of Conduct* (1990).

105. *Report of the Working Group Examining the Rights and Obligations of the Users and Providers of Electronic Funds Transfer Systems* (1985).

106. Reserve Bank of Australia, *Australian Economic Statistics 1949-50 to 1996-97: Occasional Paper No 8* (2006) <http://www.rba.gov.au/Statistics/op8_index.html> at 13 February 2006.

107. Reserve Bank of Australia, *Bulletin: The Changing Australian Retail Payments Landscape* (2003).

108. Reserve Bank of Australia, *Quarterly Statistical Release: Measures of Consumer Price Inflation* (25 January 2006) <http://www.rba.gov.au/Statistics/measures_of_cpi.html> at 13 February 2006.

109. Rosenberg, A S, *Better than Cash? Global Proliferation of Debit and Prepaid Cards and Consumer Protection Policy* (2005) Thomas Jefferson School of Law, San Diego, USA <http://law.bepress.com/expresso/eps/766> at 29 January 2006.

110. Rothchild, J, 'Protecting the Digital Consumer: The Limits of Cyberspace Utopianism' (1999) *Indiana Law Journal* 893.

111. Rothchild, J, and Silverman, G M, *Cases and Materials on the Law of Electronic Commerce* (1999).

112. Schlesinger, R B, 'The Past and Future of Comparative Law' (1995) 43 *American Journal of Comparative Law* 477.

113. Schroeder, F J, 'Compliance Costs and Consumer Benefits of the Electronic Funds Transfer Act: Recent Survey Evidence' (Report for the Board of Governors of the Federal Reserve System, 1985).

114. Searles, I, 'Self-Regulation as an Effective Alternative to Legislation and Litigation: The Case of Electronic Banking' (1990) 1 *Journal of Banking and Finance Law and Practice* 125.

115. *Second Report of the Working Group Examining the Rights and Obligations of the Users and Providers of Electronic Funds Transfer Systems* (1986).

116. Shefrin, H, and Statman, M, 'Ethics, Fairness and Efficiency in Financial Markets' (1993) *Financial Analysts Journal* 21.

117. Sneddon, M, 'A Review of the Electronic Funds Transfer Code of Conduct' (1995) 6 *Journal of Banking and Finance Law and Practice* 29.

118. Sneddon, M, 'Promises and Puzzles of Electronic Purses' (1995) *Australian Business Law Review* 469.

119. Solow, R M, 'Technical Change and the Aggregate Production Function' (1957) 39 *Review of Economics and Statistics* 312.

120. Standing Committee of Consumer Affairs Ministers, *Draft Guidelines for Consumer Protection in Electronic Funds Transfer Systems* (1986).

121. St George Bank, *Banking Services – Terms and Conditions and General Information* (09/2005).

122. Stone, C D, *Where the Law Ends: The Social Control of Corporate Behaviour* (1975).

123. 'Symposium: New Approaches to Comparative Law' (1997) *Utah Law Review* 255.

124. 'Symposium: New Directions in Comparative Law' (1998) 46 *American Journal of Comparative Law* 597.

125. Trade Practices Commission, *Finance Industry Code of Conduct on Electronic Funds Transfer Services: An Assessment by the Trade Practices Commission* (1988).

126. Tucker, G, 'Regulation of Electronic Banking' (1990) 64 *Law Institute Journal* 706.

127. Tyree, A L, *Banking Law in Australia* (2nd ed, 1995).

128. Tyree, A L, *Banking Law in Australia* (3rd ed, 1998).

129. Tyree, A L, *Banking Law in Australia* (5th ed, 2005).

130. Tyree, A L, *DigitalCash* (1997).

131. Tyree, A L, *Section 74 TPA and Payment Services* (1997) <http://austlii.edu.au/~alan/section74.html> at 5 December 2005.

132. Tyree, A L, and Beatty, A, *The Law of Payment Systems* (2nd ed, 2002).

133. *UNCITRAL Model Law on Electronic Commerce* (1996) <http://www.uncitral.org/uncitral/en/uncitral_texts/electronic_commerce/1996Model.html> at 12 March 2006.

134. *UNIDROIT Principles of International Commercial Contracts* (2004) <http://www.unidroit.org/english/principles/contracts/main.htm> at 12 March 2006.

135. Viscusi, W Kip (ed), *Regulation Through Litigation* (2002).

136. Ward, I, 'The Limits of Comparativism' (1995) 2 *Military Justice Reporter* 23.

137. Wardrop, A, and Akindemowo, O, 'Electronic Payment Systems and Electronic Banking' in Quirk, P, and Forder, J (eds), *Electronic Commerce and the Law*, (2nd ed, 2003).

138. Weerasooria, W S, *Banking Law and the Financial System in Australia* (4th ed, 1996).

139. Welsh, B, Farrington, D, and Sherman, L, *Costs and Benefits of Preventing Crime* (2001).

140. Westpac Bank, *Deposit Accounts – Product Disclosure Statement incorporating Terms and Conditions for using your Account* (01/2006).

141. Westpac Bank, *EFT Terms and Conditions of Use* (1997).

142. White, P F, *A Critique of the Self-Regulation of Electronic Funds Transfer in Australia* (MBus Minor Thesis, Victoria University of Technology, 1997).

143. Woodruffe, G, 'Government Monitored Codes of Practice in the United Kingdom' (1984) 7 *Journal of Consumer Policy* 171.

144. Zimmer, L F, 'ATM Acceptance Grows, Builds Customer Base for Other EFT Services' (1981) *Magazine of Bank Administration* 31.

145. Zweigert, K, and Kotz, H, *An Introduction to Comparative Law* (3rd ed, 1998)

Index

MIX
Papier aus verantwortungsvollen Quellen
Paper from responsible sources
FSC® C105338

FSC
www.fsc.org

If you have any concerns about our products,
you can contact us on
ProductSafety@springernature.com

In case Publisher is established outside the EU,
the EU authorized representative is:
Springer Nature Customer Service Center GmbH
Europaplatz 3, 69115 Heidelberg, Germany

Printed by Libri Plureos GmbH
in Hamburg, Germany